Exploring Issues of Continuity

The International Baccalaureate in a wider context

Edited by Mary Hayden and Jeff Thompson

A John Catt Publication

First Published 2013

by John Catt Educational Ltd,
12 Deben Mill Business Centre, Old Maltings Approach,
Melton, Woodbridge IP12 1BL

Tel: +44 (0) 1394 389850 Fax: +44 (0) 1394 386893
Email: enquiries@johncatt.com
Website: www.johncatt.com

© 2013 John Catt Educational Ltd

ISBN: 978 1 908095 47 3

eISBN: 978 1 908095 54 1

Set and designed by John Catt Educational Limited

Printed and bound in Great Britain
by Cambrian Printers

Contents

About the contributors

Nick Alchin has been teaching internationally since 1995, first teaching TOK and mathematics at the UWC of South East Asia in Singapore and subsequently at the International School of Geneva. After working as Director of IB at Sevenoaks School, UK, and Dean of Studies at the Aga Khan Academy in Mombasa, Kenya, he is now High School Principal at the UWC of South East Asia East Campus. He has been IB chief assessor for TOK (2005–2010) and vice-chair of the IB Examining Board (2007–2013), and is currently a workshop leader and consultant.

Gillian Ashworth has worked in international schools as a Head of Secondary and an MYP Coordinator, in a diversity of places ranging from India and Azerbaijan, to Africa and South America – all from a starting point of the UK. Her IB roles include that of face-to-face and online workshop leader for MYP and DP, MYP consultant and school visits team leader, senior moderator for MYP and examiner/moderator for DP. She has also taken part in aspects of MYP curriculum, assessment and workshop development for the IB.

Darlene Fisher was, until recently, Director of ENKA Schools in Istanbul for six years. Her current doctoral research focus is on educational leadership and the impact of culture. She is involved with developing courses and workshops related to training school leaders for education in an international context. Darlene is also now working as an educational consultant for the IB, ECIS and a number of independent schools. She has worked in various teaching and administrative roles in Turkey, India, Thailand, Oman, USA and Australia.

David Harrison began his teaching career in England, and in 1993 moved into the international education sphere. His previous teaching appointments have provided him with a wide exposure to curricula in an international context, including A level, Advanced Placement (AP), IB and IGCSE programmes. David is presently MYP Coordinator at The International School of Lausanne in Switzerland, is a visiting team leader for the IB MYP, and has also recently completed a master's degree in International Education.

Dr Mary Hayden is Head of the Department of Education and Director of the Centre for the study of Education in an International Context (CEIC) at the University of Bath. She is editor of the *Journal of Research in International Education* and her teaching, publishing and research supervision focus particularly on international schools and international education. She has held posts in the IB and is a trustee of the Alliance for International Education, a member of the Curriculum Advisory Board for the IPC and IMYC, and academic advisor for the ILMP.

Anthony Hemmens began attending school at the age of five and has been going to school ever since. He graduated from the University of Hull with a degree in philosophy and is presently studying for a master's degree in

Education. Anthony has lived and taught in Hungary, Portugal, Japan and the UK, and has recently taken up a position teaching DP English and TOK at the International School of Kuala Lumpur. Previous to this he spent four years teaching at Southbank International School in London.

Dr Ochan Kusuma-Powell received her doctorate from Columbia University and has developed and implemented inclusive special education programmes in the United States, Indonesia, Malaysia and Tanzania. Together with her husband, Bill, she co-authored seven books on international education. More recently, they have published articles entitled *Data at its worst, Planning for Personalization,* and *Learning to Learn: Student Metacognition.* They are both currently serving on the design team for *The Next Frontier: Inclusion* project, which supports international schools in becoming more inclusive of exceptional children.

Jamie Large is Director of Studies at Ardingly College, in West Sussex, UK, where he was previously the Head of Divinity & Philosophy and subsequently IB Diploma Coordinator. He is currently leading courses in mindfulness and metacognition for 13 year olds. Jamie has taught IBDP TOK and philosophy' both at Ardingly College and in Australia at Prince Alfred College, Adelaide, where he won an award in The Australian newspaper for most innovative educational project. More recently he has completed a master's degree in International Education.

Roger Marshman has been engaged with IB programmes since introducing the DP at Prince Alfred College, Adelaide, in 1995. He became the first IB Asia Pacific regional manager for the MYP, developing particular interest in the articulation of IB programmes. Subsequently he was Head of Secondary at St. Dominic's International School, Lisbon, and now provides consultancy to authorised IB schools and schools with IB candidate status. Roger also acts as a consultant to Flinders University, Australia, and is the author of the IB position paper on concurrency of learning.

Dr April Mattix began her teaching career as a primary grade and middle school teacher in the USA. She taught at the International School of Amsterdam and also at the Anglo American School of Moscow before studying language, literacy and culture at doctoral level at the University of Pittsburgh, USA. April is currently an Assistant Professor at George Mason University, USA, where she teaches international education, elementary education, and International Baccalaureate courses.

Richard Parker began teaching in the British comprehensive system in 1994. His first experience of the IB system was in 2001 when he moved to the International School of Brunei as a teacher of history and TOK. He was Diploma Coordinator and later Secondary Principal at St. Dominic's International School in Lisbon, one of the first schools in the world to run all three IB programmes. Richard is currently working at Victoria Shanghai

Academy in Hong Kong where he is the Secondary Principal. He is an MYP workshop leader for Heads and Administrators.

William Powell has served as an international school educator for the past 35 years in the United States, Saudi Arabia, Tanzania, Indonesia and Malaysia. He is co-author, with his wife Ochan, of *Count Me In! Developing Inclusive International Schools* (2000). More recently, he co-authored three books with Ochan: *Becoming an Emotionally Intelligent Teacher* (Corwin, 2010), *How to Teach now: Five Keys to Personalized Learning in the Global Classroom* (ASCD, 2011) and *The OIQ Factor: How Teachers can raise the Organizational Intelligence of Schools* (John Catt, 2013).

Professor Beverley Shaklee has been a regular elementary classroom teacher, teacher of the gifted, and international teacher educator for some 25 years. She is currently Professor and Director of the Center for International Education, College of Education and Human Development, at George Mason University, USA. Bev was appointed as a member of the Board of Trustees for the Alliance for International Education in 2011. Her areas of research and scholarship include international teacher education, peace education for teachers, and international mindedness in US teachers.

Professor Jeff Thompson teaches, supervises, researches and publishes through the CEIC at the University of Bath in areas relating specifically to international schools and international education. He has worked closely for many years with the IB, having held posts, *inter alia*, of Chair of the DP Examining Board, Director of Research, and Academic Director. He was founding editor for the *Journal of Research in International Education*, and is currently Chair of the Curriculum Advisory Board for the International Primary Curriculum and International Middle Years Curriculum, as well as Chair of the Alliance for International Education.

Andrew Watson is an artist, teacher and journalist who has worked across four continents. In Asia he combined his roles as a management consultant for an international schools group with contributions to television and print journalism. Between 2009 and 2011 Andrew was Diploma associate regional manager for IBAEM. He continues to lead evaluation and verification visits, and IB workshops in international mindedness, Diploma leadership, the IB Diploma core and visual arts. He also works with the Council of International Schools (CIS) and is involved in United World Colleges, particularly in Mostar.

Foreword: interpreting continuity

Although the three International Baccalaureate-related books recently published by John Catt Educational Ltd (*Taking the PYP Forward, Taking the MYP Forward* and *Taking the IB Diploma Programme Forward*) were produced as free-standing publications, we were conscious in our own editorial work (with two of them) that authors quite frequently raised issues concerning the relationship between the different IB programmes. Because the three books were not planned as a 'series', in-depth exploration of issues across the programmes was, understandably, not undertaken by those authors. In any case, some of the features identified as being relevant to the relationships between the programmes were clearly different from those associated with any one programme in particular.

It therefore seemed entirely appropriate that the emergence of interest from previous publications in what we are terming 'continuity' across the IB programmes, coinciding with intense activity within the IB organisation itself on matters relating to that topic, should lead to a publication that offers opportunity for a more extensive consideration of those features by reflective practitioners engaged in meeting the challenges of implementing continuity in their professional work, so contributing to the current debate both within the IB and in the international education sphere more widely.

The term 'continuity', which is the principal focus of this book, is itself a contested notion which is capable of a range of interpretations. It can therefore offer, through its various manifestations, an example of Wittgenstein's reference (in a different context) to the 'bewitchment of our intelligence by means of language'. As will be clear from a reading of the contributions to this book, the idea of continuity is heavily contextualised; it is therefore imperative to enter into discussion on the topic with a clear understanding of the basis upon which that discussion is taking place. As editors, we have not only been aware of the standpoints from which authors in this volume have offered their opinions, but have also gained understanding from the many teachers, administrators, curriculum developers and researchers with whom we have the privilege of working from our base in the Centre for the study of Education in an International Context (CEIC) at the University of Bath, and who have shared ideas from their practice over a long period. On that basis, it seems to us that amongst the ways in which the concept of continuity may be interpreted in an educational context, those that follow below – at least – may be identified. In attempting to interpret the concept of continuity, it should be noted that we have deliberately avoided referring to the notion of the *Continuum* that is used to describe the experience offered across the International Baccalaureate programmes. We do so because, while a number of authors here have focused exclusively on the IB programmes, others have – with our encouragement – considered issues of continuity relating to other programmes offered in the wider international education context. In that sense, for us, the IB Continuum represents one aspect of the broader concept of continuity which may be found in the sphere of international education.

Continuity and learning

Much of the debate here understandably points to the importance of continuity in the planning and implementation of a programme of student learning – after all, that's what schools are for! The notion of planned continuity in relation to the learning experienced throughout primary and secondary education is entirely consistent with what learning theorists have long professed. Effective passage from one stage of the acquisition of knowledge and skills into the succeeding stage is promoted by a clear understanding, at each stage of development, of learning that has already taken place and of the nature of the learning in which the student will next be engaged. Although such learning will often be planned on a longitudinal time basis, a version of continuity (linked with coherence and consistency) relates to the concurrency of learning within each stage of development – *ie* across the differing knowledge, skills and understandings in which the students are engaged at any one time, whether in school as part of the formal curriculum, or resulting from the totality of their learning through home, the community and the wider world (if only through the media) – a kind of 'holistic continuity'. The IB learner profile is an example of intended continuity in learning experience.

Continuity and pedagogy

Closely aligned to continuity and learning is the need for continuity in respect of the pedagogy that is offered to students to support their learning. At some stages of their learning in particular, continuity in teaching styles may be wholly advantageous, but that is not to say that continuity in pedagogy necessarily implies homogeneity in teaching approaches, chronologically or laterally. It does, however, require that the teaching presented is planned carefully to guide the development of student learning and, as such, may be characterised by deliberate heterogeneity across the differing knowledge and skills within subject areas and the acquisition of learning in the wider experiences of the formal education system. An important aspect of all three IB programmes since their inception has been the notion of the *concurrency of learning*, in which the curriculum is planned deliberately to engage learners in quite differing disciplines, with a variety of knowledge and skills, within the same time period – raising issues of interdisciplinarity and transdisciplinarity. It clearly has crucial significance for the challenge of organising pedagogy in relation to continuity.

Continuity and curriculum connectedness

The well-rehearsed distinctions used by curriculum developers in relation to the designed/delivered/learned curriculum (or other terms used to describe the same or very similar concepts) implies continuity of yet another kind. It is related to the importance of maintaining continuity in respect of the underpinning values and aims of the curriculum at each stage of its development, necessitating constant reference back, in designing and implementing new programmes in school, to the fundamental principles governing the curriculum. It is also related to fitness-for-purpose and to validity and consistency. The IB's current activity in respect of the development of the learner profile across all of its programmes is a clear expression of a search for an aspect of continuity which protects those underlying values at each stage of the separate programmes.

Continuity and improvement/progression

The importance of students, as well as teachers and parents, being able to recognise improvement in learning introduces the necessity of a form of continuity in the assessment and evaluation regimes in use. Benchmarking is an obvious example of establishing a foundation for the evaluation of achievement against which evidence of progress in the realisation of learning objectives may be collected and disseminated, which for comparative purposes will necessitate a form of continuity that is explicit and understood by all involved.

Continuity and stability

A dimension of continuity at a whole institutional level is concerned with generating, within the entire stakeholder group, a level of confidence that the appropriate quality assurance measures are not only in place but also have abiding characteristics in terms of the principles upon which the institution is based. That is not to imply that interpretation of such a form of continuity is tantamount to stagnation, for as the institution develops so will the practical ways by which those stable, fundamental principles are protected and enhanced. A further dimension of continuity relating to the notion of stability arises for those globally mobile children (sometimes described as Third Culture Kids) whose family circumstances are such that they frequently change schools and countries – with stability of educational experience varying according to the school and the programmes available in their various relocations. Stability through quality assurance and quality control systems is also evident in the numerous independent accreditation regimes used by schools. In the case of the IB, the authorisation and re-authorisation of schools to teach the IB programmes serves a similar quality assurance purpose.

These differing interpretations of continuity are by no means exhaustive, nor is any claim being made that they are discrete; quite clearly there are overlaps between them. They simply arise as significant aspects of continuity from our work with practitioners over many years.

In generating this book we have been privileged to work with a group of authors who have been willing to share with readers their reflections and views arising from wide experience with programmes of international education in general, and with the IB programmes in particular. They have also, unsurprisingly in respect of the range of interpretations of the concept of continuity, chosen to highlight differing aspects of the topic. Acknowledging the range of interpretations that the term 'continuity' generates (some of which have been identified in the brief exemplars above), for the purposes of this publication we, as editors, have chosen to organise the various contributions into three distinct, though clearly related, groups of chapters.

Thus our contributors to **Part A** of this book (Dimensions of Continuity) have each identified a major dimension of continuity which all those who have responsibility for designing international curricula at primary and secondary school levels are encouraged to consider. All represent quite fundamental features of any programme that aims to promote an understanding of international mindedness and intercultural understanding, and do so on the basis that such aspects are capable of development over time and across a range of contexts, given appropriate institutional support for the establishment of a positive learning environment. In **Part B** (Supporting Continuity), those contributing have taken up the themes of context and of support for those responsible for the implementation of programme continuity within the school, which involves an appreciation of context and the roles of leaders and appropriately trained teachers in the process. **Part C** (Programme Transitions in IB) comprises three contributions illustrating the specific processes of transition between selected IB programmes, drawing on the wide experience of the authors. These mini case studies not only link many of the fundamental topics arising in earlier chapters, but also introduce new dimensions, including brain research, and their implications for planning the transitions between separate programmes.

Across all three parts of this book it will be noted that chapters have generally been written as though for an audience who are already familiar with the context in which they are set. For those who are not so familiar with the context, background information may be found via, *inter alia*, the websites of the International Baccalaureate, International Primary Curriculum, International Middle Years Curriculum and Cambridge International Examinations IGCSE.

To all contributors we offer our gratitude for their forbearance with the length and nature of the editorial process. One of the most satisfying aspects of undertaking editorial work in the production of a book of this kind is the academic and professional learning that we, as editors, gain as a result of the interaction with such experienced and committed colleagues. Our appreciation for the high level of support we have received most certainly extends to our colleagues at John Catt, with whom it has been a pleasure to work. Our own efforts, and those of the authors and publishers, will have been justified if those who read the contributions within this book find both encouragement to add their own views to the debate, and inspiration in making effective continuity a reality within their own institutions.

Mary Hayden

Jeff Thompson

Further Reading

International Baccalaureate: www.ibo.org

International GCSE (IGCSE): www.cie.org.uk/qualifications/academic/middlesec/igcse/overview

International Middle Years Curriculum: www.greatlearning.com/imyc

International Primary Curriculum: www.greatlearning.com/ipc

Part A
Dimensions of Continuity

Chapter 1

Teaching thinking skills K–12

Nick Alchin

While it is not the business of education to prove every statement made, any more than to teach every possible item of information, it is its business to cultivate deep seated and effective habits of discriminating tested beliefs from mere assertions, guesses and opinion: to develop a lively, sincere and open minded preference for conclusions that are properly grounded, and to ingrain into the individual's working habits methods of inquiry and reasoning appropriate to the various problems that present themselves.

(Dewey, 1910: 27-28)

Introduction

Recent attention to 'teaching kids to think' is not new. It goes back many centuries, and finds clear and frequent expression in the writings of Socrates, Voltaire, Lao Tze, Plutarch, Tagore and many other educators and philosophers, especially since Enlightenment times (at least in the West). Dewey's quote is eloquent, but not especially novel. There are, however, three new factors that mean 'thinking skills' are of particular interest now.

The first is a narrow economic motivation to teach thinking skills. Once regarded as a good in its own right, or perhaps the necessary component for democratic participation, it is now also seen as necessary for economic success both for individuals and for nation states as a whole. The emergence of the 'knowledge society' makes this economic imperative a very powerful one, and then UK Prime Minister Tony Blair's sentiment expressed at the Knowledge 2000 conference – "Knowledge and skills ... are the ways by which the winners will win in the new economy" – has been heard many times from politicians of all persuasions across the world. For this reason alone, many national and international curricula now give explicit and prominent place to critical thinking, lifelong learning or higher-order thinking skills (we will examine these more carefully below).

The second, related factor is that the world is facing profoundly complex environmental, cultural and social problems which, it is frequently argued, will not be solved without the highest levels of thinking from leaders and specialists, or without an active and engaged citizenship which requires individuals to be able to assimilate, interpret and judge information from a number of competing and contradictory sources. Opening any newspaper confirms this common-place observation.

The third factor is the explosion in research from and findings in the converging disciplines of cognitive psychology, neuro-anatomy and (arguably) epistemology (see for example Kahneman (2011), Pinker (1996), Damasio (2006), and Dweck (2006)) which have done much to clarify our understanding of the central term 'thinking' and surrounding issues such as motivation, emotion and decision-making. Without underestimating the huge challenges ahead, it is fair to say that we have in the last 40 years begun to make significant advances, for the first time based on solid evidence, into how humans think.

Different drivers motivate different people at different times, and we all tend to pick and mix according to our audience; in his now famous TED talk, Ken Robinson (2010) strikingly grounded his *humanistic* appeal for encouraging creativity in an *economic* argument, asking "How do we educate our children to take their places in the economies of the 21st century, given that we cannot anticipate what the economies will look like at the end of next week?" Whether for pragmatic or idealistic reasons, taken together therefore, these drivers reflect a consensus between educators, politicians and employers that we are still facing what Resnick (1987) called 'a new challenge to develop educational programmes that assume all individuals, not just an elite, can become competent thinkers'.

The following points are, I suggest, widely if not unanimously agreed among a wide range of thinkers:

- The ability to think well and think deeply over a range of issues is one profound mark of human flourishing, and should be pursued in its own right.

- The 'banking model' of learning (where teachers deposit information into students' mental accounts) is deeply uncreative and deeply alienating to some students who do not flourish under it, and for whom education seems to have little relevance.

- This banking theory of learning, based on filling students with facts, is no longer tenable – as there is simply too much to learn. A shift from the *content* of learning to the *process* of learning is, therefore, necessary.

- The complexity of modern working life and the emergence of new jobs and careers requires individuals who can comfortably generate, adapt to and work with new information and ideas rather than stick to the known and familiar.

- The rapid pace of technological innovation and social change means that, without these individuals, a state can find its industries and workers no longer relevant in a global marketplace.

- We now know enough about the biological and psychological process of learning to be able to develop programmes that will allow learners to think better.

- Intelligence is no longer to be understood along static, unitary lines; there are several partially independent intelligences, and these are not fixed but can change over time.

The differing motivations for addressing thinking skills have, naturally, manifested in many different approaches, and even in 1990 there were over 100 such programmes in the USA alone (Nisbet, 1990). The aim in this chapter is not to explore the variety, but to consider some key issues for educators. In the next section we start by exploring the meaning of the central term 'thinking skills', before going on to see if and how these skills can be taught, and what teachers and schools should bear in mind as they attempt to do so. The focus in the latter sections on school programmes is more devoted to approaches and practices than to developmental aspects of students' thinking abilities, though there is clearly some linkage there.

How do views of mind and of learning underpin approaches to thinking skills?

Detailed exploration is beyond the scope of this chapter, but three important and inter-related ideas are needed to inform any discussion of thinking and learning; these are the constructivist model of learning, the multi-valenced notion of intelligence, and the idea that intelligence is malleable.

Piaget argued that the development of the ability to think is akin to a physical process of growth, and just as we grow to a height largely pre-determined by our genes, so cognitive skill unfolds in a developmental manner, to a set level. This view is consistent with a belief in a unitary general-purpose cognitive ability, initially described by Binet in the early 19th century as 'g', the pre-cursor to IQ. In many quarters, however, the focus has moved to social constructivist views, under which learning is seen as less of an unfolding and more of a construction; as a process of individuals making meaning with a community of co-participants. Under this approach, thinking is situated more in, and depends on, specific contexts, than it is determined by innate ability (Bredo, 2005). This view is entirely consistent with a move from a belief in a unitary general cognitive ability to a belief in multiple, largely independent intelligences – as different communities (whether these are conceived as subject specialists, classrooms or schools) will situate knowledge in different ways. Gardner (2005) writes 'We have come to believe that … [t]here is no 'pure potential' apart from some experience in working with a domain or symbol system' (p. 104).

The debate about unitary or multiple intelligences, and the implications for learning (if any) are not settled (see Willington, 2009, or Bransford, Brown & Cocking, 2002 for terrific summaries for teachers). However what is settled, at least amongst cognitive psychologists, is the belief that intelligence is malleable. While people clearly differ in intelligence, intelligence can be changed through hard work; it not fixed genetically. Darwin, of all people, was onto something when he stressed attitude over innate ability: 'men [do] not differ much in intellect, only in zeal and hard work'. Dozens of studies have found that high flyers across all disciplines learn no more quickly than those who reach lower levels of attainment – hour after hour, they improve at almost identical rates. This is a remarkable finding. High achievers do not, in general, initially learn more quickly than others; the difference is simply that high achievers spend more time talking, reading or practising in their chosen area (the evidence from Dweck (2006) should be required reading for all teachers and parents) and so develop their capacities and intelligences in such a way as to end up far more able than their peers.

The implications from these three ideas are important. They suggest that thinking skills are (a) alterable – they are not likely to be determined by a single, unalterable fixed level of intelligence; (b) closely entwined in the contexts in which they are found; and (c) about more than just intellectual prowess. So let's now consider exactly what these skills might be.

What are thinking skills?

The literature on the precise nature of thinking skills is large. There are many taxonomies (*eg* Lipman, 1991; Wilson, 2000; Scriven, 2004) which overlap to varying degrees. A particularly broad characterisation is given by Paul and Elder (2002, see Figure 1); Paul and Elder structure the model around the application of *standards* to certain *elements* to develop particular *traits*. This neat model often speaks to educators who are used to overarching standards for any curriculum area. Critical thinkers routinely apply the intellectual standards to the elements of reasoning in order to develop intellectual traits.

Any one of Paul and Elder's *standards*, *elements* or *traits* could be explored in great detail, but at a general level we can say that this and other characterisations converge on the imprecise notion that a critical thinker is one who can effectively generate, analyse and process information and, importantly, who has the dispositions and drives to do so. It is not our purpose here to explore this or any other specific model, but it is helpful to ground the discussion by making some distinctions based on a graded set of examples as follows:

1. Alex wants to be told what to do, and while he is bodily present in class his active mind is elsewhere. He does not behave poorly in the traditional sense, and is quick and able enough in conversation about general matters, but he does not care much for school, and simply never brings the spotlight of his attention to bear on the ideas he encounters in lessons. To say that he finds it difficult is not quite right – as the term *difficulty* suggests some struggle.

2. Beatrice is a highly motivated student who is eager to do well. She engages well with the ideas, and in any discursive class quickly takes a very strong position on any issue. Once she has taken a position she argues for it against other students even if it becomes clear that the

position is no longer tenable. She is, however, very quick to change her mind in an effort to reach the 'right answer' when a teacher even gently questions her views.

3. Clarence is focused, wants to succeed, and can complete good work in a structured environment. He struggles, however, to master overall principles. His ideas and skills are discrete and not joined up to form a coherent body on which he can successfully draw as needed.

4. Delfina can master ideas in one classroom setting but is unable to apply them in another. For example, she is a fine student of mathematics who cannot consistently or independently use ratios or solve equations in the science labs.

5. Edwin appears to master all the ideas he encounters. His school grades are good, but he has little confidence. When asked about novel problems he does not know how to begin, and in discussion is quick to make it clear that 'he never really got it anyway'.

6. Francis is gifted in a single subject; he has mastered a wide range of ideas, the principles behind them, and is able to routinely apply them to a variety of familiar and novel problems in a deliberate way. In his subject, he is aware of the sorts of errors he makes, always checks his own

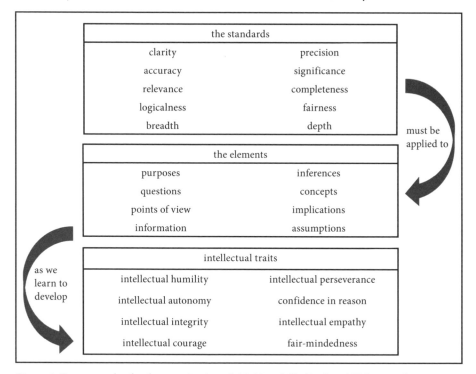

Figure 1: One example of a characterisation of thinking skills (Paul and Elder, 2002)

thinking and monitors himself against the standards he has internalised. He also tries, with mixed success, to apply the principles of his area elsewhere, though he recognises that this is not always going to work.

The students in this list, familiar to all experienced teachers, illustrate some important points:

- Alex and Beatrice both demonstrate that thinking is not just about cognitive ability but also about specific attitudes and dispositions toward thought; these attitudes and dispositions are in fact gateways to the mansions of thought. Alex's lack of motivation, and Beatrice's dogmatism and deference (a more common combination than is usually appreciated, in my view) are strong barriers to developing thinking skills.

- We recognise that Alex might be a great chess player but also an academically failing student, and that Francis might be a great historian but a hopeless artist; that is, that there are independent *domains of expertise*. In academic settings we tend to call these *subjects* or *disciplines* and they represent powerful ways of thinking which transcend specific facts or skills. Clarence is struggling to master his discipline and is, in this respect, the traditional struggling student.

- From a thinking skills perspective, Delfina and Edwin might be just as weak as Clarence, even though they may all look very different in traditional school settings. Delfina and Edwin cannot *transfer* the skills learned in one area to another; Delfina between subjects, Edwin when there is a new problem in a single subject.

Mapping these issues to conceptualisations such as those of Paul and Elder is difficult, and is perhaps one reason why thinking skills are often not embedded in school practices. Schools often look less at these models and more at issues that naturally emerge in school; one such issue is *transfer* – the ability to use one's abilities to solve new problems, rather than merely routine ones. Clearly a central part of thinking skills, it is, however, a problematic term. McCormick (1999) suggests that a pre-condition for transfer to take place is 'a match between the situation where the learning took place and the situation where the knowledge is used'. In one sense this is obvious; if there's no match, then there can be no basis on which to apply the ideas from one area to another. But near-transfer, when the match is extremely close, is not very meaningful (in the extreme case, 'transfer' from solving $2x+1=5$ to $4x+3=15$ is not really transfer, though it may be a small step in that direction) and far-transfer seems by definition to require relatively little match between the two areas – that's precisely why it is genuine transfer. The concept is, therefore, not straightforward, and it has been suggested that instead of talking about transfer *per se*, we should instead identify aspects of thought that underline all intellectual inquiry, and focus on these; such a focus would support and encourage transfer. This leads straight back to the difficult conceptualisations such as the one above, which schools find so hard to deal with. And while there are different models around, there does seem to be consensus around the notion of a core of key skills such as 'evaluating evidence', 'sound reasoning', 'and 'planning and setting goals' (McGuinness, 1999). We do, however, need to be careful that these do not lead us back to a simplistic version of a single underlying notion of intelligence, which we know is wrong. So transfer is crucial from a theoretical standpoint – but also pragmatically, transfer must be the ultimate aim of all teaching in school; firstly because students in school can only learn a tiny part of what is known; and secondly because a student who can only do precisely what they have been taught has a very bleak future. Various attempts by educators to reconcile the tensions here are the subject of the next section.

Before moving on though, it is worth stressing that the ability to transfer skills is very slippery, even from inside the classroom to just outside. Schoenfeld (1988) describes a mathematics question in a US national assessment: 'How many buses does the army need to transport 1,128 soldiers if each bus holds 36 soldiers?' That one third of eighth graders answered '31 remainder 12' shows how their ability to do division is divorced from the real issue at hand. Nor is it always easier for those who are expert. Gardner describes this vividly with respect to the MIT physics graduates who, when asked on graduation day, make basic errors on simple questions about the forces on the mortar boards they are throwing so gleefully into the air; he also describes the literature students who, though successful in their undergraduate courses, are unable to distinguish between the poems of Donne and another hack local poet except on the basis of their rhyming schemes. Such examples can be found 'from astronomy to zoology … in societies all over the world … neither Americans nor Asians nor Europeans are immune' (Gardner, 2006). Transfer from one setting to another, is very, very difficult. Gardner describes this as 'the most important scientific discovery about learning in recent years' (Gardner, 2006) because it shows that even apparent experts are often more like Clarence, Delphina or Edwin and less like Francis then we might have thought. And this is, note, experts even *within* a single given domain of expertise (the MIT physicists for example); we are not even talking about the complex multi-faceted problems mentioned in the introduction. Gardner's well-known work in education is perfectly consistent with psychological research which points to a whole set of cognitive heuristics and biases which appear to be hardwired and common across all cultures, genders and ages. Kahneman (2009), the leading psychologist in the field, has established, on the basis of decades of experimentation, that we cannot change these cognitive characteristics – they are part of the human condition; the best we can do is to be aware of them and hope to catch the errors we are bound to make. That is, Gardner and Kahneman both point us at the crucial role of metacognition and self-regulation.

This makes the case of Francis, the expert, extremely revealing. At first sight he might appear somewhat narrow, with excellent thinking skills in his own area and limited ability elsewhere. But his narrow skill-set is deep, and he is conscious of the sorts of errors he makes (the old philosophical injunction 'know thyself' takes on a new cognitive meaning here). So while he is not a polymathic genius, it is the *combination* of his (perhaps narrow) expertise with his ability to self-monitor, and to think about his thinking (that is, his ability to think metacognitively), that form the basis of what are highly developed thinking skills. If it is transfer we are looking for then we have to remember that there *has to be something to transfer* – that is, perhaps rather than seek a broad cognitive competence (*eg* 'consider competing points of view fairly', 'seek logical consistency') we should instead focus on some narrow expertise which we then seek to apply outside the usual domain. Without this subject-specific expertise, perhaps there would be little point in even seeking transfer. But to broaden from narrow expertise to broader application is not enough; transfer does not happen automatically, and this is where Francis's metacognitive ability (itself dependent on his subject-specific ability) is so important. Because he has mastered the ideas and methods of his subject so thoroughly and so consciously, he is well able to reflect on his own thinking, and to try to transfer his expertise to areas where it is not obviously applicable.

The combination of transfer and domain-specific knowledge is captured well by the developing notions of *transdisciplinarity* and *interdisciplinarity*, which are in practice how thinking skills programmes seek to promote transfer (distinctions between these and other similar terms are contested, and space prevents exploration here). Klein and Newell (1988) define the latter as a process that addresses 'a topic that is too broad or complex to be dealt with adequately by a single discipline' but that 'draws on disciplinary perspectives and integrates their insights through construction of a more comprehensive perspective'. Interdisciplinarity is perhaps itself an appropriately interdisciplinary concept (!), bridging as it does familiar traditional (but sometimes fuzzy) ideas of a cross-curricular approach with the new epistemology of thinking skills. It is a significant advance; similar ideas can also be seen in a number of other writers (see, for example Fauconnier and Turner, 2002), and thinking skills are in some quarters evolving from a focus on transfer toward a focus on interdisciplinarity. This more recent interpretation, with its emphasis on connectivity and on new perspectives, is in keeping with broader cultural zeitgeists and technological advances. Of course this trajectory of thought tells us a lot about our philosophy, but not a lot about school implementation. It is now to this aspect we turn.

What approaches to teaching thinking skills are there?

I am conscious that some educational trends catch the imagination, seem very popular for a short time but do not stand the test of time – whether tested by statistical improvement in attainment as measured by controlled experiment, or consistent, cross-cultural anecdotal evidence. The Learning Styles movement, for example, once *de rigueur*, now seems increasingly unable to find theoretical or empirical underpinning (Coffield, 2004, or Willington, 2009) and many variants of the popular Brain Gym are now wholly discredited.

Given the evidence reviewed above about the difficulty of transfer, it is hardly surprising that there is no programme that reduces thinking skills to a core set of clearly defined skills that can be as easily measured as one can measure simple recall of facts.

That said, extensive data collected around the world over the last four decades does very strongly suggest that, in several instances, thinking skills programmes do manage to achieve long-term transfer – where mathematics programmes improve attainment in language, for example. It is extremely interesting that under some programmes, while little or no immediate improvement in achievement is shown, very strong and significant effects are often seen several years later, in several disparate curriculum areas. It is this delayed benefit, and the breadth of this benefit (against control groups), that supports the claims of proponents of these programmes that far transfer and genuine cognitive advancement have taken place, because it is only if an intervention can improve the ability to think and learn – that is, the thinking skills themselves – that subsequent instruction can be made more effective.

There has been much debate over the relative merits of two types of programme:

- *Standalone curriculum-programmes* which seek to address general, sometimes de-contextualised skills.

- *Infused curriculum-programmes* which focus on developing skills in regular classroom contexts, through domain-specific skills and/or interdisciplinary approaches.

Fortunately, we can move on from this debate; reviewing 56 studies of thinking skills programmes, Cotton (1991) found that around half of the effective programmes were of each type. Either approach can and does work, and we now turn to specific methods and programmes.

The Philosophy for Children movement

The Philosophy for Children (P4C) movement (resources are available for K-12: see Figure 2) is based around the belief that thinking skills are like the skills of riding a bicycle: students must learn by doing, not by being told how to do, or by reading from a book. Thus students 'do' philosophy, rather than learn about philosophers. Lipman follows John Dewey's belief that in education we often confuse the refined, finished, end products of inquiry with the raw, crude subject matter of inquiry, and that we make the mistake of encouraging students to learn the solutions rather than investigate the problems and engage in inquiry itself. Lipman also argues that because thinking skills are a tool, they can be misused like a tool, and so it is important that we teach the skills in the context of a humanistic discipline that is committed to the furtherance of significant but problematic concepts. He suggests that the appropriate discipline is philosophy which, he argues, is to the teaching of thinking skills what literature is to the teaching of reading and writing.

THE CURRICULUM FOR EARLY CHILDHOOD

Reasoning about Personhood: *The Doll Hospital*   Reasoning about Language: *Geraldo*

THE CURRICULUM FOR PRIMARY SCHOOL

Reasoning about Thinking: *Elfie*   Reasoning about Nature: *Kio and Gus*

Reasoning about Language: *Pixie*   Reasoning about Ethics: *Nous*

THE CURRICULUM FOR SECONDARY SCHOOL

Reasoning in Ethics: *Lisa*   Reasoning about Reasoning:
Harry Stottlemeier's Discovery

Reasoning in Social Studies: *Mark*   Reasoning in Language Arts: *Suki*

Accompanying guides for teachers are available for each book.

Figure 2: the Philosophy for Children Series

The programme is based around a set of highly structured 'novels' written at age-appropriate levels. [The texts are available from the Institute for the Advancement of Philosophy for Children, Montclair State University (http://cehs.montclair.edu/academic/iapc)]. The novels contain dilemmas of rationality, ethics, aesthetics, science and civic values, have been translated into over 40 languages, and are used in over 60 countries. Set in fictional contexts, the stories raise dilemmas via the context of children's lives and lead to class discussions mediated by the teacher. The point of class discussion is to externalise the reasoning for the class, and particularly for the students themselves. The programme is delivered over a long time span and is progressive in complexity. An extensive and highly detailed teacher's guide accompanies each novel (each guide is around 400 pages in length), giving several concrete activities to help guide the discussions which follow reading a chapter. Though different novels have subject-specific foci (reasoning in science, arts, language, ethics, social studies), these are seen as expressions of domain-general reasoning through different contexts rather than as distinctly different types of reasoning. The programme was awarded 'national validity' by the US State Department in 1986.

Studies suggest that P4C is very popular with students who have taken it – though, interestingly, the few dissenting voices are from those children who are usually considered to be academically successful in the traditional sense. They are 'puzzled and resentful when they realise that philosophical questions are not amenable to simple or straightforward answers. Such children have unfortunately been trained to perceive educational value only in what can be examined and tested' (Coles and Robinson, 1991).

Research Evidence from Philosophy for Children

Experiment one: Lipman taught one class for 18 lessons of 40 minutes (Lipman *et al.*, 1980). Against a control group, students made a gain of '27 months of attainment' on standardised tests and went on to score significantly higher on a standard reading test two years later.

Experiment two: In a larger follow-up in New Jersey, 400 students in grades 5–8 were given Philosophy for Children for two-and-a-quarter hours each week. Teachers were given two hours in-service training each week (Adey and Shayer, 1993a). Post-test results showed highly significant gains against control groups, not only in reasoning but also in reading and mathematics. Unfortunately there was no long-term follow up here.

Experiment three: A validation project on 2,000 students (Sharron and Coulter, 1994) shows that, compared with control children, large gains after one year were made in mathematics, larger gains were made in English and even larger ones were made in reasoning.

These results have been replicated in other countries including Iceland (Sigurborsdottir, 1998) and in other subjects such as science (Sprod, 1998). Of particular significance is the delayed and broad improvement across the curriculum. Further, the improvements are also supported by the professional qualitative judgements by teachers familiar with the specific contexts of the students. The conclusion from Lane and Lane (1986) is typical:

> The results indicated a significant improvement for formal reasoning and in creative reasoning (the capacity to generate new ideas, to discover feasible alternatives and to provide reasons). The overall impact in improving reading and mathematics was found to be significant. The teacher's appraisal was that children were markedly more curious, better oriented towards their work, more considerate of one another, better able to reason, and that their communication skills increased. (p. 271)

The Cognitive Acceleration Movement

This project, initiated at King's College London, addresses both generic and subject-specific thinking skills. The most well-known programmes are the three Cognitive Acceleration in Science, Mathematics and Technology Education programmes (CASE, CAME and CATE respectively). Each consists of a set of practical activities for use with early secondary school students and very detailed (minute-by minute), almost scripted, lesson plans. Adey and Shayer (1993a) identify five central aspects to the movement, each of which is directly observable in each lesson plan:

- *Schema theory*. A schema is a general way of thinking that can be applied to many different contexts. CASE and CAME focus on ideas such as conservation, causality, classification, probability, ratio, proportion, variation – which, it is argued, must be internalised for significant progress, and are thus worthy of special attention.

- *Concrete preparation*. The students encounter the schema through a specific intellectual problem before explicitly identifying the schema.

- *Cognitive conflict*. Students should find new ideas puzzling as they realise that their existing mental schema are not adequate to cope with both ideas already known and the new stimulus. Students are then forced to construct a solution to the problem, leading to the next stage. [Working to create cognitive conflict is a delicate business; some puzzling ideas can be simply shrugged off as odd, or as errors, or perhaps not even seen as puzzling.] In practice, this stage will likely merge with the next, and Adey and Shayer (*ibid*) describe the two stages as 'the hammer and anvil... from which intellectual growth is shaped'.

- *Construction*. The programmes here are explicitly based in social constructivism; that is, on the basis that understanding often takes place in the social space that learners share, and is then internalised by individuals. For teachers this points to both (a) the skilled art of not telling but hinting, and allowing students to 'get it' themselves, and (b) the need to create a practice of free polylogues with peers, teasing out understanding of explanations, of articulations of difficulties and so on (like P4C).

- *Metacognition*. Throughout the activities, teachers are prompted to discuss strategies as well as ideas, and to ask questions like "why was it that this was difficult and how did you solve it?"

- *Bridging* (or in the vocabulary used here, *transfer*). At the end of each lesson, the teachers lead whole-class exploration of any general thinking skills and link them to other areas of the students' experience, including other subject areas.

Research Evidence from Adey and Shayer (1993a and 1993b)

Experiment one: CASE was implemented for two years with classes from several UK schools; in each case control classes were also run. After the two years the classes were mixed up and the individual students tracked through to GCSE (the General Certificate of Secondary Education, usually completed at age 16).

- There were some significant gains immediately after the experiments, but the biggest gains came three years afterwards, at GCSE in science, mathematics and English.

- While two thirds of the students showed significant improvements, one third showed little or no improvement over the control group. This third was not drawn particularly from either the weaker or the stronger students; there is no obvious explanation as to why some students 'took' to CASE and some did not.

Experiment two: In this experiment a whole year group undertook CAME, being taught in rotation and thus minimising teacher effects. Based on control groups, the number of students reaching the highest levels of formal thinking was expected to be 7.4% (boys) and 5.6% (girls), but actually turned out to be 19.2% (boys) and 22.9% (girls).

Experiment three: After a two-year trial, the proportion of students entering Year 9 with formal operational ability (*ie* abstract reasoning skills) was raised from 23% to 60%. The number of GCSE 'C' grades attained two years later rose from 35% to 58%. Here it is the *delayed* benefit, and the benefits in several subjects, that offer strong support for far-transfer and genuine cognitive advancement (one class showed almost no immediate gain but significant gain three years later).

The Understanding by Design Movement

The Understanding by Design (UbD) movement, originating in the USA, is quite different to the other approaches discussed here, and is widely used in US schools, districts, universities and other educational organisations. It also underpins the International Baccalaureate Primary Years Programme (PYP) and Middle Years Programme (MYP) approaches detailed below. UbD is not an approach to teaching, nor is it a school programme or a set of resources. Instead, it is an approach to *planning* for teaching. And so it says little about teaching styles, activities and so on, and it does not require a belief in any single pedagogical system or approach. Instead, it focuses on *understanding*; which is defined as a multifaceted ability to 'wisely and effectively *use* – transfer – what we know' in a flexible, thoughtful way (Wiggins and McTighe, 2006). That is, it is entirely focused on developing in students the ability to apply things learned in one context to another; which is, as we have seen, at the core of thinking skills.

The UbD method is a three step process:

- *Identifying desired learning outcomes.* We start with the end in mind, and ask 'what do we want students to know?' Recognising that we can only ever teach a tiny fraction of the known, the UbD method is to identify and address the essential ideas which are at the heart of deep, enduring understandings of value beyond the specific topic at hand, and which, it is argued, support transfer.

  A big idea is typically manifest as a helpful:

  - *Concept* (*eg* adaptation, function, perspective)
  - *Theme* (*eg* 'good triumphs over evil', 'coming of age')
  - *Ongoing debate* (*eg* nature vs nurture, conservatives vs liberals)
  - *Paradox* (*eg* freedom must have limits, leaving home to find oneself)
  - *Theory* (*eg* evolution via natural selection, manifest destiny)

- *Underlying assumption* (eg texts have meaning, markets are rational)
- *Recurring Question* (*eg* 'is that fair?', 'how do we know?', 'can we prove it?')
- *Understanding or Principle* (*eg* form follows function, correlation does not ensure causation)

(adapted from Wiggins and McTighe, 2006)

> Note that there is no tension here between these concepts and traditional content; the challenge for teachers is to structure a curriculum in such a way that the concepts arise from the content and infuse it with meaning, thus developing in students the chance to see underlying structures.

- *Determine acceptable evidence.* Having identified the ideas, UbD asks 'how will we know if the students have understood?' The UbD conception of understanding means we need to give students the opportunity to explain, interpret, apply, and reflect on the ideas; this means a variety of assessment tasks and strategies may be necessary.

- *Plan learning experiences and instruction.* Sometimes for teachers, this comes first: we know what are 'good activities'. Following the UbD method means we delay this until we know, explicitly, what learning outcomes we want, and how we will know if students have achieved them – because until these are defined, we cannot know what enabling knowledge (facts, concepts, principles) and skills (processes, procedures, strategies) are needed; in fact, we cannot know if any teaching activity is indeed good or not.

Put in this simple form, the logic behind the planning process seems obvious and, even to those new to UbD, familiar. What makes UbD so powerful are the detailed structures and guidance to help teachers follow the steps, which in practice are quite complex, and which can cause even experienced teachers to have to re-think what they do. The many books and websites available (see, for example, www.ubdexchange.org) offer a great deal of theoretical and practical support to teachers and administrators who wish to implement this approach.

Research Evidence from UbD

McTighe and Seif (2003) argued that since UbD does not have an articulated 'scope and sequence' of skills or prescribed teaching activities, it was 'impossible at this time to provide direct, causal evidence of its effect on student achievement'. However, it is clearly possible to design an experiment where controlled groups are taught similar ideas by the same teacher, one in UbD style, and another using more traditional methods; with detailed control, this should yield useful data. As far as I am aware such a study has not been undertaken, which is disappointing.

In the absence of such data the sustained growth of the movement, in what is an era of intense scrutiny, counts for something, and there is no shortage of anecdotal stories. McTighe and Seif (2003) also argue that very strong evidence is provided by the close match between UbD, current psychological understandings, other validated approaches, the Trends in International Mathematics and Science Study (TIMSS) and various research findings. These are described in detail in their paper, and the close coherences found and described there, as well as the experiences of professional educators, counts very strongly in favour of UbD as an extremely powerful tool.

The Four Programmes of the International Baccalaureate

We have not yet discussed whether approaches to thinking skills should differ according to the developmental age of the student. This is a particularly salient question for the International Baccalaureate, which offers four programmes to students of all abilities from K-12 (see www.ibo.org for overviews of each programme). The four IB programmes do somewhat differ in their approach, though there are some degrees of similarity, and an IB Continuum is in the process of being articulated with increasing precision and coherence. Ongoing emphasis on the centrality of the cross-programme IB learner profile – a set of 10 attributes that all IB learners should strive to develop – is instructive, as it contains traditional cognitive and affective attributes such as *knowledgeable* and *caring*, metacognitive aspects such as *reflective* and *open-minded* and also an explicit thinking skill as students are encouraged to be inquirers. That we can see very significant thinking skills aspects in all IB programmes is, therefore, hardly surprising.

The IB Primary Years Programme (PYP)

The PYP curriculum, for students of up to 11 years of age, distinguishes between the written curriculum, taught curriculum and assessed curriculum. Thinking skills are infused across all three, and are also particularly situated in the PYP Exhibition.

- **The written curriculum** consists of five elements, with clear elements of thinking skills embedded in each:
    - *Knowledge* is structured and conveyed not through traditional subject disciplines, but according to six transdisciplinary themes (*who we are; where we are in place and time; how we express ourselves; how the world works; how we organise ourselves; sharing the planet*). Schools develop their own programme of inquiry by approaching traditional content though the lens of one of these themes.
    - *Concepts* which cut across the transdisciplinary themes promote the exploration and re-exploration of important ideas; as these have application in any theme they should promote transfer and creative

31

thinking. The IB identifies concepts of *form, function, causation, change, connection, perspective, responsibility and reflection,* which are embedded across the PYP (in IB subject guides, and most importantly in schools' lines of inquiry); students will encounter them again and again in different guises but, understandably for this age group, not address them as abstract ideas themselves.

– *Skills* are explicitly identified as being taught in the context of the themes. While a list of specific thinking skills is explicitly identified (see Figure 3), this localisation is rather misleading as these skills appear elsewhere, as indicated. Also, equally important in light of considerations above are the other skills articulated alongside: social skills, communications skills, self-management skills and research skills.

– *Attitudes* are listed, and this affective component is a central part of both thinking skills and PYP. These are appreciation, commitment, confidence, co-operation, creativity, curiosity, empathy, enthusiasm, independence, integrity, respect and tolerance.

– *Action* might normally be considered as not directly related to thinking, but designed to 'extend the student's learning, or ... have a wider social impact' (IB 2009) and, being structured around a *reflect-choose-act*

	PYP Transdisciplinary Thinking Skills
Acquisition of knowledge	Gaining specific facts, ideas, vocabulary; remembering in a similar form.
Comprehension	Grasping meaning from material learned; communicating and interpreting learning.
Application	Making use of previously acquired knowledge in practical or new ways.
Analysis	Taking knowledge or ideas apart; separating into component parts; seeing relationships; finding unique characteristics.
Synthesis	Combining parts to create wholes; creating, designing, developing and innovating.
Evaluation	Making judgments or decisions based on chosen criteria; standards and conditions.
Dialectical thought	Thinking about two or more different points of view at the same time; understanding those points of view; being able to construct an argument for each point of view based on knowledge of the other(s); realizing that other people can also take one's own point of view.
Metacognition	Analysing one's own and others' thought processes; thinking about how one thinks and how one learns.

Figure 3: PYP Transdisciplinary Thinking Skills (IB, 2009)

model in the real world, there are clear metacognitive and affective aspects which are closely tied to thinking skills in a constructivist vein.

- **The taught curriculum** should blend these five elements through the 'exploration of conceptually based central ideas' (IB, 2009), very much along the lines of the Understanding by Design movement (see McTighe, Emberge and Carber (2009) for a PYP/UbD comparison). This is to be enacted through the central role of the precisely-defined concept of *inquiry* which Short (2009) defines as 'a collaborative process of connecting to and reaching beyond current understandings to explore tensions significant to learners'; that is, as a *stance* on the curriculum more than a set of specific practice. This is articulated in detail in IB documents (IB, 2009 and IB, 2012a) where the process of creating an integrated transdisciplinary *programme of inquiry* is set out in detail. This process is clearly, if loosely, linked to conceptions of thinking skills. The basic expectation in the PYP is that pedagogy must be actively constructivist in nature, and so naturally contains thinking skills aspects (for example, guided reflection at an age-appropriate level as a metacognitive strategy). It is worth pointing out that this is not to the exclusion of traditional learning; in the PYP 'it is recognised that there is a role for drill and practice in the classroom yet ... teaching about [concept-based] central ideas leads to the most substantial and enduring learning' (IB, 2009) which echoes recent findings from cognitive science (Willington, 2009; Bransford, Brown & Cocking 2002).

- **The assessed curriculum** has two principal thinking skills aspects. Using multiple forms of assessment strategies (*eg* observations, performance assessments, process-based assessments, tests, open-ended tasks) and tools (*eg* rubrics, exemplars, checklists, anecdotal records and continuums) means the PYP is consistent with ideas of developing multiple intelligences. Also, an emphasis on formative assessment and on developing in students the ability to recognise and work toward success criteria (which they themselves may have had a hand in constructing) is geared to developing meta-cognition in a broad sense.

- **The Exhibition** is, in IB-speak, the PYP 'culminating experience', undertaken in the final year of the programme. Collaborative in nature, it takes place under one of the transdisciplinary themes and involves in-depth, sustained inquiry, where students have a central role in the direction, scope and shaping of an investigation, and where they present the results to the wider school community.

The IB Middle Years Programme (MYP)

The MYP curriculum for 11–16 year olds is complex, with many interlocking parts, and is newly out of review. What follows will therefore be subject to the wisdom of practice, as for any developing curriculum. The MYP shares many similarities with the PYP, and thinking skills are similarly both infused in the approach to teaching and located in specific areas across the programme.

MYP Technology Aims

MYP technology aspires to develop creative problem-solvers who are caring and responsible individuals, able to respond critically and resourcefully to the demands of the increasingly technological society and to appreciate the importance of technology for life, society and the environment.

Aims

The aims of the teaching and study of technology are to encourage and enable students to:

- develop an appreciation of the significance of technology for life, society and the environment
- use knowledge, skills and techniques to create products/solutions of appropriate quality
- develop problem-solving, critical- and creative-thinking skills through the application of the design cycle
- develop respect for others' viewpoints and appreciate alternative solutions to problems
- use and apply information and communication technology (ICT) effectively as a means to access, process and communicate information, and to solve problems

---

Figure 4: IB MYP Technology Aims (IB, 2010d)

- The MYP is traditionally structured around disciplines but, like the PYP, has an approach very similar to the UbD movement with choice of subject content given to schools to develop in the service of IB-defined objectives. These objectives are very much focused on developing higher order thinking skills (see Figure 4 for example) and, like the PYP, teachers develop units of study which are centred around significant concepts and enduring understandings, rather than around specific content knowledge. The conceptually-driven nature of the MYP, while not so unusual for the primary age range, is in stark contrast to many national curricula for this age group.

- The MYP is based on three fundamental concepts, each of which reflects aspects of thinking skills:
  - *Holistic learning* in the MYP means that it is both trans- and inter-disciplinary, though the latter seems to be given much more attention in IB documents. It is interdisciplinary as at least some of the units developed by schools should be approached by more than one discipline: they literally address the same question. The very detailed IB guide (2010b) offers many fine examples, such as a unit question of 'how do instruments produce sound to create interesting pieces of music?' as an example of a transdisciplinary unit between science,

music and possibly technology. It is transdisciplinary because even entirely disciplinary units are approached through the five *Areas of Interaction* (*AoI*) which are transdisciplinary lenses through which to approach subjects; students develop deeper disciplinary understandings and thinking skills by exploring and re-exploring these ideas again and again in different disciplinary contexts. The AoI are *approaches to learning; community and service; health and social education; environments;* and *human ingenuity*. There is controversy here; though they play the same role as the PYP transdisciplinary concepts, they are very different in nature. That the current MYP review is looking to move from Areas of Interaction to (yet to be defined) *global contexts* is an opportunity to better align the programmes.

– *Intercultural awareness*, the second fundamental MYP concept, is of course a politically correct requirement of any progressive curriculum (though none the worse for that). Alongside any moral imperative, though, is the opportunity for schools to develop this into a pluralistic engagement between students and people who are in some way different. Interpreted in this way, this fundamental concept is tightly related to familiar thinking skills such as open-mindedness, awareness of other perspectives, and awareness of one's own perspective, as one of many.

– *Communication*, the third fundamental MYP concept, and alongside issues of mother-tongue, second language, intercultural understanding and so on, is the notion of language as central to 'cognitive growth as it is the means by which meaning and knowledge are negotiated and constructed' (IB, 2010b). Tight attention to language in all disciplines is therefore designed to support thinking.

• One Area of Interaction, Approaches to Learning (ATL), is a fascinating cross between study skills and thinking skills. Through this lens, students are encouraged to gently explore the nature of areas of study, and how they engage with the areas as learners. While there is, therefore, disciplinary, transdisciplinary and metacognitive benefit built in here, the focus is on learning, rather than on thinking; on process and self-awareness more than on actual cognitive benefit (the links may be close, but these are not the same things). While schools have a great deal of freedom in developing student learning expectations, the ATL categories given in IB 2010b reveal the intimate links to thinking skills; organization, collaboration, communication, information literacy, reflection, thinking and transfer are all mentioned. These are not mandated categories, however, and their location here is more transdisciplinary than standalone in nature.

• The Personal Project is the MYP culminating experience, undertaken by all MYP students over an extended period in the fifth MYP year.

Individual and transdisciplinary (since focused through an AoI) in nature, the students are assessed not against a traditional academic level of attainment but through assessment criteria which measure their abilities to pose relevant questions, define a goal, select and use information, and to communicate their reflections on the process in a report. The focus on thinking and metacognition is clear.

The IB Diploma Programme (DP)

While a strong emphasis on thinking skills has been slower to emerge in the DP than in other programmes, thinking skills can currently be identified in at least four different aspects of the DP:

- The disciplinary nature of the DP is very pronounced; in this respect the DP takes a traditional approach, and aims to develop subject experts like Francis as discussed above. Each student studies six subjects representing a breadth of disciplines, and takes three core elements (Theory of Knowledge, Extended Essay, and Creativity Action Service (CAS)). Each subject builds thinking skills into its aims and assessment objectives (see Figure 5 for the aims of Group 3, Individuals and Societies, for example) by explicit reference to higher-order thinking skills (as opposed to content) and subject methodologies (to encourage metacognition). Links to Theory of Knowledge are also made in every subject guide.

The aims of all subjects in Group 3, Individuals and Societies, are to:

1. encourage the systematic and critical study of: human experience and behaviour; physical, economic and social environments; and the history and development of social and cultural institutions

2. develop in the student the capacity to identify, to analyse critically and to evaluate theories, concepts and arguments about the nature and activities of the individual and society

3. enable the student to collect, describe and analyse data used in studies of society, to test hypotheses, and to interpret complex data and source material

4. promote the appreciation of the way in which learning is relevant both to the culture in which the student lives, and the culture of other societies

5. develop an awareness in the student that human attitudes and beliefs are widely diverse and that the study of society requires an appreciation of such diversity

6. enable the student to recognize that the content and methodologies of the subjects in group 3 are contestable and that their study requires the toleration of uncertainty.

Figure 5: Aims of IB Diploma Group 3, Individuals and Societies (IB, 2013)

- The Theory of Knowledge (ToK) programme in the Diploma Programme core is a thinking skills course. Though not the standard philosophy course of the (confusingly) same name, it shares many aspects and is essentially an exploration of what we believe to be true, and the strength of the reasons we have for our beliefs. The course examines the 'content' areas of knowledge and the 'process' ways of knowing. From 2014 the former is somewhat controversially defined as the arts, religion, natural sciences, human sciences, ethics, history, indigenous knowledge systems and mathematics, while the latter is defined as language, reason, faith, intuition, sense perception, memory, imagination and emotion. The course is constructed very much along constructivist teaching lines, with discussion and reflection playing very significant roles; assessment consists of one traditional essay and one presentation in which students explore a knowledge question of their own devising.

ToK may look like a stand-alone course, but in fact it is much more than that. ToK draws on the academic and personal experiences of the students, and provides a forum for comparison, critique and reflection. By asking 'do we have good reasons for our beliefs?' it is intrinsically interdisciplinary, as the questions cannot be answered from only one perspective; by drawing on the methods of other classes it requires metacognition and also encourages transfer. Strikingly, it can also promote these qualities in the other classes; students will ask the art teacher about *truth* in art, or the physics teacher about the scope of the scientific method.

- The Extended Essay (EE) in the Diploma Programme core is the DP culminating experience. It is a 4,000-word research project independently undertaken by all DP students. In the best cases students will identify a subject, draft and refine a focused research topic, pursue that topic via a creative and critical systematic process appropriate to the subject, and experience the excitement of intellectual discovery. The EE is a remarkably ambitious endeavour and, within a narrow area, gives students the chance to develop expertise like that of Francis (above).

- There is increasing emphasis on building upon and moving beyond disciplines, with the introduction to the DP of an interdisciplinary World Studies EE, the transdisciplinary *Literature and Performance* and *Environmental Systems and Societies* courses, and the somewhat metacognitive *Nature of Science* course.

It is also stated in the recently published *Approaches to teaching and learning across the Diploma Programme* (IB, 2012b) that 'critical and creative thinking, inquiry and managing information, understanding and applying key concepts, the development of inter- and intra-personal skills' will inform future pedagogical direction and guidance, thus further embedding thinking skills in the DP.

The IB Career-related Certificate (IBCC)

The IBCC for 16–19 year old students is made up of three components; a career-related/vocational course of study determined by the school, at least two IB DP subjects, and the IBCC Core. The fundamental aim in terms of thinking skills is to engender exactly the same skills as those addressed by the DP ToK course, but in a way that fits with the nature of the IBCC and in a way that is better aligned with the IBCC context (as opposed to the DP context). So the same outcomes are sought, but via different mechanisms, and possibly different pedagogies.

- Thinking skills are infused throughout the DP courses as detailed above, and throughout the vocational course according to the specific details of the course.

- The IBCC Core aims to blend critical thinking and intercultural understanding, through four elements:

  - *The Approaches to Learning* (ATL) course is the most obvious place to find thinking skills. Four skills areas are identified and grounded in four specific contexts (see Figure 6). As in the PYP, thinking skills are explicitly identified as one specific aspect but, also like the PYP, this location is rather misleading, as thinking skills appear in several other places across the whole programme. Interestingly the skills are more transdisciplinary than interdisciplinary in nature (this is probably inevitable given the structure of the IBCC, which does not mandate any specific discipline), and there is not a clearly articulated tight fit between these skills and either the DP or vocational courses.

	The IBCC Approaches to Learning Outline	
Thinking Skills	Ethical thinking Critical thinking Creative thinking Problem solving Lateral thinking	
Communication Skills	Interpersonal communication skills Formal writing skills Presentation skills Numeracy skills IT skills	*these areas are all explored through four contexts; workplace, environment, communities and technology*
Personal Development	Emotional intelligence Domains of emotional intelligence Process skills	
Intercultural Understanding Skills	Your culture Other cultures Language and culture Intercultural engagement	

Figure 6: IBCC Approaches to Learning

  - *Community Service* is service *learning* undertaken in a community context; it is not just volunteer work but has cognitive aspects built in; it is a vehicle for new learning that has academic value in addition to value to the community. This is a particularly powerful way of developing thinking skills, as these two examples show:

'Students may find, in consultation with the local health authorities, that there is a need to raise awareness among members of the community around important health issues. The students could then study the background to specific health problems, *eg* diabetes types 1 and 2, and then a public awareness campaign could be devised around different sectors of the community'.

'Students become aware of a sharp fall in the numbers of 'endangered species' in their local area. Students develop valuable research skills while learning about the biological and physiological make-up of different species. The students then develop a plan to provide a suitable habitat and enhance population growth. A plan is then devised to communicate the project to the local community.'
(IB, 2010a)

– *Language Development* (that is, a language other than the student's best language) can be through a DP course (if so this will count as one of the DP course requirements). The presence in the core reflects the IB belief that new languages are one means of encountering other world-views; as such the benefit may stretch well beyond the language skills themselves and allow broader development of thinking skills.

– *The Reflective Project* is the culminating experience of the IBCC. An in-depth body of work produced over an extended period, it is student-initiated and synthesises the vocational course, community and service, and critical thinking. The project involves students identifying, analysing, critically discussing and evaluating an ethical issue arising from their career-related studies; there is explicit attention to rigorous reasoning and to exploring several perspectives.

The multiple lines of emphasis here throughout all the IB programmes all point to the fact that thinking skills are woven throughout the programmes in profound, though quite different, ways. In all programmes they are both infused and have varying degrees of standalone presence. An obvious issue to explore is the degree of consistency within and across programmes; how much coherence is possible? How much is desirable? And how to go about achieving it? That these and other questions are under active consideration means this is an exciting time for thinking skills in the IB world.

Research Evidence from IB Programmes

I am not aware of any data on the thinking skills aspects of the IB programmes that has been derived from rigorous controlled experimentation similar to that undertaken for P4C or the Cognitive Acceleration movement. There is, however, a good deal of IB-commissioned research by independent bodies into the efficacy of IB programmes (see http://www.ibo.org/research/policy). Undertaken by institutions such as the Australian Council for Educational Research (ACER), and the UK National Foundation for Educational Research (NFER), the projects investigate a wide range of issues, many of which one might expect would be proxies for thinking skills (for example, longitudinal studies investigating correlations between EE grades and university academic success, or between PYP success and success in the International Schools Assessments). Much of this data is positive, but by its nature is not controlled or conclusive.

Implementation issues

I have focused on a few programmes here, but it is important to note that there are many such programmes, and not all of them work. This may not be a fault of the programmes themselves; it may be simply because implementing these programmes is so hard. Leat (1999) considers the introduction of thinking skills programs to a school where such an introduction is new, and notes that 'despite promising evidence of their effects [thinking skills programmes] usually fail to make a lasting impact or become established within school systems', likening the process to 'rolling a stone uphill'; it is tremendously hard to overcome initial resistance, every inch of the way is a struggle against gravity and you cannot rest for a moment without going backwards. This is not the place for great detail, but two pieces of research are worth noting.

In the late 1990s Californian education officials commissioned a lengthy and in-depth study into the way thinking skills are taught in Californian public schools (State of California, 1997). In detailed interviews, 89% of teachers claimed that teaching thinking skills was a primary objective, but the following facts also emerged:

- Only 19% of respondents could give a clear explanation as to what thinking skills actually were. Furthermore, by their own answers, it would appear that only 9% of respondents were actually clearly teaching thinking skills on a given day.

- 77% of respondents had little or no conception of how to reconcile content coverage with the fostering of thinking skills.

- Only a very small minority of respondents were able to use the basic vocabulary of the reasoning aspect of thinking skills. For example, only 8% differentiated between an assumption and an inference.

We have no particular reason to assume that Californian teachers are markedly different to any other group of teachers, and are thus confronted with the very real possibility that most thinking skills programmes are not articulated clearly enough for success in real, busy environments.

A second related issue to consider is the way that even expert teachers can be reduced to novices when teaching thinking skills programmes for the first time. Shulman (1986) discusses how, early in their teaching careers, teachers transform their academic subject knowledge into subject-specific pedagogical knowledge by learning a whole range of effective explanations, analogies, narratives, anecdotes, jokes, lesson starters and hooks. These are tightly tied to specific content areas, and are as much about how to (re)present ideas as they are about the ideas themselves. When the teachers are dealing with thinking skills they may well be back to developing the repertoire from scratch – an uncomfortable place for an experienced, expert teacher find himself or herself in. It is not entirely surprising that programmes are difficult to maintain here, and this raises the vital question of staff professional development.

For schools considering implementing or improving a thinking skills programme of any sort, or indeed implementing any significant change, it is always worth returning to pragmatism. Sternberg and Bhana's (1986) advice remains relevant many years on: 'The success of a given programme depends on a large number of implementation specific factors, such as the quality of teaching, administrative support, appropriateness of the programme for the student population, and the extent to which the programme is implemented in the intended manner.' Baumfield (2002) makes the following recommendations to teachers:

- Start small and aim for slow organic growth rather than trying to impose an ambitious plan on reluctant colleagues.
- Combine grass-roots enthusiasts with top-level support.
- Work across subjects to ensure focus on process rather than content.
- Ensure teachers have 'permission to fail' so that they experiment and take risks.
- Embed good practice by embedding peer observation and team teaching.
- Take time to investigate the underpinning learning theory.

These pieces of advice are more about change management than about thinking skills *per se*. So while the challenges are real, they are not new, and they are at least as much about individual teacher capacity and the capacity of individual schools to deal with complexity in a rapidly changing environment as they are about thinking skills themselves. In this, at least, thinking skills programmes share a great deal with many other school concerns.

Acknowledgements
Thanks to Ellie Alchin, Alex Holland and Naheeda Karmali for their thoughts on a draft of this chapter.

References

Adey, P. and Shayer, M. (1993a) *Really Raising Standards: Cognitive Intervention and Academic Achievement*, London: Routledge.

Adey, P. and Shayer, M. (1993b) An exploration of long-term far-transfer effects following an extended intervention program in the high school science curriculum. *Cognition and Instruction*, 11, p. 1-29.

Baumfield, V. (2002) *Thinking Through Religious Education*. Cambridge: Chris Kington Publishing.

Blair, A (2000) Address to Knowledge 2000 Conference. Available online at http://www.guardian.co.uk/uk/2000/mar/07/tonyblair (last accessed 22 April 2012).

Bransford, J. D., Brown, A. L., and Cocking, R. R. eds. (2002) *How People Learn: Brain, Mind, Experience, and School*, Washington DC: National Academy Press.

Bredo, E. (2005) Reconstructing Educational Psychology. In: Murphy, P. ed. *Learners, Learning and Assessment*. London: Paul Chapman.

Coles, M. J. and Robinson, W. D. eds. (1991) *Teaching Thinking: A Survey of Programmes*. London: Bristol Classical Press.

Coffield, F. (2004) *Should we be using Learning Styles? What Research has to say to Practice*. Newcastle: Learning and Skills Research Council.

Cotton, K. (1991) Teaching Thinking Skills. Schools Improvement Research Series: North Western Regional Educational Laboratory. Available online at http://hppa.spps.org/uploads/teaching_thinking_skills.pdf (last accessed 2 August 2013).

Damasio, A. (2006) *Descartes' Error: Emotion, Reason and the Human Brain*. New York: HarperCollins.

Dewey, J. (1910) *How We Think*. Lexington: Heath.

Dweck, C. (2006) *Mindset: The New Psychology of Success*. New York: Random House.

Fauconnier, G. and Turner, M. (2002) *The Way We Think: Conceptual Blending and the Mind's Hidden Complexity*. New York: Basic Books.

Gardner, H. (2005) Assessment in Context. In: Murphy, P. ed. *Learners, Learning and Assessment*. London: Paul Chapman.

Gardner, H. (2006) *Five Minds for the Future*. Boston: Harvard Business School Press.

International Baccalaureate (2006) *The learner profile booklet*. Cardiff: International Baccalaureate.

International Baccalaureate (2008) *MYP: From principles into practice*. Cardiff: International Baccalaureate.

International Baccalaureate (2009) *Making the PYP happen: A curriculum framework for international primary education*. Cardiff: International Baccalaureate.

International Baccalaureate (2010a) *Career-Related Certificate Guide*. Cardiff: International Baccalaureate.

International Baccalaureate (2010b) *MYP guide to interdisciplinary teaching and learning*. Available online at http://occ.ibo.org/ibis/documents/myp/m_g_mypxx_mon_1005_1_e.pdf (last accessed 1 May 2012).

International Baccalaureate (2010c) *Quality and Research in the IB: Overview of Research within the Schools Division*. Available online at www.ibo.org/research/ (last accessed 8 May 2012).

International Baccalaureate (2010d) *Middle Years Programme Technology Guide.* Available online at http://occ.ibo.org/ibis/occ/home/subjectHomeMYP.cfm?subject=techm (last accessed 8 May 2012).

International Baccalaureate (2011) *Personal Project Guide.* Available online at http://occ.ibo.org/ibis/occ/home/subjectHomeMYP.cfm?subject=persp (last accessed 8 May 2012).

International Baccalaureate (2012a) *Developing a transdisciplinary programme of inquiry.* Cardiff: International Baccalaureate.

International Baccalaureate (2012b) *Approaches to teaching and learning across the Diploma* Available online at http://occ.ibo.org/ibis/documents/dp/d_0_dpyyy_amo_1204_1_e.pdf (last accessed 1 May 2012)

International Baccalaureate (2013) *Group 3 Aims.* Available online at http://ibpublishing.ibo.org/live-exist/rest/app/tsm.xql?doc=d_3_wldre_gui_1105_1_e&part=1&chapter=4 (last accessed 5 May 2013).

Kahneman, D. (2011) *Thinking, Fast and Slow.* London: Allen Lane.

Klein, J. T. and Newell, W. H. (1998) Advancing Interdisciplinary Studies. In Newell, W. H. ed. *Interdisciplinarity: Essays from the Literature.* New York: College Entrance Examination Board.

Lane, N. R. and Lane, S. A. (1986) Rationality, Self-Esteem and Autonomy through Collaborative Enquiry. *Oxford Review of Education*, 12 (3), p. 263-275.

Leat, D. (1999) Rolling the Stone Uphill; Teacher Development and the Implementation of Thinking Skills Programmes. *Oxford Review of Education*, 25 (3), p. 387-403.

Lipman, M. (1991) *Thinking in Education.* Cambridge: Cambridge University Press.

Lipman, M., Sharp, A. M. and Oscanyan, F. S. (1980) *Philosophy In The Classroom* (2nd ed). Philadelphia: Temple University Press.

McCormick, R. (1999) Practical Knowledge: A View from the Snooker Table. In: McCormick, R and Paechter, C eds. *Learning and Knowledge.* London: Paul Chapman.

McGuinness, C. (1999) *From Thinking Skills to Thinking Classrooms.* Nottingham: DfEE Publications.

McTighe, J., Emberger, M., and Carber, S. (2009) UbD and PYP: complementary planning frameworks. In: Davidson, S. and Carber, S. eds. *Taking the PYP Forward.* Woodbridge: John Catt.

McTighe, J. and Seif, E. (2003) *A Summary of Underlying Theory and Research Base for Understanding by Design.* Available online via http://assets.pearsonschool.com/asset_mgr/current/201032/ubd_myworld_research.pdf (last accessed 5 August 2012).

Nisbet, J. (1990) *Teaching Thinking: An introduction to the research literature* (Spotlight no. 26) Edinburgh: Scottish Council for Research in Education.

Paul, R. W. and Elder, L (2002) *Critical Thinking.* New Jersey: Prentice Hall.

Pinker, S. (1998) *How the Mind Works.* London: Penguin.

Resnick, L. (1987) *Education and Learning to Think.* Washington, DC: National Academy Press.

Robinson K. (2010) Changing Education Paradigms. Available online at http://comment.rsablogs.org.uk/videos/ (last accessed 22 April 2012).

Schoenfeld, A. (1988) Problem Solving in Context(s). In: Charles, R. and Silver, E. eds. *The Teaching and Assessing of Mathematical Problem Solving.* Reston, VA: National Council for Teachers of Mathematics.

Scriven, M. (2004) *A Working Definition of Critical Thinking.* Available online at http://lonestar.texas.net/~mseifert/crit2.html (last accessed 11 May 2004).

Sharron, H. and Coulter, M. (1994) *Changing Children's Minds: Feuerstein's Revolution in the Teaching of Intelligence.* Birmingham: Questions Publishing Company.

Short, C. (2009) Inquiry as a Stance on Curriculum. In: Davidson, S. and Carber, S. eds. *Taking the PYP Forward.* Woodbridge: John Catt.

Shulman, L. (1986) Those Who Understand; Knowledge Growth in Teaching. *Educational Researcher,* 15, p. 4–14.

Sigurborsdottir, I. (1998) Philosophy with Children in Foldaborg. *International Journal of Early Childhood* 30 (1), p.14–16.

Sprod T. (1998) "I can change your opinion on that": Social Constructivist Whole Class Discussions and their Effect on Scientific Reasoning. *Research in Science Education* 28 (4), p. 463-480.

Sternberg, R. G. and Bhana, K. (1986) Synthesis of Research on Effectiveness of Intellectual Skills programmes: Snake-Oil Remedies or Miracle Cures? *Educational Leadership* 44 (2), p. 60–67.

State of California (1997) *California Teacher Preparation; Instruction in Critical Thinking.* Sacramento: State of California, Commission on Teacher Credentialing.

Wiggins, G. and McTighe, J. (2006) *Understanding by Design* (2nd ed). Pearson Education: New Jersey.

Wilson, V. (2000) *Can thinking skills be taught?* Scottish Council for Research in Education; Spotlight Series. Available online at www.scre.ac.uk/scot-research/thinking/ (last accessed 11 May 2004).

Willington, D. (2009) *Why don't students like school?* Jossey Bass: San Francisco.

Chapter 2

Continuity in international education: the case for metacognition

Ochan Kusuma-Powell and William Powell

A common thread running through the mission statements of many international schools is the assertion that our schools teach students to 'learn how to learn'. It appears clear that international schools around the world recognize that this is one of their most important purposes. Less clear, however, is what exactly schools *do* to teach students to learn how to learn, and how consistently and effectively they do it. The questions that arise include: what are some of the definitions being used to guide practice in this area?; to what purposes are the efforts being put?; and to what degree are we finding consistency and effectiveness of approach with respect to metacognition in international schools?

In this chapter, we will review the current literature on metacognition and make the case for supporting student metacognitive development. We will also present a picture of current practice from individual schools and give overviews of what specific curricular programs, such as the International Baccalaureate (2013), the International Primary Curriculum (2013), and the Common Ground Collaborative hope to achieve in developing student metacognition within their current frameworks. This will hopefully give readers an idea of the continuity in international education that exists in developing student metacognition, specifically for those students transferring from one international school to another. Finally, we will discuss our own thoughts on the purposes of developing student metacognition, and how schools might deconstruct and apply those purposes in developing, implementing and assessing programs supportive of student metacognition.

What we say and what we do: the gulf

Although the wording may not be exactly the same, most international schools strive to develop in children the means to become lifelong learners and critical thinkers. A quick review of a number of international school mission statements shows a common theme:

'Our mission … will strive to advance the value of learning, growth and self-awareness as life-long endeavors'

'(Students) … will become smart about their own learning processes, understanding what does and does not work for them as learners'

'... (we) challenge each student to develop the attitudes, skills, knowledge and understanding to become a highly successful, spirited, socially responsible global citizen'

'... (we work) together to achieve our goal of developing independent learners and international citizens'

'We respect students' individual and cultural identities, encouraging them to become independent learners eager to carry on learning throughout their lives'

'(Our) students strive for academic excellence by learning how to learn'

'Our mission is to encourage students to be independent, lifelong learners who strive for excellence'

Each one of these statements in its own way advances the cause of teaching students to become aware of (and thus in greater control of) their thinking and learning. As we will suggest later in this chapter, there may however be a significant gulf between what many schools are saying and what they are doing in a deliberate and planned fashion.

Current thinking on metacognition: where we are

Awareness and knowledge about our own thinking and learning has evolved since Flavell's (1979) work in this area in the late 1970s. One indication of increased consciousness surrounding metacognition has been its specific inclusion in the revision of Bloom's *Taxonomy of Educational Objectives* (Anderson *et al.*, 2001). Metacognitive knowledge is now a separate category under the Knowledge dimension, indicating a distinct type of knowledge (separate from Factual, Conceptual and Procedural Knowledge) that was not widely known or recognized at the time of publication of the original *Taxonomy* (Krathwohl, 2002).

There are currently many definitions and differing frameworks on metacognition. However, there is agreement that metacognition consists of two elements: cognitive knowledge and cognitive regulation. There are several related components to 'cognitive knowledge', including the individual's knowledge of 'self as learner'; knowledge of the demands of a given task; and knowledge and application of strategies, or how the individual might bring together knowledge of self as learner and knowledge of appropriate cognitive processes to achieve a goal. For example, a Middle School student with a writing assignment may realize that while she has the content knowledge needed to reply to an essay question, she has difficulty getting started with written assignments, and may recognize further that a thesis statement needs to be crafted in order to get the essay started.

Cognitive regulation refers to the processes of planning, monitoring and evaluating strategy use and individual performance against a goal; thus, being *intentional* about one's learning (Bransford *et al.*, 2000). In the example above, the same Middle School student may decide that she needs to stop procrastinating, focus on isolating her opinions about the writing topic and draft an initial thesis statement. Metacognition has been linked to critical thinking, including problem analysis, and making inferences and judgments (Ennis, 1985), motivation, and self-regulated learning (Schraw *et al.*, 2006) – that is, the capacity to control and direct one's own learning. Students who are aware of different strategies and approaches to learning tasks are more likely to use them. Similarly, students who recognize they have difficulty performing specific operations – say, in mathematics – will have the opportunity to study for tests in an appropriate manner. As such, metacognition is strongly associated with academic achievement (Bransford *et al.*, 2000; Hattie, 2009). In his meta-analysis of educational research, Hattie (2009) actually ranks the influential factors that promote or interfere with student achievement. Among the top 20 that promote student achievement, many have a metacognitive component; metacognition by itself ranks 13th from the top.

Whereas earlier research in the area of metacognition concluded that young children were incapable of metacognitive thought, more recent studies have shown that children as young as three to five years of age are able to comment on their thinking and learning at simple levels (McLeod, 1997; Whitebread *et al.*, 2009). In addition, studies suggest that metacognitive development can improve with maturity. In a recent visit to a Pre-Kindergarten–Grade 1 multi-age classroom, the authors overheard two children discussing the task demands of their assignment. The older of the two noted that the assignment would require both reading and thinking, to which the younger student, a four-year-old, replied 'OK, you do the reading and I'll do the thinking, because I can't read'.

Metacognition can also be enhanced through deliberate instruction (Hattie, 2009). This implies the need to teach for metacognitive knowledge *explicitly*, and to label it as such (Pintrich, 2002). For example, in teaching the persuasive essay, teachers may wish to point out different ways in which arguments might be set out, and to what effect on the reader. This invitation to take on the perspective of a potential audience requires a degree of empathy and flexibility of thought. This process makes metacognitive discourse deliberate. Being explicit about these different approaches to argumentation and their effects provides students with a window into the thinking and reasoning behind their decisions, and may help them to make connections between their writing and their prior knowledge of readers.

Thus, our knowledge of metacognition suggests strongly that while the selection and prioritization of academic content is important, the deliberate teaching and development of student metacognition – learning how to learn – is critical to continued learning. We may hope or assume that students will learn how to learn on their own, but many will not. Given its close relationship with successful learning, student metacognitive development is not something that should be left to chance. However, at this time, there is no generally agreed curriculum for metacognition and no widely accepted scope and sequence chart for learning to learn. In fact, some schools may equate metacognition with classes in isolated study skills. Pintrich (2002) emphasizes that effective metacognitive instruction needs to be deliberately explicit and embedded in content.

Metacognition in international curricula

The International Baccalaureate Programmes

The International Baccalaureate Diploma Programme (IBDP) was founded in 1968 in order to address a number of idealistic and practical educational concerns. Perhaps the most pressing practical concern was the development of a widely recognized university entrance qualification for international school students. There was a great need for this, and the early IB understandably placed high priority on its credibility with universities. This translated into a strong emphasis on rigorous curricular content and assessment. The IBDP includes the Theory of Knowledge (ToK), which contains a strong element of critical thinking and could incorporate elements of metacognition if the teacher were so inclined. In the academic subjects of the IBDP, the concept of 'learning how to learn' is paid lip-service, but the implementation is very much at the discretion of the individual school and teacher, and we have heard many IBDP teachers comment that curriculum overload prohibits such a focus. It is probably fair to say that the early IB emphasis on content rigor and assessment was, to some extent, at the expense of other areas such as pedagogy and metacognition.

In 1994 the IB introduced the Middle Years Programme (IBMYP) and three years later the Primary Years Programme (IBPYP). The IBMYP has an explicit emphasis on Approaches to Learning (ATL), which includes a number of metacognitive elements such as thinking skills, social skills, and self-management skills. The ATL include an organized approach to developing these skills. The IBPYP was based on the International Schools Curriculum Project (ISCP) developed by Kevin Bartlett and others, which included a draft student learner profile. It contained important metacognitive dimensions including the outcomes for IB learners to be open-minded, balanced, risk taking, and reflective. The IBPYP also focuses on Transdisciplinary Skills, one of which is explicitly metacognition: 'Analysing one's own and other thought processes; thinking about thinking and thinking about how one thinks and how one learns.' At this point, the three IB programmes had grown up independently and did not represent a coherent learning continuum, especially in the area of developing student metacognition. In 2006, however, the IB adopted the PYP learner profile for all three programmes, thus for the first time making explicit that the attributes of the profile were a desirable outcome for all IB students irrespective of which programme they were undertaking.

There is, of course, the perennial difference between the written curriculum and the taught curriculum (what is intended and what happens in practice) and it is our observation from communication with many international schools that, with a few notable exceptions, little is currently being done in schools in a coherent and systematic fashion to support students in learning how to learn. And while expectations regarding student metacognition have been expressed in PYP and MYP documents, the deconstruction of what this means and how to apply and implement it has been left up to individual schools. The IB has recognized this omission and has embarked on two initiatives. The first is a major re-examination of the ATL in the MYP as part of the program review known as *MYP: The next chapter*. The documents are still in draft form and will not be published until 2014. However, they contain a clear statement on the need for ATL and a systematic approach to include:

- Learning skills (*eg* time management, goal setting, self-verbalization, memory techniques);

- Metacognitive skills (*eg* planning, monitoring, and evaluating outcomes – content and process);

- Cognitive skills (taking effective notes, using structural writing planners, calibrating own learning preferences, self-assessment); and

- Affective skills (persistence and perseverance, focus and concentration, overcoming distractions, reducing anxiety and delaying gratification).

There is, obviously, overlap in these areas, but the overarching outcome is to support students in building 'resilience in learning'; learning how to deal effectively with setbacks and difficulties … how to bounce back, make changes and persevere – the skills of the self-regulated learner (Nicolson, 2012). These skills are being amalgamated into five categories across the three IB programmes:

thinking skills;
social skills;
research skills;
self-management skills; and
communication skills.

The second initiative is the extension of ATL into the Diploma Programme. In early 2012, the IB prepared an executive summary of what it is calling 'Approaches to Teaching and Learning Across the Diploma Programme'. This document sets out to describe purposeful strategies, skills and attitudes that permeate the teaching and learning environment. Metacognition appears to be at the heart of this initiative: 'Driven by inquiry, action and reflection, IB programmes aim to develop a range of skills and dispositions that help students effectively manage and evaluate their own learning' (IB, 2012: 2). The authors recognize that IB pedagogy is more explicit in the PYP and MYP though implicit in some of the DP subject guides, and that 'we need to bring these ideas together into a broad, agreed set of principles for the programs' (IB, 2012: 4). The specific outcomes for the ATL initiative at DP level include students understanding how judgments about learning are made, and becoming aware of and understanding how they learn. This initiative also seeks to 'empower teachers as teachers of learners as well as teachers of content' (IB, 2012: 2).

These are indeed welcome initiatives. However, at the present time there is a co-mingling in the documentation of teacher and student outcomes that may prove confusing to the end users. There is also an emphasis on behavioral skills (*eg* note-taking, graphic organizers), which could be misinterpreted to be the teaching of isolated study skills at the expense of values and beliefs – the cultivation of a self-reflective learner identity.

The authors of the Diploma Level ATL Executive Summary appear to recognize that what gets assessed gets taught, and they state 'since ATL skills may well be assessed and pedagogy of teachers is so linked to subject assessment demands in DP assessment, colleagues will also wish to be fully involved' (IB, 2012: 1) in the development of the scope and sequence of ATL at the Diploma level.

International Primary and Middle Years Curriculum (IPC and IMYC)

The IPC and IMYC are products of Fieldwork Education and are used in more than 1400 national and international schools in over 65 countries worldwide. Both the IPC and IMYC are based around three guiding questions, one of which has a clear metacognitive focus. It asks: 'What kinds of learning will our children need and how should they learn it?' Martin Skelton, co-founder and director of Fieldwork Education, understands that an effective curriculum in the 21st century must go beyond the acquisition of knowledge. He writes 'Knowledge is not enough … Because a curriculum based on knowledge alone cannot bear the weight of expectation we should be placing upon it'. Skelton then goes on to emphasize the acquisition of skills: 'Skills are the essence of what it is to be able to do something. And because skills are developmental over time … it is during good skills learning that students develop the rigor, resourcefulness and endurance that, we are rightly told, matters so much' (SecED, March 1, 2012: 7).

The IPC is organized around three clusters of learning goals: subject goals, personal goals, and international goals. All the IPC learning goals include the development of knowledge, skills and understanding. The personal goals have a metacognitive dimension and the outcomes include students being at ease with the continually changing context of their lives, being able to cope with unfamiliar situations, approaching tasks with confidence, and moving between conventional and more fluid forms of thinking. The IPC promotional literature states that there are personal goals for enquiry, resilience, morality, communication, thoughtfulness, cooperation, respect and adaptability. There is also an emphasis in the IMYC on promoting self-reflection and assessment *for* learning.

In our conversations with educators from schools using the IPC there is recognition of the metacognitive dimension of the curriculum, though teachers expressed concern that, if metacognition is an explicit learning outcome, they were provided with little practical support or guidance for its implementation in the classroom setting. A number of teachers suggested that IPC and IMYC consider developing a 'metacognitive tool box' for teachers' use.

Common Ground Collaborative (CGC)

The Common Ground Collaborative is a curriculum initiative of the International School of Brussels (ISB), spearheaded by Kevin Bartlett and Gordon Eldridge. There are a number of innovative and welcome aspects to this project. The first is that it places cognition and metacognition at its heart. The second is that Bartlett and Eldridge recognize that teachers are extremely busy people and they have attempted to keep the curriculum framework as simple as possible (without being simplistic) and to make it as teacher friendly as possible (without losing sight of the ultimate purpose – student learning). They have also backed it up with the training and tools necessary to 'do the learning business', seeing all of this as part of their overall goal to 'define, design and deliver' learning.

Unlike other curricular programs that may start with a philosophy, mission or even standards, CGC starts with a definition of learning itself. This simply expressed definition recognizes three facets: conceptual learning, competency learning and citizenship learning, each of which drives one element in a coherent three-part curriculum design. Competency learning is the facet which captures the metacognitive element of the CGC curriculum. Within the CGC, this facet is designed to equip students to own and manage their own learning processes and is expressed through four cognitive learning standards:

- Learning through guided inquiry
- Language for learning
- Learning relationships
- Learning for innovation

At the center of these four cognitive learning standards is a metacognitive cycle that outlines a process that a student might move through in order to become an increasingly independent and self-directed learner. The learning cycle includes five stages, all of which are student driven, as seen in Figure 1.

The cognitive learning standards and metacognitive cycle are also reflected in matching teaching and learning standards, bringing a common language and practice to the classroom as well as a coherence of expectations and understanding. The CGC has developed rubrics for each of the cognitive learning standards, each with indicators of seven increasingly complex levels of attainment. Embedded into these cognitive learning standards are metacognitive traits. In its 'genesis school', the International School of Brussels, teachers are providing feedback to students, and reporting to parents

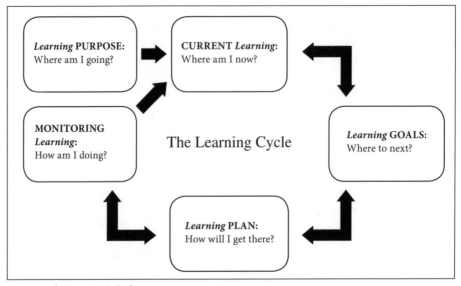

Figure 1: the Learning Cycle

on progress in cognition and metacognition; they now have sufficient recorded data to be engaging in meaningful analysis and refining practice accordingly. The CGC has informally influenced curriculum development in a number of flagship international schools. It is still being developed, but Bartlett and Eldridge promise a website during 2013 as well as a 2013 roll-out for other interested schools.

External examination programs

Many international and national schools use external assessments of student learning such as the University of Cambridge International General Certificate of Secondary Education (IGCSE), English A level examinations, or the American Advanced Placement tests. These are subject-based examinations that focus on content knowledge mastery and, to varying degrees, on critical thinking and skills acquisition. While individual syllabi may contain reference to metacognition, they do not represent fully developed courses of study in the sense that there are specific curricula to be followed; nor do these examinations emanate out of a guiding educational philosophy with explicit values and beliefs. As such any classroom emphasis on metacognitive development is left entirely to the teacher's discretion; it is not required or embedded or designed into the assessment products.

International schools: where are we in developing student metacogntion?

Our interest in metacognition led us to try to ascertain what is being done in international schools to promote student metacognition, and what opportunities there might be for students transferring from one international school to another to experience continuity in this regard. In April 2012 letters of inquiry were sent, via AISHnet (the Academy for International School Heads network) and HEADnet (the network of heads of schools offering one or more of the IB programmes), to heads of schools around the world to find out what international schools are doing in the area of student metacognition. Three basic questions were asked:

In what ways does your school emphasize the teaching of metacognition?

What kinds of skills are being taught, and how is metacognition being assessed?

At what age/grade does this begin?

There was a very poor return from schools, perhaps for a number of reasons: the timing of the inquiry which, for some schools, occurred towards the end of their academic year; the implied complexity of the issues involved; and perhaps a lack of formalized activity in the area of student metacognition. Of the 22 returns received, five responded straight away by acknowledging that while they recognized the importance of developing student metacognition, their schools were not yet engaged in any systematic approach to the teaching of metacognitive skills and that, in many cases, the explicit teaching of metacognition was teacher-dependent. Other responses suggest that some work is being done in this area, particularly at the Elementary and Middle school levels, especially in those schools offering the PYP and MYP.

For example, Atlanta International School has drafted a scope and sequence chart for ATL in Grades 6–8. Their rubric includes categories on reflection, thinking and transfer. In the PYP programme at Beijing City International School, specific units of inquiry explicitly target how children learn. In a Grade 5 unit, for example, the central idea spells this out: 'exploring ways we learn helps us to understand ourselves and maximize our learning capacity.' Lines of inquiry include the different learning styles and intelligences, the unique challenges we face as learners, and how to optimize our learning capacity. This is similar to the work being done at Qatar Academy where, for example, a third grade unit focuses on 'Who we are'. 'Here, the students reflect on themselves as learners, focusing on SMART (specific, measurable, attainable, relevant and time-bound) goals and attributes of the PYP attitudes and the learner profile. These SMARTs are drawn and highlighted throughout the rest of Grade 3 and provide scaffolding for the students in later grades ... Awareness and understanding of different learning styles is focused on throughout the grades, and becomes part of our differentiation' (Hedger, 2012). At Qatar Academy, students use e-portfolios that begin in the primary school and are continued into the senior school. Students at this level begin to focus their thinking around the Areas of Interaction and develop SMART goals to measure their own learning. They also self-assess against rubrics based on the IB learner profile. At Nanjing International School (NIS), teachers embed metacognitive learning in their Units of Inquiry as part of the planning process, effective scaffolding of tasks and focused feedback. Metacognitive strategies include self-assessment, individual goal setting, monitoring of progress, and reflection on the achievement of the goals. In the PYP programme at NIS, metacognitive development is based around the following key principles:

- Students will be given clear and consistent scaffolds to help them understand the learning process.
- Students will develop a common vocabulary to discuss the learning process.
- Students will both receive and give feedback on their learning process, not just a finished product.
- Student reflection will always be valued.
- Students will constantly be challenged to think about what they need to do to improve.

Both students and teachers have responsibilities for the achievement of student goals.

Other international schools have also accomplished noteworthy progress in the area of explicitly developing student metacognition. As mentioned earlier, the International School of Brussels is the pilot school for the Common Ground Collaborative, and they have implemented, taught, assessed and reported on student metacognitive development. At the International School of Bangkok, where student metacognitive development is an explicit part of the school's mission, a school-wide task force has been meeting for the last two years to develop a working definition and a continuum of skills. Their ultimate goal is to embed explicit skill development across all subject areas and at all grade levels. They recognize that, in order for this to happen, they need to create a developmental continuum to target, assess, and show growth over time in each of the learning phases (what they are calling 'direct, monitor and evaluate'). They will pilot this continuum in the 2013-2014 academic year.

At the International School of Manila, educators have developed school-wide transdisciplinary skills, with one of the five such skills being 'critical thinking' and another 'personal management and reflection'. These skills are embedded in unit planners throughout the school and at all grade levels, and the rubric is incorporated into assessments. The work on metacognition was spearheaded by the Elementary School in 2006 when units of study were created for 'learning about learning', and included topics such as collaboration and learning styles. While these units are usually the first to be taught during the academic year, a focus on 'learning about learning' is embedded throughout the school year. At the Middle School level, the English department has developed reading strategies around understanding how you read, making students aware of the thinking strategies they use in the process of reading (*eg* using background knowledge, creating mental images, questioning, inferring, determining importance, synthesizing, and monitoring for meaning). Teachers regularly pose questions to students such as 'How do you know when you don't understand?' as a means of supporting students in monitoring their thinking and comprehension. The International School of Manila continues to support teacher metacognition through the provision of in-service training.

Work on student metacognition at the American International School of Johannesburg (AISJ) is division-specific; explicit work in this area is well underway. In the Elementary School, teachers are expected to develop thinking and reading/writing skills simultaneously through mini-lessons, guided reading lessons, and strategy lessons that focus on specific skills. The literacy coach has developed a set of question prompts that teachers can use to support student thinking during reading and writing. These are age- and grade-appropriate, and include such questions as 'You said _____. Does that sound right?'; 'You are nearly right. Try that again and think 'what would look right, sound right, or make sense?''; 'What evidence did you find to draw that conclusion?'

At the high school level at AISJ, metacognition is promoted in three primary ways: through the teaching of the IBDP Theory of Knowledge, through the development of reflective practice, and by promoting self-regulated learning. Reflective practice is supported through both formative and summative assessments, and students are asked to reflect on product, process, content, purpose, applicability and personal growth. Teachers help students to strive for self-regulated learning by promoting learner independence together with the use of technology. As one teacher wrote, 'Everything about education has changed. This is a paradigm shift on a scale not seen since the influence of the Industrial Revolution. And if everything is changing – from the physical appearance of a school to the type of learner we need to create – then we need to change, too. The push is towards self-regulation, and we need to teach metacognition accordingly'. The Teaching and Learning Team at AISJ is actively promoting teacher consciousness on developing metacognition by placing it on the agenda as an area of inquiry for their professional learning communities.

The technology leadership group at the United World College of South East Asia (UWCSEA) is also working hard to embed the use of technology in the development and explicit teaching of metacognitive skills. As a group, they are very clear that technology is there to support learning goals, and not the other way round. Andrew McCarthy and Jeff Plaman, digital literacy coaches at UWCSEA, recently introduced an assessment idea they call 'learning talks'; they wanted to 'make visible' what students were thinking about their learning. Several teachers across the two campuses developed exciting examples of classroom practice. Some examples were at the reflection stages of a project, thus providing students with an opportunity for input at the summative assessment stage. There were other examples at the formative assessment stage. Guy Roberts, an IB Diploma Level English teacher, uses 'Educreations' and 'Show Me', both available on the iPad, for students to create screencast movies of their annotations on a text along with their reasoning and thinking: 'It used to be that by the time we got to the commentary, it was too late to help students to practice their skills in developing a commentary. Using 'Educreations' I can 'listen in' on what they are saying and doing, and I can catch the misconceptions ahead of time. Or I can ask them to explain something in a different way. All of this is ahead of doing the 'official' IB oral commentary, so that by the time that event rolls around, the students are already well-versed in this skill.'

It is evident, for the moment, that there is no commonly accepted definition or understanding among international schools of what metacognition is or the skills and knowledge that might comprise it. An accepted understanding is that metacognition means 'thinking about thinking' but, beyond that, schools are working – often in isolation from one another – to come to an understanding of what this means and how to implement it within curricula. Hopefully, this will change to some extent when the new MYP ATL is rolled out in 2014. However, at the current time, a student who transfers from one international school to another may not experience the same focus on metacognitive development (if any), from one school to another. More seriously, other than in a few flagship international schools, students moving between grades and teachers will probably also find differences in focus with reference to metacognitive development.

Assessing metacognition

There are many challenges in assessing a complex construct like metacognition. One of the most common methods used by teachers is sometimes to provide 'reflection' sheets asking students about their thinking and learning at the end of a unit. Clearly, this poses difficulties in ascertaining a student's metacognitive development: in the first instance, the reflection protocol is provided to the student in retrospect rather than during the learning of the unit itself. Quite often, many teachers will hand out reflection sheets towards the end of term, and students have been heard to say they have been 'reflected out' after a day of encountering one reflection sheet after another as they move from class to class. Thus, not only is it too late for the teacher to act on the information that may be gleaned from such reflection sheets; the level of metacognition presented may not reveal true levels of student thinking.

In addition, the reflection protocol touches upon only a narrow part of what is a large and complex construct. The reflection protocol also relies on written expression and self-report and may thus underestimate the student's metacognition. It also poses problems for children in the early years and elementary schools, and children for whom written language may pose a problem. We have not yet come across a method of assessing metacognition that relies on other than the verbal expressive/linguistic facility of the child. While reflection can be an invaluable way to take learning beyond the episodic, and while it may provide opportunities for students to generalize their thinking and learning to new and novel future situations, many teachers are often ill-equipped to teach students how to reflect; most reflection sheets do not go beyond three basic questions: How did it go? What makes you say that? What did you learn? These questions by themselves are insufficient to provoke the depth of thought necessary for new learning or insights that might be carried into future situations. International school leaders and those responsible for leading adult learning in international schools may wish to invest time and energy in providing teachers with opportunities to learn how to engage in structured reflection (*eg* from the Cognitive Coaching model developed by Costa and Garmston, 2009) in order to support students in doing the same.

Our thoughts on metacognition

Thirty five years ago, when we began our careers as international educators, international schools were perceived as 'outposts of progress' and parents were fortunate if they stumbled across one that was accredited, had qualified teachers and had a coherent written curriculum. Much has changed. Today, the flagship international schools are amongst the finest and most innovative schools anywhere in the world and have an enormous amount to teach national systems. Thus it is disturbing that there is not greater continuity and consistency in the important business of student metacognition, of learning to learn. When teachers value the process that students use to select learning targets, to plan and complete a task, and to reflect on their learning, they will teach the required skills. Thus, we notice a correlation: teachers who are themselves conscious of their thinking and learning are also likely explicitly to support students in the development of metacognition.

We perceive metacognition as the discovery and development of our identity as a learner. We emphasize discovery in the sense that metacognition is an exploration of self, but it is not just mapping what exists; it is also the deliberate development of attitudes, beliefs, values, and skills that will serve to make us effective and efficacious learners. To this end, we also see an absence of specific reference in the literature to knowledge of emotions and emotional self-regulation as a component of metacognitive knowledge. Krathwohl outlines metacognitive knowledge as 'Knowledge of cognition in general as well as awareness and knowledge of one's own cognition' (2002: 214) and lists the components of metacognitive knowledge as strategic knowledge, knowledge of cognitive tasks – including appropriate contextual and conditional knowledge, and self-knowledge. Emotional knowledge and emotional self-regulation is missing.

Research from neuroscience (Damasio, 1994; LeDoux, 1998) underscores the connections between emotion and cognition; that emotions, both positive and negative, guide our decision-making and our behavior. As we in schools are all aware, if a child experiences a negative emotional interaction during the day, any learning for that child will also be negatively impacted for the remainder of the day. Emotions have a powerful influence over all learning, and students need to learn a vocabulary for their emotions and learn strategies for regulating them. This will serve them well in developing the attitudes, beliefs, values, and skills that will serve to make them effective and efficacious learners.

We cannot expect to be metacognitive without also exploring how our emotions affect our learning. This is particularly true when it comes to difficult learning challenges. There are two kinds of challenges that learners face: technical challenges and adaptive challenges. Technical challenges require informational learning. For example, if we want to use a new and unfamiliar computer application in the design of a lesson, we need to engage in informational learning. Perhaps we will read the instruction manual, take a specific online tutorial or ask a knowledgeable colleague for help. The mastery of the new computer application is a technical challenge that requires informational learning. This tends to focus on developing behavioral skills or capabilities and content knowledge acquisition. Informational learning probably does not require deep emotional self-analysis. Adaptive challenges, however, require transformational learning that focuses not just on behaviors and capabilities, but on values, beliefs and even our identity (Dilts, 1994). Learning how to learn is an adaptive challenge that requires transformational learning. This is not just a cognitive exploration; it is also a deeply emotional one.

In order to engage in the discovery and development of ourselves as learners, we need a framework or model from which to work. We need to begin with a profile of the metacognitive learner. We believe that such a profile would include attributes such as resilience, self-directedness, emotional intelligence (Powell & Kusuma-Powell, 2010), insightfulness and strategic reasoning. Schools need a curricular framework for metacognition and we believe that such a model emerges from the Five States of Mind from Cognitive Coaching (Costa & Garmston, 2002). Readers familiar with Costa's Habits of Mind will see that they are, for the most part, embedded within the States of Mind. The five States of Mind are internal capacities that can be developed over time. They are efficacy, flexibility, craftsmanship, consciousness, and interdependence. 'These basic human forces drive, influence, motivate and inspire our intellectual capacities, emotional responsiveness, high performance and productive human action' (Costa & Garmston, 2002:124). The five States of Mind form an organizing model through which we can design explicit instruction and support students of all ages as they come to discover and develop their learner identities.

Efficacy

Efficacious students believe in themselves and are self-confident learners. They are optimistic and self-assessing and self-correcting. They have internalized achievement motivation and accept responsibility with a proverbial 'can do' attitude. Efficacious students have an internal locus of control and show initiative in controlling their environment. They are able to control impulsivity, gather data, persevere, and take responsible risks. According to Costa and Garmston, when compared with individuals who have an external locus of control, they are less hostile, less aggressive, more trustful and less suspicious of others.

Flexibility

Flexible students are able to perceive a situation from another person's point of view. They are cognitively empathetic. Flexibility requires a student to step beyond and outside of him or herself. It requires the individual to view a situation from a multitude of different perspectives. Flexible students are comfortable with doubt and tolerant of ambiguity. They challenge the habitual, question the known and stretch the cognitive frontiers of self and others. Students who exhibit flexibility are empathetic and reflective listeners; they ask themselves if there is another way to view or interpret the present situation; and they gather data with all the senses, often responding with wonder and awe.

Craftsmanship

Craftsmanship is both an attribute and an energy source. The constant striving for improvement is certainly a quality of the lifelong learner, but it is more than a static characteristic. It is also a dynamic motivating force that compels the student towards greater refinement, greater skillfulness and greater precision. We see craftsmanship when our students communicate with coherence and accuracy. Effective learners construct clear visions and set specific goals. They understand how these goals may be attained and carefully monitor their progress. They are self-assessing and self-modifying. The craftsman-like student is not without failures, but these are perceived as valued opportunities for further growth.

Consciousness

Consciousness is the construction of meaningful knowledge about the world around us, our immediate environment, school and family. It is also the interior knowledge of ourselves, our thoughts, feelings, hidden anxieties and fleeting impressions. In short, consciousness is deliberate and careful attention to events that are both internal and external. Consciousness is the path to self-knowledge and without it there can be no impulse control or self-direction. Self-consciously 'conscious' people delight in the subtleties of complex interaction. They explore their own reactions, they monitor their values, thoughts and behaviors, and they will articulate the internal criteria behind decisions that are to be made. They are politically sensitive and are able to predict problems and misunderstandings.

Interdependence

Interdependence is a state of reciprocity in which people have common goals and work together for the furtherance of those goals. Interdependent students are idealistic, altruistic and optimistic. They are able to suspend the pursuit of their own ego gratification in order to focus their energy on the achievement of group goals. Interdependence is not a naturally occurring state but a series of sophisticated and complex learned behaviors. It is nothing less than an explicit statement about how we choose to perceive, value and interact with the rest of our species and, in doing so, how we choose to define ourselves.

These States of Mind can be used by schools and individual teachers to forge a framework for embedding a robust and meaningful metacognitive strain in every unit of study that we design. We have also come to the conclusion that, in order to encourage or foster the development of metacognition in students, teachers must themselves be conscious of their own thinking and learning. They must engage in self-reflection on these States of Mind. In other words, teachers need to be trained to be self-consciously aware of the processes they engage in as they learn: during planning, monitoring during the task itself, and later in reflection; and then model this metacognition for their students. This is an important area for professional learning that has been largely overlooked in the past.

Conclusion

At the present time there is valuable metacognitive work being done by some international school teachers and some schools, but for the most part this work tends to be undertaken by individuals or schools in isolation from each other. While there is widespread lip-service paid to 'learning to learn', many schools – perhaps most – treat this in practice as a discretionary aspect of the student's learning experience. For many international schools there seems to be a regrettable, if tacit, understanding that some students will 'get it' through mere exposure, and others will not. For high quality schools with an authentic commitment to fostering lifelong learning, this is an unacceptable state of affairs. The development of metacogntive awareness is simply too important to be left to chance.

References

Anderson, L. W. and Krathwohl, D. R. eds., with Airasian, P. W., Cruikshank, K. A., Mayer, R. E., Pintrich, P. R., Raths, J., and Wittrock, M. C. (2001) *A taxonomy for learning, teaching and assessing: A revision of Bloom's Taxonomy of Educational Objectives (Complete edition)*. New York: Longman.

Bransford, J. D., Brown, A. L., and Cocking, R. R. eds. (2000) *How people learn: Brain, mind, experience and school (Expanded edition)*. Washington D.C.: National Academy Press.

Costa, A. and Garmston, R. (2002) *Cognitive Coaching: A foundation for Renaissance schools, Second Edition*. Norwood, Mass.: Christopher-Gordon.

Damasio, A. (1994) *Descartes' error: Emotion, reason and the human brain*. New York: Harper Collins.

Dilts, R. B. (1994) *Effective presentation skills*. Captola, Ca.: Meta.

Ennis, R. H. (1985) A logical basis for measuring critical thinking skills. *Educational Leadership*, 43 (2), p. 44–48.

Flavell, J. H. (1979) Metacognition and cognitive monitoring: A new area of cognitive developmental inquiry. *American Psychologist*, 34 (10), p. 906–911.

Hattie, J. (2009) Visible learning: *A synthesis of over 800 meta-analyses relating to achievement*. Abingdon: Routledge.

Hedger, G. (2012) (former Director, Qatar Academy), *Private Correspondence*, May 2012.

International Baccalaureate (2013) Available online at www.ibo.org (last accessed 29 March 2013).

International Baccalaureate (2012) *Approaches to teaching and learning across the Diploma Programme: Executive summary*. The Hague: International Baccalaureate.

International Primary Curriculum (2013) Available online at www.greatlearning.com/ipc (last accessed 29 March 2013).

Krathwohl, D. R. (2002) A revision of Bloom's Taxonomy: An overview. *Theory Into Practice,* 41 (2), p. 212–218.

Lai, E. R. (2011). Metacognition: A literature review. *Pearson Research Report*, Available online at www.pearsonassessments.com/hai/images/tmrs/Metacognition_Literature_Review_Final.pdf(last accessed 17 June 2012).

LeDoux, J. (1998) *The emotional brain*. New York: Touchstone.

McLeod, L. (1997). Young children and metacognition: Do we know what they know they know? And if so, what de we do about it? *Australian Journal of Early Childhood*, 22 (2), p. 6–11.

Nicolson, M. (2012) Personal communication, 14 February 2012.

Pintrich, P. R. (2002).The role of metacognitive knowledge in learning, teaching, and assessing. *Theory Into Practice*, 42 (4), p. 219–225.

Powell, W. and Kusuma-Powell, O. (2010) *Becoming an emotionally intelligent teacher*. Thousand Oaks, Ca.: Corwin.

Schraw, G., Crippen, K. J., and Hartley, K. (2006) Promoting self-regulation in science education: Metacognition as part of a broader perspective on learning. *Research in Science Education*, 36, p. 111–139.

SecED. (2012) "Hopes and Fears" interview with Martin Skelton, p. 7, 1 March 2012.

Whitebread, D., Coltman, P., Pasternak, D. P., Sangster, C., Grau, V., Bingham, S., Almeqdad, Q. & Demetriou, D. (2009) The development of two observational tools for assessing metacognition and self-regulated learning in young children. *Metacognition and Learning*, 4 (1) p. 63–85.

Chapter 3

International to the core: developing international mindedness in the IB continuum

Anthony Hemmens

The IB continuum and its programmes

The International Baccalaureate (IB) continuum is a sequence of three adjacent educational programmes providing a continuous international education from early childhood to school graduation, ages 3 to 19 (IB, 2008a). As of April 2013, the IB is providing international curricula to over 3,500 schools in 145 countries, with more than a million students (IB, 2013a) receiving education through one, or a combination, of its programmes: the Primary Years Programme (PYP), the Middle Years Programme (MYP), and the Diploma Programme (DP). With no requirement that schools offer more than one of the programmes, each stands independently and is self-contained; offered consecutively, they are intended to form a coherent and meaningful sequence of learning (IB, 2008a).

Developed and introduced at different times (the DP in 1968, the MYP and PYP in 1994 and 1997 respectively) (IB 2013c), the programmes evolved in response to needs and opportunities in the global educational marketplace (Hallinger *et al.*, 2011). The IB does not envisage that students will experience a seamless transition through its programmes, but asserts that there is sufficient coherence to the continuum to give it a recognizable identity (IB, 2008a). According to Bunnell, differences in the structure of each programme 'arguably hinders any articulation of a continuum' (2011: 264). Possibly, this is truest of the DP which, in its function as a pre-university preparatory course providing certification, consists of a prescribed curriculum with examinations and externally assessed or moderated coursework. This contrasts to the PYP and MYP which are both frameworks of educational provision that are internally assessed. Stobie (2005) identifies these differences in curriculum design and assessment models as sources of transitional tension between the MYP and the DP. However, irrespective of these programme disparities, commonality in components and features provides consistency to the programmes of the continuum; all three have a commitment to language learning, learning to learn, and learning through experience; they promote subject connectivity; they emphasise development of the whole child; each culminates in an assessment task to synthesize learning: in the PYP an exhibition, the MYP a personal project and a research-based extended essay of 4,000 words in the DP.

Most salient of all, however, the continuum is bound by a common philosophy of international education, central to all three programmes, expressed in the IB mission statement and learner profile. The consistent philosophy and cohesive force of the PYP, MYP and DP is two-fold; to develop the whole child, focusing on intellectual, personal, emotional and social growth; and to develop international mindedness (IB, 2008a).

The IB takes a holistic view of knowledge, in which all knowledge is interrelated, and a holistic view of learning, with an emphasis on discovering relationships both between areas of knowledge, and between the individual, communities and the world (IB, 2008a). For learners aged 3-12, the PYP is a transdisciplinary educational model (IB, 2008a) where knowledge, concepts and skills are treated not within discrete subject areas but through themes which transcend those subjects. Approached through units of inquiry the six transdisciplinary themes of the PYP are:

- Who we are
- Where we are in place and time
- How we express ourselves
- How the world works
- How we organize ourselves
- Sharing the planet

Inherently international in their scope, these themes promote an understanding of human commonality and shared experience considered essential in the context of international education (IB, 2008a). Working collaboratively, students explore the themes from the shared perspectives, personal experiences and cultural backgrounds of their fellow class members. The sharing of personal experience is deemed important as it 'increases the students' awareness of, and sensitivity to, the experiences of others beyond the local or national community' (IB, 2007: 6). In this, the IB identifies a critical starting point for the effective development of international mindedness, the student's ability to 'consider and reflect upon the point of view of someone else in the same class' (IB, 2007: 6); empathy is an essential element in both the development and definition of international mindedness.

Organized into eight subject groups and undertaken by students aged 11-16, interdisciplinary learning in the MYP is achieved through its distinctive core: the five areas of interaction. As with the PYP themes, the areas of interaction focus on human commonalities and the real world connections of subject content (IB, 2008a). Described as a context for learning (IB, 2008a) and addressed within subject disciplines, the areas of interaction are:

- Approaches to learning
- Community and service

- Human ingenuity
- Environments
- Health and social education

In contrast to the PYP transdisciplinary themes and the DP Theory of Knowledge (ToK), which 'abounds with topic questions relating to intercultural understanding' (Hill, 2002: 23), promotion of international mindedness is not explicitly embedded in the areas of interaction. In the MYP, more than in the other programmes of the continuum, the extent to which international mindedness is successfully promoted through its core is dependent on how it is implemented and utilized, with the school and its teaching faculty needing to actualize the IB international objective through collaborative vertical and horizontal planning (IB 2008b).

Studied over a two-year period by students aged 16-19, the DP consists of six academic areas of study, including science, first and second languages, humanities, mathematics and the arts, and three compulsory core components completed by all students: creativity, action, service (CAS), the extended essay, and ToK. As might be expected from an educational programme with prescribed curriculum content, of all the continuum programmes direct reference to the IB international objective is most prevalent in the DP where 'subject aims, objectives, content and assessment criteria are written in order to develop international mindedness' (IB, 2009: 6).

International mindedness and the learner profile – a relationship considered

If we take the view that 'the product of a successful international education is international mindedness' (Hill, 2012: 246) then international education becomes less defined by what it is and more defined by what it does and what it seeks to achieve. This definition circumvents the complexity of context and locus of international education: national schools offering international curricula, international schools offering national curricula, national schools with multicultural student bodies, international schools with predominantly monocultural student bodies. Whether international education is perceived as enabling the children of globally mobile expatriates to experience educational continuity (Cambridge and Thompson, 2001), or providing global and globalized local elites with international credentials to maintain their socio-economic advantage in the face of educational competition (Lowe, 2000), it can be asserted that all education is international education when it leads to international understanding and international mindedness.

For the IB, the ultimate purpose of education is to develop young people who have an international understanding and help to make a better world (IB, 2013b). In this way education is transformative, schools are seen as instruments of social change, and the curriculum has a social constructionist orientation

(Eiser and Vallance, 1974, cited by Marsh, 2009). The IB makes direct reference to its international objective in its mission statement, which it considers to be the driving force behind the continuum (IB, 2008a):

'The International Baccalaureate aims to develop inquiring, knowledgeable and caring young people who help to create a better and more peaceful world through intercultural understanding and respect. To this end the organization works with schools, governments and international organizations to develop challenging programmes of international education and rigorous assessment. These programmes encourage students across the world to become active, compassionate and lifelong learners who understand that other people, with their differences, can also be right.' (IB, 2013b)

The international objective of the IB, expressed as intercultural understanding in the mission statement, is repeated and rephrased as international mindedness in the introductory statement of the learner profile. Described as the mission statement in action (IB, 2008a) the learner profile is a list of ten attributes of the kind of learner who will help realize the international intentions of the mission statement, with learners striving to be 'inquirers, knowledgeable, thinkers, communicators, principled, open-minded, caring, risk-takers, balanced and reflective' (IB, 2008c). Just two of the learner profile descriptors make direct reference to international, or intercultural, understanding; knowledgeable learners 'explore concepts, ideas and issues that have local and global significance' while open-minded learners 'are open to the perspectives, values and traditions of other individuals and communities' (IB, 2008c: 5). The IB describes international mindedness as 'an attitude of openness to, and curiosity about the world and different cultures' (IB, 2009:6), presumably necessitating an internationally-minded individual to be open-minded and an inquirer, the first and sixth attributes of the learner profile. However, the exact correlation between the learner profile and the international objectives of the IB, as expressed in the mission statement, is ambiguous. Certainly, understanding is not enhanced by descriptions such as '[the learner profile is] a map of a lifelong journey in pursuit of international mindedness' (IB 2008c:2).

In an attempt to define international mindedness the IB asserts it is typified by a person who demonstrates the learner profile attributes (2007). However, are the ten attributes of the learner profile the exhaustive set? Are they all of equal importance? Might an internationally-minded person be internationally-minded but not a risk-taker? How communicative does an internationally-minded person need to be; is listening or speaking competence of primary importance? Ultimately, the attributes of the learner profile are not sufficient to differentiate between the internationally-minded and the non-internationally-minded; all the values of the learner profile can, with equal validity, be argued to embody what it means to be nationally minded. Alternatively, the relationship could be understood not as the attributes of the learner profile defining international mindedness, but as international mindedness developing from these attributes. The IB alludes to this when it states that the attributes of the learner profile are those of the kind of student who 'in the struggle to establish a personal set of values … will be laying the foundation upon which international mindedness will develop' (IB 2008a: 3). Exactly how the attributes of the learner profile lead to international mindedness is not made explicit. While it is true that an internationally-minded individual will possess personal attributes and values, it is certain neither that those values are the cause or source of their international mindedness nor that the particular attributes listed in the learner profile are the definitive set required. As Wells argues, there needs to be 'rigorous theoretical justification to substantiate the premises on which the values for the IB learner profile were chosen' (2011:177).

For this author international mindedness is too elusive a quality to define with precision, yet easily identified by those in possession of it, readily gauged from the attitudes people hold and the statements they make about life and the world. As a state of mind and a state of character, international mindedness is a level of personal identity that transcends the boundaries of a national conceptual framework. Neither precluding nor excluding identities founded upon smaller geo-cultural regions, the internationally-minded locate themselves in a global context and identify with the global mass of humanity, recognizing common ancestry and common purpose. An internationally-minded person is an interculturally literate person possessing 'the understandings, competencies, attitudes and identities necessary for successful living and working in a cross-cultural … setting' (Heyward 2002:10); in our highly and increasingly globalized world such cross-cultural settings need to be understood as intra-national as well as international entities.

The IB states that international mindedness 'is concerned with developing a deep understanding of the complexity, diversity and motives of human actions and interactions' (IB 2009:6). Herein lie two critical facets of international mindedness. Firstly it 'develops', secondly it is an 'understanding'; the international objective of the IB is achieved when learners develop an understanding of themselves through an understanding of the world, both at and beyond the local and national level. International mindedness is not a body of knowledge and cannot be transmitted through traditional didactic teaching methods; instead, as a personal identity, it is mentally constructed by each individual learner.

Constructing intercultural understanding – pedagogy and the continuum core

Much of the subject content and many of the aims, targets and procedures of an international curriculum will be common also to a national curriculum (Skelton, 2002). A curriculum largely focused on national issues with little emphasis on empathy is unlikely to foster greater intercultural understanding

(Wells, 2011), while a curriculum with international objectives will be one that de-emphasizes the study of academic subjects from a single national perspective (Gellar, 2002) and promotes international mindedness. As an understanding of personal identity, international mindedness develops from and through the IB pedagogical emphasis on constructivist learning; the common pedagogical approach in the three IB programmes (Hill, 2012), which itself lends yet further coherence to the continuum.

In keeping with constructivist theory, the IB regards learning as a 'developmental path of constructing, testing and revising mental models of how the world works, [enabling] each student to make meaning of their lives and the world around them' (IB, 2008a:12). Students, therefore, develop an understanding of the world leading to international mindedness when they actively engage in the cognitive process of critical evaluation of subject content and personal experience – their own and that of others – that transcends the cultural perspective of their national origin and dominant national reference. Learning is a process achieved through a combination of knowledge, skills and understanding (Skelton, 2002). The starting point is the position of understanding the learner already possesses, with skills of inquiry, critical thinking and metacognition applied to new knowledge, subject content and personal experience, to build the connections that facilitate the active construction of new meaning (IB, 2008a). The core components of the continuum programmes (the PYP units of inquiry, the MYP areas of interaction and ToK [particularly but not exclusively] in the DP core), in their transdisciplinary/interdisciplinary function of encouraging students to make connections between academic disciplines and with the real world, are the pivotal source of the development of international mindedness in the IB continuum. Furthermore, it is from and in these core components, at age-appropriate levels, that the skill set necessary for this learning process is derived and developed.

Both the skills developed in the continuum core components, and the conceptual understandings developed through their use – including international mindedness, develop over an extended period of time (Marshman, 2010). Skills proficiency develops through regular and repetitive practice; it is learning by doing, knowledge through experience (Mackenzie, 2000), while intercultural understanding requires 'regular, planned exposure to ideas and their analysis, revision and connection' (Marshman 2010: 9). The time required is afforded the learner through participation in the programmes of the continuum, taking the learner through ages 3-19, but also beyond into adulthood. Metacognition, thinking about knowledge itself, is seen by the IB as fundamental to the thinking strategies, attitudes and competencies necessary for learners to monitor and control learning, and to become effective lifelong learners (IB, 2008a). It is developed through the IB emphasis on assessment for learning, where students produce their own formative feedback on performance, in the MYP area of interaction 'approaches to learning', and the

DP ToK. An awareness of the influences that shape thinking enables learners to select, develop and defend their position of understanding in a self-critical way (Woolfolk *et al.*, 2008), allowing learner autonomy. The IB does not stipulate a timeframe in which its objective of international mindedness will be achieved; the formation of identity is an ongoing 'lifelong' process, with the skill of metacognition enabling learners to continue to develop international mindedness after their formal school experience is complete.

Defined broadly by the IB as the process that moves learners from their current level of understanding to a new and deeper level, inquiry includes – among other activities – speculation, research, problem solving, analysis, evaluation and considering alternative explanations (IB, 2008a). Shifting in approach from the transdisciplinary PYP model to the more disciplinary models of the MYP and DP, inquiry in the IB learning experience is structured, with the teacher employing strategies and support to facilitate purposeful and productive student inquiry (IB, 2008a). Learning with understanding requires cognitive engagement necessitating dialogue, both internal to each individual learner and social among class members. In a context of learning for international mindedness the conversation is critical, as through it 'self-awareness and identity can be cultivated' (Alchin 2011: 35). Typically, lessons conducted in and through the continuum core components follow the Socratic model whereby the teacher poses questions and students offer their ideas and opinions. This is instructional conversation, where classroom discussion is designed to promote learning and 'the teacher's goal is to keep everyone cognitively engaged in a substantive discussion' (Woolfolk *et al.*, 2008: 414).

Functioning to initiate and maintain the momentum of dialogue, guiding questions are central to learning for understanding (IB, 2008a), needing to be carefully chosen to guide learners towards important understanding (Woolfolk *et al.*, 2008). Guiding questions frame learning in the PYP units of inquiry, focus learning through the areas of interaction, and structure learning in ToK (IB, 2008a). However, in practice a teacher cannot merely provide a list of questions, albeit international in focus and promoting higher order thinking skills, and expect that meaningful discussion at a depth of enquiry which leads to learning with understanding will automatically follow. Discussion orchestration can be unpredictable, with effectiveness and participant engagement affected by many factors including class dynamics and personal interests. Often the teacher needs to wait for the crucial moment of 'bite' when students collectively 'turn on' to a topic and begin to discuss and evaluate at a deep and sophisticated level. This being the case, teachers cannot be completely certain when or how discussion that promotes the development of international mindedness in a meaningful way will surface, necessitating that they are able to identify when it becomes the focus of the lesson and to orchestrate the debate effectively once initiated by students, responding to them and helping to direct the flow of discussion so that understanding is enhanced. The IB states that 'the challenge of excellent teaching is to help students achieve genuine and sophisticated understanding' (2008a: 13); sophisticated understanding of the world is an intercultural understanding. Excellent teaching, in the context of international mindedness, facilitates this understanding where it is actively realized by the learners themselves.

In a ToK lesson at Southbank International School (SIS) in London, two students, from Kuwait and Botswana, proposed that 'the history of Europe is one of a terrorist state' – a provocative statement from which an impassioned discussion ensued. In their response, all the students – particularly those from European backgrounds – needed to assess carefully the role and impact of European colonialism and how this was, and is, perceived by the peoples European countries colonized. Many of these students were forced to consider and re-evaluate their understanding of themselves and their cultural identity. The learning focus with which the lesson began had transposed to a focus on international perspectives, significantly challenging the level of understanding and mental model of many in the class. Learning outcomes were identified at the end of the lesson. This was learning for international mindedness. Teachers must be able and willing to adapt or abandon planned learning outcomes and lesson structures in order to allow student autonomy and authentic learning. In the context of learning for international mindedness, the teacher's skill of responding to students and the immediate classroom situation, drawing out learning in real time, is more important than the predictive skill exercised in planning.

The idiosyncratic nature of constructivist learning in the context of international mindedness means that the plenary stage of a lesson, when students reflect on and record what they have actually learned, becomes of paramount importance. When classroom discussion is rich and varied, covering myriad academic and cultural issues resulting in new understandings, what a student has actually 'learned' may not be immediately obvious. Sufficient time needs to be allotted at the end of a lesson for students to reflect on, and to record, *their* learning outcomes. Furthermore, students need to keep a note of their ideas throughout a lesson as discussion progresses; a series of mini-plenary statements. Through these study habits, the ideas students develop in a lesson are consolidated and a permanent record produced that can be referred to later as a means of both refreshing memory and continuing the process of evaluation and reflection itself.

The above example from SIS also serves to illustrate how international mindedness is not effectively developed by comparing and contrasting the perspectives of people from the same or similar cultural background(s), even if from different countries. International mindedness is not significantly advanced, if advanced at all, by comparing and contrasting the perspectives and cultures of countries as similar as Portugal and Spain, Laos and Thailand, the USA and Canada. Van Oord (2005) suggests it is preferable to describe differences between nations with closely linked and similar cultures as differences in social custom or habit. For international mindedness to be effectively served, a comparison and contrast of perspectives across a wider diversity of cultures is necessary, between regions of the world with vastly different cultural frameworks. Cultural diversity is a core feature of international education (Thompson, 1998) as from it international mindedness is enabled. Students need meaningful exposure to different cultures, and meaningful engagement with the people of those cultures, if the development of international mindedness is to be enhanced. This is achieved in two ways: through engagement with the cultural diversity in the students' immediate educational environment; and by extending exposure to cultural diversity through travel experience.

International mindedness through cultural diversity in and outside the classroom

Research by Hayden and Thompson indicates that of 'prime importance [is] student exposure to other students of different cultures within the school' (in Thompson, 1998: 284). For the development of international mindedness, the multiple perspectives inherent in a culturally diverse student body are an essential learning resource. The international focus of guiding questions is not, in itself, sufficient to promote international awareness. Students construct their own meaning with social engagement between classmates acting as stimuli, and knowledge being individually constructed through social mediation (Windschitl 2002, cited by Woolfolk *et al.*, 2008). For the purpose of developing international mindedness, this process is both enabled and enhanced when the learners in the classroom represent a diversity of cultural perspectives which, expressed and exchanged in response to guiding questions, allow individual learners to reconstruct their own mental models of intercultural understanding.

It does not follow, however, that a wide mix of nationalities and cultures represented in any particular class will automatically translate into the development of international understanding or that this resource will be effectively utilized. The quality of student interaction is paramount. Engineered at school level, this begins with acknowledgement, respect and understanding of the cultural diversity present. Teachers need a keen understanding of this diversity and how best to exploit it as a learning resource, knowing which perspectives to draw out (and at which instances) to maximize cultural contrast and the challenge to established models of intercultural understanding. Effective orchestration of class discussion is of the utmost importance, with the teacher directing questions and eliciting responses so as to encourage international awareness and promote international mindedness.

Action and service in the context of experiential learning is an important component of education with an international emphasis (Cambridge 2010). Common to all three programmes of the continuum, the IB commitment to 'learning through experience' is realized in the PYP through 'action', the MYP through 'community and service' (one of the five areas of interaction of its core) and through CAS in the DP core (IB, 2008a). Requirements from the students in each programme vary in accordance with their level of development and maturity. At age-appropriate levels of activity, the continuum 'learning through experience' components develop, among other skills, critical thinking and the making of connections between academic subjects and real life; both key elements to constructivist learning. Seen by the IB as identity forming, this feature of the continuum encourages learners to consider the human condition in the immediate, wider and global community; the setting becoming wider as the learners progress through the programmes.

Exposure to people from different cultures within their own cultural setting, where travel experience takes learners beyond their cultural reference and comfort zone, exposing them to cultural diversity and challenging their cultural assumptions, provides essential stimuli leading to intercultural mindedness. Many CAS projects in schools across the world promote intercultural understanding (Hill, 2012), with learning through CAS largely resulting from reflection on interactions with other people (Alchin, 2011). CAS is a valuable vehicle for engagement in cultural diversity outside the classroom. In February each year the majority of IB1 (first year IB Diploma) students at SIS participate in a 10-day excursion to the Mwereni School in Tanzania as part of their CAS programme. While in Tanzania they engage with different tribal groups and participate in activities beyond the scope of usual travel experience. On their return, students reflect on their experience when completing CAS documentation and in a series of CAS/ToK integrated lessons that examine experiential knowledge. The students are always greatly moved by what they have experienced, substantiating the IB claim that for many 'CAS activities include experiences that are profound and life-changing' (2008a: 35). As a result of this trip all the students claim to have a deeper understanding of the world and their place in it, of other cultures (those experienced in Tanzania) and of their own. The Tanzania CAS trip takes the students well beyond their cultural reference and out of their comfort zone, and international understanding is served. However, if students as intellectual tourists (Roman, 2003, cited by Bates, 2012) are to achieve an accurate and complete understanding of the culture and people they visit, in order to avoid superficiality, misinterpretation and the reinforcement of cultural stereotypes (Bates, 2012), they need to be knowledgeable of the factors that have formed that culture and defined those people; experiential knowledge gleaned through travel needs to be combined with socio-political, economic and historical contextualizing knowledge. The internationally-minded need to be knowledgeable about the world if they are to understand it.

Conclusion

While the development of international mindedness permeates every aspect of the IB programmes and is itself the binding force of the continuum, ultimately it is realized in the continuum core components. Through these core components learners are equipped with the necessary skills and dispositions, and provided with the necessary opportunities of discussion, inquiry and experience, that facilitate the learning for understanding which promotes international mindedness and forms personal identity. As learners progress through the continuum their intercultural understanding develops through increasingly aware stages (Hill, 2012), with more sophisticated levels of understanding achieved as they engage with more demanding content and more advanced intercultural perspectives, and become more proficient at utilizing the cognitive skills essential to this process.

Arguably, however, the core components of the continuum are not all equally effective in their role of promoting international mindedness, with the MYP areas of interaction possibly representing the least effective learning structure for this purpose. Is it sufficient that students in the MYP '*should* develop international mindedness [and] *should be encouraged* to consider issues from multiple perspectives' (IB 2008b: 10, this author's emphasis)? Perhaps the IB needs to make its commitment to international mindedness and intercultural understanding more explicit in the MYP by including it directly as an area of interaction, with 'intercultural awareness setting the context for big ideas and informing the unit question' (Phillips, 2011: 39). However, even if this measure were taken, it is not certain that international mindedness would be promoted effectively through the areas of interaction; as Bunnell argues, connections made through the areas of interaction can 'become superficial and forced, rather than meaningful and natural' (2011: 265). Furthermore, fully engaged in their own subject content, many teachers view the areas of interaction as artificial and unnecessary constructs that detract from subject specific teaching and learning (Phillips, 2011). Without being fully understood and supported by the teaching body, the areas of interaction are unlikely to deliver the necessary promotion of international mindedness. Arguably, the international objective of the IB needs to be more explicit in the MYP, employing a more transdisciplinary approach, either structuring the programme predominantly around the promotion of international mindedness as with the PYP, or providing a component to the programme with a specific objective of promoting international mindedness, as with ToK.

International students do not constitute a homogeneous group; their cultural, national and linguistic backgrounds vary (Hayden, 2006). For some students, at various stages of the IB continuum, the promotion of international mindedness is a challenge not so much to previously established personal identity as to the creation of a personal cultural identity in the first instance. 'Where are you from?' is a meaningless enquiry for many international students, with globally mobile children often unable or unwilling to identify a single country as the foundation of their cultural identity. However, while they may inhabit a world between nations, is it really the case that they necessarily live, as Eidse and Sichel (2004, cited by Hayden, 2006) suggest, unrooted lives? For many globally mobile students (the so-called 'third culture kids' or 'global nomads'), the IB focus on international mindedness will constitute the very cultural foundation into which they root their own identities. For international students, international literacy is crucial not only for success in the globalized world (Heyward, 2002) but also for successful participation in international education itself. If a justification were ever needed for the international dimension and objective of the IB continuum, this alone would surely suffice.

References

Alchin, N. (2011) The Identity of the IB Diploma Programme Core. In: Hayden, M. and Thompson, J. eds. (2011) *Taking the IB Diploma Programme Forward*. Woodbridge: John Catt Educational, p. 24-41.

Bates, R. (2012) Is Global Citizenship Possible, and Can International Schools Provide It? *Journal of Research in International Education*, 11 (3) p. 262-74.

Bunnell, T. (2011) The International Baccalaureate Middle Years Programme after 30 Years: A Critical Inquiry. *Journal of Research in International Education*, 10 (3) p. 261-74.

Cambridge, J. (2010) International Curriculum. In: Bates, R. ed. *Schooling Internationally: Globalisation, Internationalisation, and the Future for International Schools*. London: Routledge, p. 121-47.

Cambridge, J, and Thompson, J. (2001) A Big Mac and a Coke? Internationalism and globalization as contexts for international education, Unpublished paper available online via http://staff.bath.ac.uk/edsjcc/intedandglobaldoc.pdf (last accessed 6 May 2013).

Gellar, C. A. (2002) International Education: A Commitment to Universal Values. In: Hayden, M., Thompson, J. and Walker, G. R. eds. *International Education in Practice: Dimensions for National & International Schools*. London: Kogan Page, p. 30-35.

Hallinger, P., Lee, M. and Walker, A. (2011) Program Transition Challenges in International Baccalaureate Schools. *Journal of Research in International Education*, 10 (2), p. 123-35.

Hayden, M. (2006) *Introduction to International Education: International Schools and Their Communities*. London: Sage.

Heyward, M. (2002) From International to Intercultural: Redefining the International School for a Globalized World. *Journal of Research in International Education*, 1 (1), p. 9-32.

Hill, I. (2002) The History of International Education: An International Baccalaureate Perspective. In: Hayden, M., Thompson, J. and Walker, G. eds. *International Education in Practice: Dimensions for National and International Schools*. London: Kogan Page. p. 18-29.

Hill, I. (2012) An International Model of World-class Education: The International Baccalaureate. *Prospects (UNESCO)* XLII, p. 341-59.

IB (2007) *Making the PYP happen: A curriculum framework for international primary education*. Cardiff: International Baccalaureate.

IB (2008a) *Towards a Continuum of International Education*. Cardiff: International Baccalaureate.

IB (2008b) *Middle Years Programme (MYP): From principles into practice.* Cardiff: International Baccalaureate.

IB (2008c) *IB Learner Profile Booklet.* Cardiff: International Baccalaureate.

IB (2009) *The Diploma Programme: From Principles into practice.* Cardiff: International Baccalaureate.

IB (2013a) Facts and Figures. Available online via www.ibo.org/facts/fastfacts (last accessed 20 April 2013).

IB (2013b) IB Mission and Strategy. Available online via www.ibo.org/mission (last accessed 20 April 2013).

IB (2013c) *IB Fast Facts.* Available online via http://www.ibo.org/facts/fastfacts/index.cfm (last accessed 20 April 2013).

Lowe, J. (2000) International Examinations: The New Credentialism and Reproduction of Advantage in a Globalising World. *Assessment in Education: Principles, Policy & Practice,* 7 (3), p. 363-77.

Mackenzie, J. (2000) Curricular Interstices and the Theory of Knowledge. In: Hayden, M. and Thompson, J. eds. *International Schools and International Education: Improving Teaching, Management & Quality.* London: Kogan Page, p. 42-50.

Marsh, C. J. (2009) *Key Concepts for Understanding Curriculum.* London: Routledge.

Marshman, R. (2010) Concurrency of Learning in the IB Diploma Programme and Middle Years Programme, *IB Position Papers.* Cardiff: International Baccalaureate.

Phillips, E. (2011) International mindedness and Intercultural Awareness in the MYP: A Relationship Reviewed. In: Hayden, M. and Thompson, J. eds. *Taking the MYP Forward.* Woodbridge: John Catt Educational, p23-45.

Skelton, M. (2002) Defining 'international' in an International Curriculum. In: Hayden, M., Thompson, J. and Walker, G. eds. *International Education in Practice: Dimensions for National & International Schools.* London: Kogan Page, p. 39-54.

Stobie, T. D. (2005) To What Extent Do the Middle Years Programme and Diploma Programme of the International Baccalaureate Organization Provide a Coherent and Consistent Educational Continuum? *International Schools Journal,* 25 (1), p. 30-40.

Thompson, J. (1998) Towards a Model for International Education. In: Hayden, M. and Thompson, J. eds. *International Education: Principles and Practice.* London: Kogan Page, p. 276-90.

Van Oord, L. (2005) Culture as a Configuration of Learning: Hypotheses in the Context of International Education. *Journal of Research in International Education,* 4 (2), p. 173-191.

Wells, J. (2011) International Education, Values and Attitudes: A Critical Analysis of the International Baccalaureate (IB) Learner Profile. *Journal of Research in International Education,* 10 (2), p. 174-88.

Woolfolk, A., Hughes M. and Walkup, V. (2008) *Psychology in Education.* Harlow: Pearson Longman.

Chapter 4

Continuity in international education: a case study of students' views

Jamie Large

The context: Ardingly College

Ardingly College is an independent co-educational school situated in West Sussex, UK, and founded on Christian principles by Nathaniel Woodard in 1858. The stated aim of the College is 'to enable all our boys and girls to develop their love of learning, academic potential and individual talents in a caring community which fosters sensitivity, confidence, a sense of service and enthusiasm for life' (Stapleton, 2011: 1). The College is composed of a Pre-preparatory School including a nursery (ages 2½-7), a Preparatory School (ages 7-13) and a Senior School (ages 13-18) on one site. The Christian ethos of the College is central to its character, and an atmosphere of care and respect for each other pervades the College and is regularly commented upon by visitors and inspectors.

As at May 2013 there are 535 students in the Senior School. Between the ages of 13 and 16, students study a broad range of General Certificates of Secondary Education (GCSEs), the national examinations taken in England, Wales and Northern Ireland. In the same age group students study for International GCSEs (IGCSEs) in some subjects. In the Sixth Form (ages 16-18) students choose from one of two educational programmes. Approximately 40% choose the International Baccalaureate Diploma Programme (IBDP), a two-year linear programme with terminal examinations and a core of Theory of Knowledge (ToK), an Extended Essay of 4000 words, and activities in Creativity, Action, Service (CAS) (IB, 2013). 60% of the Sixth Form choose the national Advanced Subsidiary (AS) and A2 modules, the combination of which results in A level qualifications.

Aims of the case study

This chapter is based on a small-scale study undertaken during 2012 at Ardingly College with a view to understanding Senior School students' perceptions of the concept of international education. Beginning with an exploration of a number of authors' thoughts on this topic, the chapter will go on to explain the implementation of the case study before discussing the findings. The chapter will conclude by considering possible implications of the findings for continuity of international education across the K-13 age range.

The main aims of the case study were twofold:

1. To understand what senior school students understood by the term 'international education', with a view to informing discussion within the college more broadly about what constitutes that concept.

2. To understand how senior school students themselves thought we might improve international education at the college and thus inform teachers' consideration of how best to improve the implementation of international education.

(Large, 2012: 8).

The focus of this research was therefore on the perceptions of students rather than on those of other stakeholders such as teachers, parents or governors. As a teacher and senior manager at Ardingly, I was interested to compare student perceptions of 'international education' with those found in literature, and with the working definition I derived from engaging with that literature (see below). In addition I hoped that the case study would provide those of us in the senior management team with some ideas on which to base the improvement of international education at the college.

International education: some definitions

Attempting to define international education is rather like trying to sweep leaves into a pile on a windy day. With each attempt to collect together the leaves into a single pile the wind shifts or distorts it. In the same way each attempt to define the term 'international education' is vulnerable to attack and each definition is likely to be in some way imperfect. Since at least the ideas of Shane (1969), the term international education has been a 'basket term' in that it has meant different things to different people in different contexts (cited in Sylvester 2005: 129).

Smart (1971) wrote 'what international education *is* depends primarily on what it is *for*" (p. 442), and the context in which international education is perceived is arguably vital for understanding the term. It is likely that different definitions of international education have been made for different purposes and within different social, economic and educational contexts. Wylie (2008) supports this idea by defining international education as 'the 'internationalization' of message systems and formal educational knowledge' (p: 7). Wylie has produced a matrix of contexts of international education to show how theory and practice mix to produce different conceptualisations of the term (p.12). He plots the theoretical perspectives of colonialism, post-colonialism, global economy, global ideology and global civil society alongside the practices of mechanism of learning and control (ICT and teachers) and message systems (assessment, pedagogy and curriculum) to produce a complex matrix of ways in which to contextualise an understanding of international education. This is a good attempt to provide a multiple-perspective conceptualisation of international education. However, it could be criticised for being too focused around social theory rather than educational theory, although admittedly these concepts are likely to be closely related since any meaningful definition of the term 'society' is likely to involve processes of education within it. A pragmatic response to Wylie's matrix may lead to another criticism of his approach, namely that his matrix of 20 contextualised understandings of international education might be considered too varied and unwieldy to be helpful, or indeed meaningful. Nonetheless as a moderate constructivist ontologist myself, I believe that Wylie's approach will certainly get us to think in a deeper way about a variety of contexts in which the term 'international education' is defined (Large, 2012).

Husén (1994) defined the term as follows: 'International education refers both to the objectives and content of certain educational pursuits and to the institutionalisation of such activities. In the former case it deals with the role education plays in bringing about certain competencies, such as the mastery of foreign languages, of knowledge about other cultures, or certain attitudes conducive to international understanding. In the latter case it refers to certain institutions, projects, and curricula within or outside the formal educational system' (p. 2972). This definition is quite similar to a helpful summary of many key elements to international education found in Hayden and Thompson's 'universals of international education':

- Exposure to others of different cultures within the school;
- Teachers as exemplars of 'international mindedness';
- Exposure to others of different cultures outside the school;
- A balanced formal curriculum;
- A management regime which is value consistent with an institutional international philosophy.

(Thompson 1998: 285)

There are many other definitions of international education, which there is not space to discuss here, but drawing on ideas from Hayden, Thompson, Hill (2007) and Husén in particular, I arrived at my own working definition of international education as follows:

An intended, embedded and realised educational experience in which students develop the knowledge, skills and attitudes which equip them to understand and find connections between the cultures and nations of other people and their own, and which prepares them for a globally competitive workplace.

This working definition formed the basis for the implementation of the case study, described overleaf.

The case study at Ardingly College

Data collection

I chose a mixed methods approach to collecting data, using online questionnaires and focus groups. Focus groups allowed me to follow up from the questionnaires to get a detailed and insightful understanding of student ideas, and to check that I had understood the questionnaire responses accurately. The case study involved purposive sampling (Bryman, 2008: 458) in that I had chosen students from three year groups: 13-14-year-olds in Year 9 (also known as 'Shell' at Ardingly), 15-16-year-olds in Year 11 (also known as the Fifth Form) and 17-18-year-olds in Year 13 (also known as Upper Sixth). This cross-section (Bryman, 2008: 44) of the overall students available at the college helped to gain a reasonable range of responses from students of different ages.

The aim of this was to see whether there was any consistency in perceptions between students of different ages and therefore if any general conclusions could be made across the year groups, or whether instead students of different ages had different perceptions. Either way, taking account of student perceptions would have implications for us at Ardingly College in terms of how we might best develop international education.

Responses from the focus groups and from the online questionnaire, which included questions requiring both written responses and responses involving the creation of pictures or diagrams, were collected and coded to enable some analysis of the responses. Questionnaire results consisted of 14 students in Year 9/Shell, 12 students in Year 11/Fifth, and 17 students in Year 13/Upper Sixth; thus 43 students in total. In addition, focus groups were undertaken with four students in each of the three year groups.

Data analysis

Analysis of the data gathered can be summarised as falling into four categories: defining international education, the value of international education, reasons for views of international education, and suggestions for improving international education at Ardingly College.

Defining international education

Written responses to the question asking students to define international education were coded as follows, with the same codes being used for both the questionnaire and focus group responses:

- Education in which students come from a mixture of countries
- Education in which students come from a mixture of cultures
- Education in which students learn about other countries
- Education in which students learn about other cultures
- Education in which the curriculum draws upon a variety of beliefs

- Education in which the curriculum is broad and recognised across national boundaries
- Education in which skills for future careers are developed: school, university, jobs
- Education in which attitudes are developed: respect, care, tolerance, understanding
- Education which promotes learning of other languages
- Education in which teachers come from a mixture of countries
- Education in which a student travels from his/her home country to learn in another country
- Education for all people

Shell/Year 9 students as a group considered an important feature of international education to be 'Education in which students come from a mixture of countries'. Eight of the Year 9 students included this within their definition. One Year 9 student wrote "It is where people from different parts of the world learn in one school". A second important element for Year 9 students was 'Education in which a student travels from his/her home country to learn in another country' (six Shell students included this in their definition). One Year 9 student wrote 'children from other countries gaining scholarships and such to go to school in a different part of the world'.

Fifth/Year 11 students on the other hand were far more concerned than other year groups to define international education as 'Education in which the curriculum is broad and recognised across national boundaries'. All 12 of the Year 11 students included this in their definition of international education. One Year 11 student wrote 'An exam which is recognised all over the world e.g. the IB programme'. Year 11 students considered the following two elements also to be features of international education: 'Education in which attitudes are developed: respect, care, tolerance, understanding' and also 'Education for all people'. One Year 11 defined international education as 'Education for everyone around the world wherever they live'.

Upper Sixth/Year 13 students defined international education with a focus on 'Education in which attitudes are developed: respect, care, tolerance, and understanding'. Eleven of the Year 13 students included this in their definition. One of the Year 13 students wrote of international education that it 'emphasises the importance of seeing the world not just from one's own perspective that will be influenced by the culture in which one is raised but also to try to see the world through the eyes of others'.

In terms of overall student responses *across* the year groups the most frequently mentioned element of international education in the questionnaire was 'Education in which the curriculum is broad and recognised across national boundaries'. Twenty-two of all 43 students referred to this in their definition.

This was also mentioned in Year 11 and Year 13 focus groups although not in the Year 9 focus group. The second most regularly mentioned element of the definition of international education across year groups was 'Education in which attitudes are developed: respect, care, tolerance, understanding' (19 students) and the third was 'Education in which students come from a mixture of countries' (17 students).

It seems that despite some common ground across year groups about what defines international education there was significant difference between year groups as outlined above. Why this was is not easy to say. Perhaps students looked at each other's responses within each group, thus resulting in greater consistency of results within each year group than between them. Perhaps younger students with no experience of the IBDP, which some consider to be a programme of international education, had a different understanding of the term than older students who were either studying the IBDP or were in the same year group as those who were studying it. Older students may have simply matured with age in their understanding of the term. It is likely that any concept as nebulous as international education will be understood differently by different people, and no claim is being made here about how these results might be reflected in a greater sample of students of the same age within the same school, let alone students of similar ages in other schools. Perhaps the experience of Year 13 students actually learning alongside students from a greater range of national and cultural backgrounds than younger students (as is the case at Ardingly College) influences the results. This of course is mere speculation, since the origin of the beliefs of students is well beyond the scope of this case study, and the samples for each year group are small, but it certainly raises interesting questions about how best to explain and develop international education for different age groups.

Pictorial representations of 'international education' included as responses to some questions were perhaps more consistent across the year groups than were the written definitions of international education. The following codes were used:

- Many hands holding up a globe
- A globe composed of many flags or with many flags attached to it
- People of different countries holding hands
- People holding hands around a globe or a map of the world or a jigsaw of the world
- Map or globe of the world with visual reference to teaching, learning or academic mortarboard
- Flags with reference to teaching or learning
- Hand-drawn picture of two people connected across the sea by thought clouds
- The IB logo

- A head in profile showing a brain which is a globe
- A picture of Ardingly College with many flags superimposed on it

For all year groups the most common features were coded as 'A globe composed of many flags or with many flags attached to it' (eight of the Year 9 responses; five of the Year 11 responses and four of the Year 13 responses respectively) and 'People holding hands around a globe or a map of the world or a jigsaw of the world' (four of the Year 9 responses; five of the Year 11 responses and three of the Year 13 responses respectively). 'The globe' seemed to be a common theme to all images chosen and a number of the codes were of similar nature so the statistics mentioned earlier in this paragraph perhaps tend to disguise the common agreement between images, most of which were composed of some or all of the same elements. We cannot of course be certain as to what these pictures were intended to convey, and the fact that Google searches using terms such as 'international' and 'education' are likely to lead students to have chosen similar images may well have artificially drawn students to picture international education in limited ways. Nonetheless the images chosen seem to convey a sense of people from different nationalities coming together around the world. This seems to fit well with the overall analysis of written definitions across the year groups. Furthermore the images which were different to the majority of images chosen, including those images which were hand-drawn, seemed to fit with the majority of images chosen from the internet. Overall then we can say that these common images fit well with the written definitions students gave, and that the main emphasis was on connections between different groups of people around the world, learning together. This element of the research process was very subjective since images are so open to interpretation, but combined with the written definitions I was able to come to a fairly clear understanding of how students defined international education.

What is clear is that although students had different understandings as to what the term means at different ages, they did have a grasp of the central elements of international education which have to do with connecting with people from a multitude of backgrounds and developing knowledge, skills and attitudes which equip them to do so, and which fitted well with the working definition of international education.

The value of international education

There was significant agreement on the value of international education across the year groups. In both questionnaires and focus groups students considered international education to be important. In questionnaires 19 students gave it a rating of 4 out of 5 in terms of importance, and 19 students gave it a rating of 5 out of 5 (Very important): a total of 38 out of the 43 students therefore rated international education as either 4 or 5. Perhaps this was due to the fact that students partly come to the college because of its stated concern for international education. Alternatively, perhaps students rated international education highly because they felt under pressure to do so by the very fact of my asking them. The questionnaire was anonymous, however, so hopefully this reduced that particular influence. The implication for management of the college is that, at least in this sample, international education is valued highly by students so we should do what we can to develop and enhance it, given that the senior management of the college believe it is important too.

Reasons given for views on international education

This part of the research, both in the questionnaire and the focus groups, supported the high rating students made of international education, and also reinforced ideas about their definitions of international education. Year 9 and Year 13 students largely agreed with each other. Seven of the Year 9 students and 12 of the Year 13 students included as part of their reason for rating international education comments that 'It is important to learn about other cultures' whereas only one Year 11 student included this element within his/her reasons. One Year 9 student wrote 'It helps our generation learn about others and communicate with them'. Similarly four of the Year 9 responses and 12 of the Year 13 responses included 'It helps to improve tolerance of others and peace in the world and it brings people together'. These emphases reflected the tendency of Year 9 students to focus their definition of international education around education in which students from different countries mix, and the Year 13 tendency towards defining international education in terms of developing positive attitudes towards others. In addition 9 of the Year 13 students included in their reasons 'It helps you maintain your own culture as well as appreciating other cultures'. One Year 13 student wrote that 'From experiencing other cultures, we learn to appreciate our own culture'. This was the only year group who gave this reason, which was interesting and showed a mature understanding of international education, which fitted well with the final element of the working definition. Year 11 students were concerned with the belief that international education was important because 'It will reduce poverty and world inequality' (five students) and 'All people deserve the same chances and international education is an education for all' (four students); again this fitted well with Year 11 emphases in their definitions. By and large there was agreement between questionnaire responses and focus groups responses per year group on reasons for rating international education. Why the Year 11 students had such a focus on equality rather than other reasons is unclear, but again this focus fitted closely to their definitions.

When taken as a whole across the year groups, the sample of responses seemed to show two main reasons: improving attitudes such as tolerance towards others (17 out of all 43 students), and that it is important to learn about other cultures (20 students). Again this seems to fit with the working definition of international education and showed students to hold a wide-ranging yet coherent understanding of the term international education.

Improving international education at Ardingly College

Suggestions for improving international education are of course predicated on what defines international education in the first place, but it seems that there were some useful ideas from students that might help us as a college to improve international education. This section was the most difficult to code as student responses varied so much, yet analysis was still possible. Six of the Year 9 students and six of the Year 13 students included 'Encourage students to learn a greater range of languages and ensure language teachers are native speakers' amongst their suggestions, whilst only two of the Year 11 responses included this suggestion. One Year 13 student wrote 'A better understanding of languages would be greatly beneficial'. Five of the Year 11 responses, seven of the Year 13 responses and four of the Year 9 responses suggested 'Teach more about other cultures in the curriculum'. As an average across all year groups this was the most frequent suggestion, included by 16 of the total of 43 students. The analysis above may however be influenced by the fact that so many disparate concepts (*eg* overseas literature, international issues) were put together under the umbrella term of 'Teach more about other cultures in the curriculum' in order to make coding possible. Nonetheless this was justified since students used these examples in combination. Year 13 and Year 11 students also frequently suggested 'Facilitate exchanges to schools abroad and more trips abroad (*eg* Continue with service trips to Kenya and Gambia to build and teach)' with three of the Year 11 responses including this suggestion and six of Year 13 responses including this suggestion. One Year 11 student wrote 'We could be linked to another school in another country and do exchanges with them for students and even teachers'.

Overall the main suggestions were that we should increase international education through a variety of elements of the curriculum; the facilitation of more international exchanges; and the improvement of languages provision at the college. It is perhaps these overall ideas across the years that are the most pressing for the college to consider.

Conclusions and implications for K-13 continuity of international education

Visitors to Ardingly College regularly praise the positive and caring atmosphere experienced when meeting students and staff. The Christian foundation, predicated on compassionate love for others, may be an important element in creating this atmosphere. This foundation explicitly encourages attitudes of respect and care for others, and so it is not so surprising that in this context international education is valued by the students.

It seems that, although there is a great deal of variation as to what international education means to different ages of students at Ardingly College, there is nonetheless some agreement within each year group, and also some agreement on a number of key terms across the year groups as to the meaning of international education, namely:

- Education in which students come from a mixture of nationalities
- A broad internationally recognised curriculum
- Education in which tolerance and respect are developed

The complexity and contextual meaning of the term international education will continue to make international education a difficult concept to embed within schools, but I also suggest that those schools which have a considered and properly embedded philosophy already aligned to attitudes of respect and care for others will find it easier to do so. It is likely that many if not all schools will claim that these attitudes are central to their educational philosophy. It is however the real, lived character of the place that, I would suggest, makes the difference.

In relation to the second aim of the case study, students suggested a wide range of ideas as to how international education could be improved, which will help to inform our own thinking as teachers about this area of development. There was less consistency within year groups than there was for the definition of international education, but there was still some broad agreement that international education would be improved at the college by: increasing the focus on cultures within the curriculum; facilitating more international exchanges; and improving the range of languages provided at the college. This fits with Hayden and Thompson's idea that international education is to be embedded in a balanced formal curriculum (Hayden and Thompson, 1996), although it falls short of the more subtle features of 'interstitial' and 'institutional' learning (Thompson, 1998), which relate more directly to the 'real, lived character of the school' mentioned in the preceding paragraph. It also fits well with Hill's and Skelton's ideas that international education relates to the context of individuals and to others within and outside one's own culture (Hill, 2007; Skelton, 2002). As such this case study hopefully contributes to the ongoing debate as to how best to implement international education in schools.

The reader will have observed that the focus of this case study was Years 9-13, yet international education needs to begin at a much younger age than this. Whilst it is difficult to project from the data gained in the case study to what younger students might think about international education at Ardingly College, it is likely that the roots of good international education should start much younger. I have already touched upon the idea of knowing one's own context as a starting point for understanding others. In addition to the more obvious ways in which our younger students come to understand the cultural and religious context of the college and its wider locality within West Sussex, England, students in the early years are now spending some of their time following the Forest Schools approach to the curriculum for part of the week (Forest Schools, 2013). This enables students as young as three years of age to understand and value learning in their own immediate local environment, in our case the woodlands contained in the school grounds. By learning in and from this environment, students come to respect and enjoy the natural surroundings which partly make up what it means to be living in West Sussex. From this they can explore values of caring for the environment and for others, and thence they are encouraged to develop a care for those from other cultures. We aim to roll out the Forest School approach appropriately in all years in due course. Other examples of international education in the pre-preparatory age range include learning about Chinese New Year, inviting an African Chief into school, an exploration of other faiths in Religious Education lessons, learning about other cultures through an imaginary journey of a penguin travelling overland from the North Pole to the South Pole, and Sixth Form students informing the children about their work teaching in Kenya and Gambia (see below).

The curriculum for 11-14 year olds, which spans the Preparatory and Senior schools, focuses around key themes across the subject areas of divinity and philosophy, geography and history. In Year 7 the theme is the UK, in Year 8 the theme is Europe and in Year 9 the theme is the world. Heads of department in each subject area across both schools have worked together to produce a curriculum which focuses around what it means to be British, European and international. This curriculum is intrinsically related to the development of international education, which starts from the local and moves outwards towards the global. Other departments are encouraged to contribute to these themes in their own way, for example through art and science.

In Year 9 we have also included lessons on metacognition and meditation to increase self-awareness, awareness and respect for others, to enhance learning, and to promote positive well-being in students. Whilst this is less obviously related to international education, it is hoped that time for reflection amongst students and staff will help us as a community to be more aware and more compassionate, and this fits well with international education. Each of these projects within the curriculum, of which there are many others, has its ultimate aim in developing human flourishing in our students, or what Aristotle referred to as Eudaimonia (Jowett, 2011), part of which is a more mature understanding of and appreciation for the interdependence an individual has with others not only within our community, but also in the wider UK context and ultimately in the world as a whole. It is the progression of various elements across the years which is vital to embedding international education in schools. There are also trips aboard, for example students fundraise for and teach in Kenya and Gambia, and various sports and cultural trips organised to Spain, South Africa and elsewhere. In addition 52 nationalities are represented by students at the college and 13 nationalities by the teaching staff, with a careful balance being made so that normally around 15% of the student population come from a range of national backgrounds rather than many coming from just one or two national backgrounds. There is an international committee of students to consider how international understanding can be developed across the school; the boarding houses celebrate contemporary cultural events from different nations, and students are prepared for a global workplace with careers education. Students go on to study at universities around the globe, especially in Europe, Hong Kong, America and Canada as well as within the UK, and a wide range of first and second languages is taught across the school. In short, students learn about and from others, and they grow in their appreciation of those from other backgrounds as well as their own.

As the world continues to change rapidly, the vexing questions of what defines international education and how it can best be embedded in schools within different contexts will remain live issues. I believe that, though small in scale, this case study has been helpful at Ardingly College in giving us an insight into students' perceptions about international education. It has encouraged students and staff to reflect on the question of how to define and improve the facilitation of international education, and it has fed into continuing strategic developments at the college. I hope that the findings of the case study, and its implications for continuity across the age range, might also be of interest and relevance to other schools that can relate to the Ardingly College context.

References

Bryman, A. (2008) *Social Research Methods*. Oxford: Oxford University Press.

Forest Schools (2013) Available online via www.forestschools.com (last accessed 5 May 2013).

Hayden, M. and Thompson, J. (1996) Potential difference: the driving force for International Education. *International Schools Journal*, 16 (1), p. 46-57.

Hill, I. (2007) International education as developed by the International Baccalaureate Organization. In: Hayden, M., Levy, J. and Thompson, J. eds. *The Sage Handbook of Research in International Education*. London, Sage Publications, p. 25-37.

Husén, T. (1994) International Education. In: Husén, T. and Postlethwaite, T. N. eds. *The international encyclopaedia of education*, 2nd Ed, Vol 2, Oxford, Pergamon, p. 2972-2978.

IB (2013) The IB Diploma Programme. Available online via http://www.ibo.org/diploma (last accessed 5 May 2013).

Jowett, N. (2011) *Translation of Aristotle's 'Politics'*. Available online via http://classics.mit.edu/Aristotle/politics.mb.txt (last accessed 21 November 2011).

Large, J. (2012) *International Education at Ardingly College: A case study*. Submitted as an MA dissertation for Master of Arts in Education (International Education) at the University of Bath.

Skelton, M. (2002) Defining 'international' in an international curriculum. In: Hayden, M., Thompson, J. and Walker, G. eds. *International education in practice: dimensions for national and international schools*. London, Kogan Page, p. 39-54.

Smart, R. (1971) The Goals and Definitions of International Education: An agenda for discussion. *International Studies Quarterly*, 15, (4), p. 442-464.

Stapleton, P. (2011) *Ardingly College Staff Handbook*. Ardingly College, Hayward's Heath.

Sylvester, R. (2005) Framing the map of international education (1969-1998), *Journal of Research in International Education*, 4 (2), p.123-155.

Thompson, J. (1998) Towards a model for international education. In: Hayden, M. and Thompson, J. eds. *International education. Principles and Practice*. London, Kogan Page, p. 276-290.

Wylie, M. (2008) Internationalizing curriculum: Framing theory and practice in international schools. *Journal of Research in International Education*. 7 (5), p. 5-19.

Chapter 5

Intercultural understanding: continuity in the international secondary school

David Harrison

The 'internationalist' and 'globalist' dichotomy that exists in international schools, as expressed by Cambridge and Thompson (2004), is one that deserves attention. In the one corner is the 'moral development of the individual' including responsible citizenship and international understanding, while in the other is the importance of 'economic and cultural globalisation' (p. 165). One organisation that attempts to reconcile these forms of education is the International Baccalaureate (IB), considered to be a leader in the provision of curricula which aim to emphasise the 'internationalist' concept of intercultural understanding.

The IB offers a continuum of education starting with its Primary Years Programme (PYP) followed by the Middle Years Programme (MYP) and finally the Diploma Programme (DP). These programmes provide an age-appropriate curriculum to students aged 3 to 18 years by varying the approach according to the developmental phase of those involved. The PYP is multidisciplinary and employs units of inquiry that blend together a variety of subject areas, from languages to mathematics, arts to sciences. The MYP is more interdisciplinary with eight distinct subject groups, while encouraging the formation of links through interdisciplinary units, and areas of interaction which are shared by all subjects and act as the context for learning. The DP is largely disciplinary with subject content, defined by the IB, upon which final examinations are based.

The MYP is a relatively complex curriculum package which has its own programme model (see Figure 1). Not shown on the schematic are the three fundamental concepts that underpin the programme:

- Communication
- Intercultural Awareness
- Holism

Typically covering the first five years of secondary school, MYP is followed by students who are 11-16 years old.

Figure 1: IB Middle Years Programme (MYP) Curriculum Model

The Diploma Programme caters for students who are 17-18 years old, and the curriculum model (see Figure 2) shares several identical aspects with the MYP, such as the student positioned in the centre immediately surrounded by the Approaches to Learning, which are the lifelong skills required for students to be effective in their studies.

Figure 2 : IB Diploma Programme Curriculum Model

The IB continuum is designed to encourage students to experience a smooth flow as they pass through any of the 207 international schools that (as at May 2013) offer all three programmes (IB, 2013). However, there are also other considerations. The IB programmes were developed in three different locations, by three different groups of people at different moments in time. The most well-established of the programmes, the DP, was initially conceived in the 1960s with significant input from the International School of Geneva and other international schools/colleges. Initially spearheaded by the International Schools Association (ISA), the IB was at that stage 'idealistic, pedagogic and pragmatic' (Hill, 2007: 26). The MYP, meanwhile, started its life as the International Schools Association Curriculum (ISAC) quite separately from the IB, which took it over in 1992 before offering it to schools under its present name in 1994. Similarly the PYP emerged from an initiative known as the International Schools Curriculum Project (ISCP) and Hill, a major force within the IB, acknowledges that 'the link with the MYP was not ignored but was not the priority.' (ibid: 30). The picture in 1997, when the addition of the PYP completed the continuum, was certainly not without its flaws and the IB has worked diligently ever since in adapting the individual programmes to emphasise key aspects. The organisation now highlights the same standards and practices for programme evaluation, a more clearly articulated approach to assessment, and well-defined culminating activities in all three programmes: the PYP Exhibition, the Personal Project in the MYP and the Extended Essay within the Diploma Programme.

Additionally, in 2008 the IB elevated the PYP student profile to become the IB learner profile, now used in all three programmes. This is an attempt by the IB to identify attributes possessed by all effective IB learners, whether they be a three-year-old, a secondary student or even an adult. This was a significant development as the learner profile also claims to express a 'clear and concise statement of the aims and values of the IB, and an embodiment of what the IB means by 'international mindedness'.' (IB, 2008: 1). The concept of international mindedness is connected to the notion of intercultural understanding, and between them they surely represent key areas of importance in the arena of 'internationalist' education. Yet the planned delivery of them is too often found wanting.

In the literature can be found a plethora of terms connected to international schooling, which led Marshall (2007: 38) to conclude that 'teachers and global educationalists are currently drowning in a sea of seemingly similar terms.' Excluding intercultural understanding, a few examples are international mindedness, international understanding, international education, internationalism, global citizenship, world-mindedness and cosmopolitanism. Even within the focused area of culture, terms abound such as multiculturalism, intercultural competencies, intercultural awareness and cultural tolerance. When reading many of the authors who employ these terms it seems the eventual goal is often similar – the delivery of a meaningful education to the students – even if this is not always clearly stated. The real issue is not the terminology, but what is being conveyed in the classroom; a sentiment echoed by Haywood when he says 'it is, I suggest, time that we face these issues and move towards identification of what our educational objectives should really be, since the absence of a more articulate position is not helpful to schools or to students.' (2007: 80). Being clear about what we do and, perhaps just as importantly, what we do not incorporate into any discussion about intercultural understanding is vital if the final conclusions are to be valid.

In an attempt to rationalise some of the principal concepts, a diagram can be created to represent some of the interactions between them (see Figure 3, later). The progression towards this model will focus on three terms; international mindedness, intercultural understanding and global citizenship. Clearly this is not an exhaustive list, but it will serve the purpose of covering the substantive issues.

International mindedness

The term that has perhaps received the most attention in schools over the last decade is international mindedness. Although initially used many years ago, international mindedness has experienced a renaissance of late. Ongoing debate at the end of the last century centred on what exactly international education consists of and whether it was solely found within the realm of international schools. The answer from Hill was very clear: 'International schools are not the only providers of international education.' (2000: 24). Indeed, Hill goes on to suggest that some international schools can be less international than national schools if they do not exploit the 'rich cultural diversity' present in their student body (2000: 26). Continuing, he suggests that trying to create a link between international schools and international education is a folly, and that time and thought instead should be given to other dimensions. His suggestion is to consider 'international mindedness', which he famously expressed as being 'an attitude of the mind' (2000: 33), his suggestions mirroring the sentiments of Hayden and Thompson in the same year when they discussed the concept of an 'international attitude' which 'would be related as much to the affective domain as to the cognitive domain of educational objectives.' (2000: 53). Hill sees the main advantage of this articulation as the prevention of becoming bogged down with practicalities: 'Thinking about being international (the end result of an international education) elicits different responses from asking people to identify the characteristics of an international education ... it lifts the respondents' considerations from the pragmatic to the behavioural.'

Whilst Hill's argument helped in avoiding the trappings of the term international education, international mindedness itself is open to interpretation and no clear definition for it exists. However, the idea that the term 'international' is best thought of in an abstract manner has gained considerable support. Roberts talks in a similar vein when he says that 'translocation of the body to another country does not produce internationalism, which has to do with hearts and minds.' (2003: 71). Like Hill, Roberts concludes that an international education can happen anywhere: 'the country, the type of school, and the national or ethnic mix of the student body is unimportant' (2003: 72).

The concept of international mindedness has grown to such an extent that it is now a part of many established procedures. This includes the revised IB standards and practices which insist that, 'The school develops and promotes international mindedness and all attributes of the IB learner profile across the school community.' (IB, 2010).

Some feel such an abstract notion needs to be firmly rooted in something more tangible or even that international mindedness should be replaced with yet another term. This led Wilcox to ask 'should we replace the term internationally-minded with a different term that conveys the intent, commitment and belief in particular universal values?' (2009: 46). A more practical step is taken by Haywood (2007) in his attempt to construct a typology for international mindedness (IM). Haywood likens his approach to that of Gardner's multiple intelligences, and devises several types of IM:

- Diplomatic IM – respect for the nation and culture
- Political IM
- Economic and Commercial IM – interpersonal interaction, communication skills, cultural understanding
- Spiritual IM
- Multicultural IM
- Human Rights IM
- Pacifist IM
- Humanitarian IM
- Environmentalist IM

This is a noticeable shift, as Haywood identifies not only types of international mindedness but also skills and attributes that are no longer abstract but *could* be measured – even though he expressly would not wish for IMs to become overly specific by saying that they are 'not in themselves objectives we should in any way identify as learning outcomes in their own right' (p. 85). However, as is also the case with Gardner's multiple intelligences, there are now tests on the market for translating this abstraction into quantitative data.

Intercultural understanding

When expressed in the manner noted above, the overlap between international mindedness and intercultural understanding is clear, and shows a vision of international mindedness encompassing many different elements. Intercultural understanding as a subset of IM is consistent with the ideas of Hill and the IB.

Hill's own classification is a little different from that of Haywood, although several similarities exist:

'the IBO conception of international education focused on developing international mindedness and it comprised the following:

- educating the whole person with academic breadth and CAS
- citizenship education via service, preferably in the community external to the school
- critical reflection, dialogue and research skills
- intercultural understanding
- learning more than one language
- lifelong education: learning how to learn
- values to enable wise choices for the good of mankind.' (2007: 33)

Of some interest, and contradictory to Hill's stance, the IB has repeatedly used the terms intercultural understanding and international mindedness in a way that suggests they are separate (see, for instance, the IB document *Language and Learning in the IB Programmes*), but nowhere can a clear distinction between the two be found (IB, 2011). The recently modified programme models (as in Figures 1 and 2) add to the confusion in that they separate the learner profile from international mindedness, which is inconsistent with their previous stance. In an attempt to clarify the situation, the IB stated that 'international mindedness was previously represented in the models by the learner profile, but as it is about much more than the individual learner, it is now positioned on the outside of each model, underpinning the programmes' (IB, 2012). Exactly what these extra facets of international mindedness may be is not clear.

Reinforcement of the notion of intercultural understanding being a subset of international mindedness is expressed by other prominent authors. Skelton sees globalization as the driving force for change, but links intercultural understanding to IM when he notes that 'Increasing globalization is perhaps the single most important reason why we need to develop internationally-minded curricula. ... it is already essential to understand, relate to and coexist with other cultures whilst at the same time remaining a part of one's own' (2002: 43).

Global citizenship

Of the three terms considered here, the third is global citizenship. As with international mindedness, this is an established term that has been brought to the foreground over recent years. An advocate within the context of international education is Boyd Roberts, who sees a principal role of international education as being the production of global citizens 'and good ones at that' (2003: 73). He views global citizenship as clearly related to international mindedness, arguing that 'global education is internationally-minded and concerns itself with global issues such as the environment, the distribution of wealth and resources, and so on.' (ibid: 70). In his *Practical Guide for Schools*, Roberts makes a coherent comparison between the concepts of international, intercultural and global, and in doing so reveals how he perceives the relationships between the three (see Table 1).

Perspectives in educational programmes		
Intercultural	International	Global
Concerned with differences and diversity, as well as with underlying common characteristics and features		Concerned with issues that relate to all people, to our common humanity, and with interdependence
Related to characteristics of different cultures (including practices, beliefs and values, languages and religions) Necessarily concerned with human culture	Related to characteristics of different countries/nations/states Concerned with defined parts of the world, and how they differ and interrelate	Concerned with global issues and systems that relate to all countries and people, across national and regional boundaries: economic, political, environmental, cultural, technological Concerned with the whole world-all people; the whole planet
Example of areas of concern and interest		
Different religions, customs and rituals, literature, culture	Political systems of different countries; national economies and their interactions; conflict, trade and relationships between countries	Globalization itself, climate change, finite world resources, global poverty, global infectious diseases

Table 1: Comparison of international, intercultural and global educational programmes (Roberts, 2003)

In this sense, Roberts partially sees global education as a fusion of intercultural and international education, although his definition of international education could be seen as quite narrow. However, what seems to be apparent is that in Roberts' view there is a substantial overlap between global citizenship and intercultural understanding. With this in mind, a model emerges to show how the terms intercultural understanding, international mindedness and global citizenship fit together (see Figure 3).

There is no intended significance attached to the size of the overlap between the different terms. Aspects of international mindedness may exist, it is proposed, which do not fall within the realms of either global citizenship or intercultural understanding. Global citizenship and intercultural understanding embrace the larger scale of human civilization; issues that affect global populations

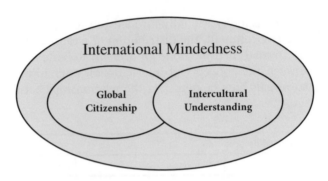

Figure 3: Proposed relationship between key terms of international education

and what can happen when cultures interact. Overarching these, international mindedness also accounts for the individual and the day-to-day behaviour of students at school. The key point with Figure 3 is that a relationship exists between all three concepts. Neither international mindedness nor global citizenship can be ignored, therefore, when contemplating intercultural understanding.

Intercultural understanding is often assumed, unquestioningly, as being necessary and it is commonly found in the mission statements and aims of international school websites around the globe. Several reasons are put forward for intercultural understanding having a special role in international schools, some of which are identified at a student level by Pearce. The first point, and perhaps the most important to practising teachers, is the direct effect on education, in that 'any differences in culture will be barriers to communication and hence to learning' (2001: 44). A second point is the effect that it has not just on the student but on the whole family. An inversion of the expression 'happy children mean happy parents' comes to mind when Pearce writes that 'a move to another country brings a change of every element except the parents ... if the new way of life takes all the parents' attention the children are indeed alone' (ibid: 55).

Other reasons presented for the important role of intercultural understanding relate to the larger stage. Writing in a UNESCO document, de Leo sees an increased responsibility resting with schools due to the changing nature of children's lives when he says:

'In the past it may not have been as important to foster intercultural understanding or to affirm, strengthen, celebrate and develop pride in one's own cultural identity and heritage through schooling, because learners were surrounded by their culture in every aspect of their lives ... The situation is very different today, as children are exposed to cultures constantly within their own community and through the presence of the media, necessitating education in intercultural understanding to strengthen their own culture and to gain deeper understanding of others' (2010: 5).

International schools are often seen as institutions supporting students dislocated from their own culture. The question of how to accommodate such a large mix of individual cultures is so complex that often the issue as a whole is largely ignored.

A final point, which is more relevant to many international schools than to those found within national systems, is the eventual destination of international school students. Having lived abroad, in my experience the general trend has been for students to remain away from their host nation and culture. This results in students living much of their lives in a different cultural environment which requires that, to be successful, they must learn to integrate or remain on the periphery of society. This trend has been seen over a considerable part of the history of international schools, but the pattern is now changing as the clientele of international schools shift towards richer citizens of the host country rather than the globally mobile expatriates of the past. As Brummitt (2010) estimates, 'overall, 70-80% of international school students are now from local families, a complete reversal over the last 20 years'. It should be noted that the total number of international school students has risen rapidly over those two decades so, although the percentage of non-host country international students may have decreased, the net total has still increased several-fold. Further information from higher education adds weight to the perception that students who study abroad are more likely to stay away from their host nation. Analysis carried out by Wiers-Jenssen (2008: 101) concludes that 'mobile students – particularly those who graduated abroad – more often than non-mobile students search for and gain work experience abroad ... In the domestic labour market, mobile students hold jobs with more international assignments than non-mobile students'.

International curriculum and intercultural understanding

If there is a need to educate for intercultural understanding, then the question arises as to what this would look like in schools using the MYP and DP. Borrowing from international mindedness and global citizenship initiatives, a general scheme could be one that is context-based and delivered through the curriculum.

Roberts has completed much of the framework required when approaching such a task. Working through the curriculum, he suggests one of four options to consider (2009: 80):

- 'Add a curriculum component specifically dealing with these issues
- Select, substitute or modify an existing element of the curriculum
- Permeate or infuse
  - one or more existing subjects, or
  - the entire written curriculum

> – Introduce a new curriculum that addresses global issues and the development of global citizenship more effectively'

The same approach to analysing international programmes for global citizenship adopted by Roberts could be applied to intercultural understanding. As a precursor to this exercise, the school would need first to identify the requirements for such a programme, something that Haywood considered when proposing his conceptualisation of international mindedness. Haywood's suggestion, which could be adapted to intercultural understanding, has two components (2007: 86):

'Essential components are the minimum a school must provide ... They may be universal in nature, while 'supporting' features ... are fundamentally located in the local culture of the school.'

This marries well with the holistic fundamental concept of the MYP, which places a high degree of importance on the relationships between different areas of knowledge and the context in which they are applied.

A further consideration of intercultural understanding within secondary school students is their developmental stage, *ie* what should be taught and when. Intercultural education is, by its very nature, value-laden. This is something Gellar (2002: 31) says we should not shy away from, when he says of internationally-minded schools that their 'ethical aim is actively to espouse and uphold certain 'universal' values and to make them an integral part of the life of the school'. We may debate whether it is possible to identify universal values, but Pearce believes that 'what we may morally do is consent together to agree and follow one value-system' (2003: 64).

Values form at a young age, with Hofstede's research leading him to say that, by the age of 10, 'most children have their basic value system in place, and after that age, changes are difficult to make' (1991: 8). Pearce (2003: 62) expanded on this argument by differentiating between foundation values, which he asserts are in place by the approximate age of seven, and an adult framework which is relatively stable by the age of 14. If true, this has implications for the development of intercultural understanding during the early MYP years; great thought needs to be given to the values being transmitted by the school as the student's thoughts are still relatively pliable. Subsequently, within the DP and the upper years of the MYP, presenting students with dissonant situations will have less of an effect. From this angle the MYP can be seen as 'moulding' – where students are perhaps more likely to incorporate new perspectives – whereas the DP is more 'instructive' as teachers challenge students' existing values.

Assessing intercultural understanding

Once a programme for intercultural understanding has been proposed it would be appropriate to check if it is successful. Despite the convictions of some that intercultural understanding is not quantifiable, many attempts have been made at assessing aspects of this concept. Claiming to be one of the most comprehensive tools is the Intercultural Development Inventory (IDI) which is 'a statistically reliable, cross-culturally valid measure of intercultural competence' (IDI, 2012). The IDI stems from work carried out by Bennett and Hammer, and aims to position individuals on an intercultural development continuum (see Figure 4).

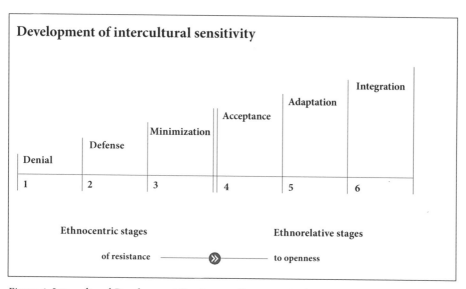

Figure 4: Intercultural Development Continuum (Bennett, 1993)

This scale is based on earlier work by Bennett, who devised the developmental model of intercultural sensitivity (DMIS) which postulates that intercultural understanding, or 'sensitivity', develops sequentially from one phase to another. According to the DMIS, as understanding develops the most significant change occurs during the two-stage shift from ethnocentricity to ethnorelativism, which Bennett views as having key characteristics that are opposites of one another: ethnocentricity refers to 'the experience of one's own culture as 'central to reality' ... the beliefs and behaviors that people receive in their primary socialization are unquestioned' (Bennett, 2004: 2). Alternatively, in the ethnorelative stages a person accepts that their culture is only one of many.

The ethnocentric orientation is divided into three stages, which share the commonality of avoidance of cultural difference. This may be done by refuting the existence of other cultures (denial), being resistant to other cultures (defence) or downplaying the importance of cultures other than one's own (minimization). A characteristic behaviour of those within the denial stage is a general lack of interest in cultural difference even when it is presented to them, as well as an inability to distinguish between different cultures. The defence stage acknowledges the existence of other cultures, but sees one culture as dominant or 'most evolved'. Bennett sees people within this stage as most likely to complain about immigrants and to feel attacked when their values are threatened in any way. When people expect similarities between their culture and another, they are within the minimization stage and they often believe that people of other cultures will want to be more like them once they have experienced their culture.

On the other hand, ethnorelative dispositions aim to seek cultural difference. In order to move into these stages, a person must be able to understand their own culture. As Bennett states, 'Only when you see that all your beliefs, behaviors, and values are at least influenced by the particular context in which you were socialized can you fully imagine alternatives to them' (2004). Similarly divided into three stages, ethnorelativism starts with acceptance, followed by adaptation and finally integration. Those within the adaptation stage not only acknowledge the values of others but also realise that they are equally as real as their own; whether they agree with them, or like them, is irrelevant. In adaptation, 'one's worldview is expanded to include relevant constructs from other cultural worldviews' (ibid), with the associated changes in behaviour that result. Integration is mainly a matter of identity, so that a person may move in and out of different 'world views' seamlessly.

An important final point is made by Bennett in saying that:

> I would also like to disavow any idea that more interculturally sensitive people are generally *better* people. To say so would imply that there was one universally good kind of person and that this particular model just happened to describe that goodness. On the contrary, this model describes what it means to be good at intercultural relations. (2004: 9)

The transition between stages is marked by 'evolutionary strategies'. For example, to move from denial to defence there must be an *awareness of difference* as a strategy, whereas to move from acceptance to adaptation the individual must go through intensive research and exploration to know the new cultural framework (Bennett, 1993). The IDI itself is administered as a survey including a series of 50 or 60 statements, depending on the version used, to which participants respond on a five-point scale of responses from disagree to agree. The IDI has been used with many groups of both students and teachers. The role of teachers is argued to be crucial, as 'all school education depends totally upon the views and capabilities of teachers, and especially those aspects of intercultural education which depend upon permeated values and concerns' (Costa, 1997: 183).

One of the largest student studies using the IDI was conducted by Straffon (2003) and involved 336 high school students in an international school in Kuala Lumpur. Referring to intercultural sensitivity (ICS), Straffon noted that 'the length of time that a student had attended an international school was found to have a statistically significant relationship with the level of ICS in these students' (p. 498) as well as that the students' overall scores were high, placing 97% in the ethnorelative stage. Davies (2010), meanwhile, used the IDI to sample 86 teachers against a number of factors such as gender, international school experience, experience of living with other cultures, and the specific effect of taking a professional development course in the local culture – in this case Thai. Of interest is that the mean score for these teachers was in the minimization range, much lower than for the high school students mentioned above. Also in contrast to the Straffon study, there was little correlation between international school exposure and an increased IDI score. One conclusion that could be drawn from this study is that adults and students respond differently when exposed to a new culture. Another possible explanation is that the specific culture the cohorts experience has a different effect. Put in another way, the students from Straffon's investigation might be more able to express and develop their intercultural sensitivity in the new culture of Kuala Lumpur than the teachers are in Thailand.

In a different study Taylor surveyed 50 teachers at his own school in Germany. Similarly to Davies, he says that 'in all the ... studies, the participating teachers were in the minimization stage. This is a surprising result' (2012: 19). Taylor suggests three reasons why this may be: teachers having a low level of intercultural understanding, teachers 'seeking minimization', or the IDI being an invalid measurement technique for that context. If the first of Taylor's propositions is indeed true, then students may be advancing their own intercultural understanding through interaction with other sources, such as family, friends and situations outside school, or the curriculum is at least partially independent of the teachers delivering it. This indicates the importance of a well-designed programme (which can promote intercultural understanding even if teachers themselves do not show high levels of this trait) as well as the more obvious need to consider intercultural education from a broader perspective rather than it being promoted in the classroom alone.

It is debatable whether the IDI can be used within the MYP. As Davies states, 'the IDI is not intended for middle school aged students' (p. 49) and, maybe for this reason, Pederson (1998, in Davies) decided to use a modified version of the IDI when analysing the intercultural sensitivity of grade 7 students (12-13-year-olds). Despite this, a major benefit of this measurement technique is that it is based on a concrete continuum. Rather than being an inventory merely ticking off a number of desirable traits, it forms a larger picture which allows respondents to see themselves within a framework. This has the advantage of allowing individuals (students in this case) to see what the next step could be. This view is shared by Paige *et al.,* speaking from a more theoretical standpoint (2003: 469):

'Interculturalists have also been interested in scales that could be used to measure intercultural sensitivity for research purposes as well as in intercultural education, training, and personnel selection. A number of instruments do exist, two of the best known and most widely used being the Culture Shock Inventory (Reddin, 1994) and the Cross-Cultural Adaptability Inventory (Kelley & Meyers, 1992). While both measure specific human characteristics thought to be associated with intercultural sensitivity (eg, flexibility and openness, emotional resilience, cultural knowledge), neither purports to measure intercultural sensitivity as a developmental construct. The IDI ... was designed to assess intercultural sensitivity along the lines of the constructs embedded in the DMIS.'

Conclusion

Intercultural understanding is a vital element of good international education. Within the IB programmes there is a philosophical framework for its implementation and, despite the relative paucity of concrete guidance – and even elements of confusion, there is an intent that should not be ignored. Indeed, international school teachers have an obligation to consider intercultural understanding as we may be some of the few in a position to do so:

> While there is a growing realization of the limitations of the organizational culture of public education to cope with the global culture to create conditions that would lead to the reconfiguration of cultural identities, national policy initiatives during the last two decades across the world have hardly led to any significant systemic change in public education. In contrast, it is the community-based, non-formal and non-government sectors of education and the emerging open learning systems that have been formed to break new ground to create the learning opportunities for a wide cross-section of the population. (Jalaluddin, 2002: 101)

Good schools will devote the necessary time and resources to identifying, developing and assessing all aspects of the education they deliver. Within the IB secondary school programmes, intercultural understanding requires not only identification of what each school deems to be the 'essential' values and topics, but also an appreciation of the changes taking place within the students themselves.

References

Bennett J. M. (1993) Toward ethnorelativism: A developmental model of intercultural sensitivity. In: Paige, R. M. ed., *Education for the intercultural experience.* Yarmouth, ME: Intercultural Press, p. 21-71.

Bennett, J. M. (2004) Becoming Interculturally Competent. In: Wurzel, J. S. ed. *Toward multiculturalism: A reader in multicultural education.* Newton, MA: Intercultural Resource Corporation.

Brummitt, N. (2010) The Changing Face of International Schools. Available online via www. iscresearch.com/isc-research-newsletter/?id=5#story_1. (last accessed 22 December 2011).

Cambridge J. C. and Thompson, J. J, (2004) Internationalism and globalization as contexts for international education. *Compare*, 34 (2), p. 161-75.

Costa, X. B. (1997) Intercultural education and teacher training. In: Woodrow, D. *et al.* eds. *Intercultural Education. Theories, Policies and Practice.* London: Ashgate.

Davies, A. (2010) The Applicability of the Intercultural Development Inventory for the Measurement of Intercultural Sensitivity of Teachers in an International School Context. Thesis (Doctor of Education (EdD)). University of Bath.

De Leo, J. (2010) *Education for Intercultural Understanding.* Bangkok: UNESCO.

Gellar, C. A. (2002) International education: a commitment to universal values. In: Hayden, M.C., Thompson, J.J. and Walker, G.R. eds. *International Education in Practice: Dimensions for National and International Schools.* Kogan Page, London, p. 30-35.

Hayden, M. C. and Thompson, J. J. (2000) International education: Flying flags or raising standards? *International Schools Journal* Vol XIX (2), p. 48-56.

Haywood, T. (2007) A Simple Typology of International-Mindedness and its Implications for Education. In: Hayden, M., Levy, J. and Thompson, J. eds. *The Sage Handbook of Research in International Education.* London: Sage, p. 79-89.

Hill, I. (2000) Internationally-minded schools. *International Schools Journal,* Vol XX (1), p. 24-37.

Hill, I. (2007) International Education as developed by the International Baccalaureate Organization. In: Hayden, M., Levy, J. and Thompson, J. eds. *The Sage Handbook of Research in International Education.* London: Sage, p. 25-38.

Hofstede, G. (1991) *Cultures and Organisations* London: HarperCollins.

IB (2008) *IB Learner Profile Booklet.* Cardiff: International Baccalaureate.

IB (2010) *Programme Standards and Practices.* Cardiff: International Baccalaureate.

IB (2011) *Language and Learning in IB Programmes.* Cardiff: International Baccalaureate.

IB (2012) *Coordinator's Notes November 2012.* Cardiff: International Baccalaureate.

IB (2013) *IB World School Statistics.* Available online via http://www.ibo.org/facts/schoolstats/progcombinationsbyregion.cfm (last accessed 5 May 2013).

IDI (2012) Developing Intercultural Competence. Available via http://www.idiinventory.com/about.php. (last accessed 3 March 2012)

Jalaluddin, A. (2002) Education in a culturally diverse world. *International Schools Journal,* Vol XXI (2), p. 98-102.

Kelley, C. and Meyers, J. (1992) *The Cross-cultural Adaptability Inventory.* Yarmouth, ME: Intercultural Press.

Marshall, H. (2007) The Global Education Terminology Debate: Exploring Some of the Issues. In: Hayden, M., Levy, J. and Thompson, J. eds. *The Sage Handbook of Research in International Education.* London: Sage, p. 38-51.

Paige, M. R., Jacobs-Cassuto M., Yershovaa Y. A. and DeJaeghere, J. (2003) Assessing intercultural sensitivity: an empirical analysis of the Hammer and Bennett Intercultural Development Inventory, *International Journal of Intercultural Relations,* 27 (4), p. 467–486.

Pearce, R. (2001) Developing Cultural Identity in an International School Environment. In: Hayden, M. and Thompson, J. eds. *International Education: Principles and Practice.* London: Kogan Page, p. 44-65.

Pearce, R. (2003) Cultural values for international education. *International Schools Journal,* XII (2) p. 59-65.

Reddin, W. J. (1994) *Using Tests to Improve Training.* Englewood Cliffs, NJ: Prentice Hall.

Roberts, B. (2003) What should international education be? From emergent theory to practice. *International Schools Journal*, XXII (2), p. 69-79.

Roberts, B. (2009) *Educating for Global Citizenship.* Cardiff: International Baccalaureate.

Skelton, M. (2002) Defining 'international' in an international curriculum. In: Hayden, M., Thompson, J. and Walker, G. eds. *International education in practice - dimensions for national & international schools.* London: Kogan Page.

Straffon, D. A. (2003) Assessing the intercultural sensitivity of high school students attending an international school. *International Journal of Intercultural Relations*, 27 (4), p. 487–501.

Taylor, S. (2012) Globally-minded students: Defining, measuring and developing intercultural sensitivity. Unpublished International Education: Philosophy and Practice unit assignment (Doctor of Education (EdD)). University of Bath

Wiers-Jensson, J. (2008) Does Higher Education Attained Abroad Lead to International Jobs? *Journal of Studies in International Education*, 12 (2), p. 101-130.

Wilcox, A. (2009) The emergence of "internationally-minded" national schools in Australia. *International Schools Journal*, XXIX (1), p. 33-49.

Part B
Supporting Continuity

Chapter 6

Implementing continuity: context is everything

Andrew Watson

Introduction

> Mission statement, learner profile and interdisciplinary curriculum design provide the intellectual integrity of the International Baccalaureate (IB) programmes. The IB is explicit in recognising that: 'Schools should be aware that there is no one-formula-fits-all approach to developing the IB Diploma Programme. Each school is unique and needs to consider its own context and the community it serves before deciding on the best way forward (IB, 2009a).

This chapter explores what this can and does mean for IB World Schools and argues that, in order to implement continuity with coherence and consistency in IB World Schools which offer the IB Diploma Programme, understanding of context is crucial. I identify three essential and interdependent elements in context:

- Local values, traditions and environment
- The philosophy of the International Baccalaureate
- The curriculum and the integrative role of the IB Diploma core

The chapter first establishes and reflects on the original vision of the International Baccalaureate and the IB Diploma, a programme with moral purpose at its heart, and proposes that the original vision and educational philosophy of the IB, born in 1968, is increasingly valid as we look ahead. Second, the chapter attempts to articulate some of the challenges of 21st century education, suggesting that we cannot carry on doing what we have been doing. Third, it considers the contextualised application of the essential elements identified above to three continental case studies, taken from my professional experience:

1. The first case study, based in the Middle East, reflects on the moral purpose of a school meeting the needs of its population in a situation of conflict.

2. The second case study, set in South-East Asia, considers an IB Diploma Programme which found itself in no-man's land, caught between a western educational framework (British), and an international imperative.

3. The third case study is set in the heart of Europe and reflects on how becoming an IB World School can drive whole school improvement when the values and traditions of a school can be successfully fused with the practices and beliefs of the IB.

The chapter concludes that, as the IB grows, it continues to learn from its experiences and is actively addressing concerns related to quality assurance and consistency across the world. Two steps in particular, the new authorisation process and the global programme of continuing professional development, reflect a renewed commitment to the original vision of the IB and the importance of understanding context in implementing continuity.

My professional experience has afforded me the privilege of working with and visiting a large number of schools all over the world. Whilst there might be notable similarities between them, I try to be sensitive to and develop understanding of the context of every one of them. By context, I mean the sum of the parts; the unique composition comprising a history, traditions, socio-economic setting, geography, population, demographic, languages, board, principal, teachers, students and parents; in short, everything that sustains the organisation. No amount of pre-reading and research can fully prepare me for the nuances, the character of the school and its community. Contexts need to be read *and* experienced. Whilst patterns may emerge between schools, especially those in similar contexts, there is always a surprise somewhere, which is one reason why school consultation and verification visits are such an important part of the new IB authorisation and evaluation processes. Assumptions about context, like stereotypes about people, are best avoided. Educational ethnocentrism is as dangerous as any other kind of ethnocentrism (which is not, by the way, an argument for relativism). The school needs to be given a chance to tell its own story.

Nonetheless, one pattern that has emerged which surprises me is that schools sometimes seem reluctant to spend time reflecting on their own context and potential. In different countries, I have witnessed the phenomenon of boards and school principals, in particular, misreading their own context, and imposing their views on the people at the sharp end: the teachers and students. Often it seems these ideas come from a romantic or nostalgic view of their own education experience – in the board's case sometimes dating back 30 years or more – and an apparent desire to replicate their rose-tinted memories with unsuspecting school communities. The third case study, for example, takes a school in the heart of Europe which, whilst international by any other name, was so determinedly British that instead of remaining at the school for their IB Diploma years, high achieving students would be sent off to well-established British boarding schools by parents who yearned for the 'real thing'. They perceived the local experience as a pale imitation of their memory of what a school should look and feel like, but the comparison was at best fallacious. Misreading one's own context is a bit like trying to run a marathon (which is hard enough) with shoes on the wrong feet, making continuity at best painful, at worst impossible. It is a tough and brave decision to say half way through, "Ah, our shoes are on the wrong feet, let's put them on the right feet and try again." But as Julia Middleton (2007) observed:

> Too often, leaders have not understood the world they were moving into and tried to introduce an order that is familiar to them. Or they have taken too long to understand the world they have walked into – and missed the boat as a result. (p. 36).

If it seems unkind to refer to 'misreading context', perhaps it is more of a case of 'underestimating the potential of opportunities'. And it is by no means always to do with boards and principals, although it does have something to do with leadership.

A special kind of triangulation

Consider the proliferation of British private schools abroad over the past 20 or so years (Davidson, 2009) which, rather than assimilate, seemed to desire to create a transplanted cloned satellite of their British mothership. Reminiscent perhaps of American Robert McCulloch, who bought and rebuilt London Bridge in Arizona where, originally, it spanned a chasm of dune rather than a river, British branded schools abroad remain 'Forever England' (ibid). We should, at any rate, be wary of the kind of 'hegemonic benevolence' to which Thomas refers (1998), disparaging as he is about the last hundred or so years of educational history which are, in his view, 'strewn with the relics of well-intentioned programmes'.

Davidson (2009) attributes this proliferation to English being the *lingua franca* of banking and business, and an associated market-driven demand for British schools. More recently in this brave new world, largely through a process of sometimes painful trial and error (symptoms include regular and irregular changes of leadership and the mothership withdrawing its satellite franchise), many 'branded' schools now seem to understand a great deal more about the need to develop a special kind of triangulation which, in order to best meet their aspirations, blends local values, traditions and environment with the philosophy and curriculum of the International Baccalaureate. The latter is particularly important because IB provides programmes with international mindedness at their heart, ready to be moulded so that form can reflect function (Jacobs, 2010). Reading context to find the balance between these interdependent elements is crucial to implementing continuity.

And where does the IB Diploma programme stand in these market-driven, product-branding times?

The original vision of the International Baccalaureate and the IB Diploma; a programme with moral purpose at its heart

The International Baccalaureate can be said to have been born out of a fusion of pragmatism and ideology; the former to provide for increasingly mobile and transient communities, and the latter to create an education for peace and a sustainable world. Whilst the educational context has changed dramatically in the last 60 years, the IB vision is just as relevant to the 21st century as it was in the latter part of the 20th. Far from being just educational products, the IB Diploma Programme – and subsequently the Primary and Middle Years Programmes – arose out of a philosophy of life. They are value-rich and value-driven. Understanding what this can and does mean is critical to realising the potential of being an IB World School in general, and of the Diploma Programme in particular, as a means of implementing continuity.

It seems to me that the journey through life is tough enough, so if it is possible for the experience of education to make it easier to navigate that journey, then it is worth trying. It is most especially worth trying if, as G. K. Chesterton (1924) proposed, 'Education is simply the soul of a society as it passes from one generation to another'. There exist great utopian dreams of what education can and does mean to the world, articulated by visionaries such as Kurt Hahn, who wanted to create 'an intellectual international force for peace' (in Walker, 2012) underpinned by service learning. Hahn's dreaming led to the formation of the United World College (UWC) movement, a force for positive change if ever there was one. Delors unequivocally describes education as 'The Necessary Utopia' (1998) and Tsolidis (2002) 'imagines the best' as they argue for idealism over pragmatism as a starting point for education. Walker (2011) tempers the vision with acknowledgement of the 'huge challenge of designing an education that prepares for an uncertain future' and the implications for the twin arts of teaching and learning. The IB organisation, over which he presided with such distinction, remains ideally placed to meet such a challenge. After all, the IB, as Walker himself suggests, translated:

> all those high-flown aims into a realistic international curriculum that commanded the respect of universities and the support of governments (2011: 3).

The IB Diploma Programme is, as Walker (2011: 5) observes, 'A rare example of educational stability and continuity', perhaps for two reasons. First, because it was the product of intelligent, considered compromise as visionary teachers sought to unite the best of a number of worlds from which it was drawn – including the French Baccalauréat and English A levels. The second is the apolitical nature of the IB, which allows the curriculum to undergo a remarkably inclusive and creative process of cyclical review and modification, remaining 'free of national assumptions and prejudices' (McRae, 2010). Nevertheless, as Walker (2011: 5) goes on to point out, 'it has not proved easy for the DP to accommodate both the pragmatic and the visionary aspects of the IB'. One reason for this might be that discomfort can be found when an 'unapologetically idealistic' (IB, 2002) international programme is launched in an environment not used to 'foreign' or, at the very least, unfamiliar ideas.

In 2006 a local school board in Upper St Clair, Pennsylvania, 'banned' the IB for being 'un-American, Marxist and anti-Christian' (Younge, 2006). A teacher was suspended for caricaturing a President Bush speech and drawing parallels between Bush and Hitler, whilst the Republican party referred to the IB in their 2004 election campaign as though it were part of an 'international conspiracy', alluding to the fact that the IB had been 'developed in a foreign country ... and we have to be careful about what values our children are taught' (ibid).

The IB ideology is explicit and unapologetic in seeking to change the world 'for the better', which raises the question of what corporate IB understands by 'for the better'. It would be erroneous to suggest that a shared understanding exists beyond IB. I just happen to agree with IB. But it has been argued (McRae, 2010; Bocchi, 2009) that its curricula represent collective conversion to a western neo-liberal paradigm. McRae (2010: 243) writes of students finding 'irksome' the 'ethos of liberal tolerance that runs through the way the curriculum is taught'. Just as British Schools abroad can be seen as a form of hegemonic benevolence, can the IB mission statement be seen as an instrument of indoctrination and, if so, how is it any different from any other extremist ideology? If values are the expression of culture, then as Hofstede (1997: 8) points out, they are 'feelings with an arrow to it; they have a plus and minus side' or as the Japanese proverb has it: 'the reverse side also has a reverse side'.

The counter argument can point to a Diploma Programme curriculum design which empowers ethical decision making with a global perspective. The IB does not promote tolerance of intolerance; rather it encourages judgements which reflect a sense of searching for ethical absolutism, as opposed to cultural relativism. This subtle but vital distinction is one which many, both those in education and those observing IB from the outside, seem to miss. The IB Diploma's Theory of Knowledge (ToK) for instance, is all about substantiating and justifying a position; using the tools of ToK, it just so happens that most extreme arguments are impossible to substantiate if they are explored in sufficient depth. This is important, because with a sense of moral purpose comes responsibility for standing up for things like social justice and trying to behave ethically. As the new IB ToK syllabus reflects:

> Much of the disagreement and controversy encountered in daily life can be traced back to a knowledge question. An understanding of the nature of knowledge questions can allow a deeper understanding of these controversies (IB, 2012: 20).

Continuity within the IB over the last 45 years has meant evolution rather than revolution but, as it has grown in size and strength, so has its boldness.

Increasingly it now echoes Bronowski (1973) in calling for action beyond contemplation. In writing of the rights and responsibilities of global citizenship, George Walker (2011) speaks of a 'duty' to act. For McRae the IB represents:

> A set of ideas about how young people should be educated to become effective, successful and honourable global citizens. If, in this ever more global world, the most important form of capital is human capital, the IB is the most important common force shaping the ideas of the next generation who will help run the world (2010: 233).

It is important to note in passing that, with the IB's significant growth over especially the last ten years, come two issues in particular. First the issue of quality control; second, the question of to what extent the IB is, in actuality, ready, prepared and able to 'meet its mission'. Can it remain true to its original ideology? The IB claims that it:

> [p]roactively engages like-minded donors, schools, universities, non-governmental organizations, and ministries to develop specialized educational programmes that promote concept-based, student-centred, and internationally-minded education (IB, 2013a).

However, whether due to a lack of project finance, initiative or vision, there are examples of countries in need of IB's help, notably Bosnia and Herzegovina as one example, where the IB has turned down opportunities to make a significant and meaningful impact. Such apparent reluctance does not sit easily with a 'duty to act'.

For a school embarking on its IB journey, there is an explicit expectation that it will be buying into the philosophy of the IB (2011) and into a culture; a shared way of doing things. A potentially uncomfortable challenge appears with the real or imagined prospect of old certainties being shaken. 'The call to action' can sound uncomfortable indeed. How does such a thing fit into a school's context? Understanding the philosophy of the IB is the key to unlocking potential in the IB Diploma Programme and it is fundamental to its successful implementation. It also has broader implications for the success and the continuity of the whole school, even if a school offers only one of the IB programmes.

Some of the challenges facing 21st century education: We can't carry on doing what we've been doing.

i.   The past isn't necessarily the best foundation for the future

ii. What we really need for our life's journey; an holistic approach that allows us to take in the view

iii. What kind of future are we imagining?

i. The past isn't necessarily the best foundation for the future

A common starting point of the workshops I lead is a proposal that on our journey through life we should develop a sense of healthy scepticism towards education as we know it. The past is not necessarily the best foundation for the future; to revisit G. K. Chesterton, we need to have nurtured a soul to pass on. In the recent history of humanity, the results of organised education have by no means always yielded results in which we can rejoice; gas chambers built by learned engineers or educated Eichmanns, for instance. We should be suspicious of the role that 'education' has played in creating an increasingly complex environment in which our children are sentenced to 20 years or more in schooling, just so that they can learn how to survive in it (Uys, 1980). The human incubation period is getting longer, not shorter. In school, it appears that we first ask students 'to master the accepted way of doing things before they are permitted to deviate' (Menand, 2011). Where then is the thrill of the chase, and what price the risk-taker? Where is the IB learner profile in the education equation? Does continuity equate with conservatism? Does continuity require conformity, maintaining the *status quo*? I say no; by all means deviate, just make sure you take your moral compass with you. If we keep our children bound in cotton wool, how will their experience of education best prepare them for life after the longest incubation of any animal?

How does the curriculum and a student's experience of school prepare them for the rest of their life? Do teachers teach 'for real life'? (Perkins, 2010). Are we teaching *from* real life? What does that mean anyway? Perhaps it means developing and refining focus on the key issues facing humanity in the 21st century? And what are these if not sustainability (in the broadest sense of the word) and conflict resolution, as recognised by the United World College movement? Where, as the global population explodes, is awareness in schools of the horrors of modern slavery and human trafficking? To what extent does any curriculum allow, encourage and facilitate focus on such utterly vital issues? These are not remote; they are essential. What kind of world are schools imagining? How far ahead do they think? Is it just to the next contrived 'stage' that society has formed for them, jumping through the next invisible hoop or sitting the next artificial examination? And how do we measure success? In the IB Africa Europe and the Middle East (IBAEM) region, where I live and work and where the disparity between rich and poor countries and within countries (some more than others) is unfathomable, 'success' can, in some circumstances, be measured in very simple and literal terms: getting all the students to school at all, for example or, at the end of the day's shift, getting back home alive. In some places, technology is not represented by a mobile phone, but by a water pump. The urgent concern generated by understanding the reality of the condition of people's lives around the world is not something we can allow to be peripheral to school experience; it must also lead to action.

ii. What we really need for our life's journey; an holistic approach that allows us to take in the view

Perhaps I should have mentioned my bias earlier; I am a painter. When people ask me 'what kind of painter?', I have learned to respond that I am a 'romantic colourist'. I think this means that I try to see and capture the beauty and aesthetic in all things. Usually this involves a great deal of meditation and learning to see and understand colours, often where and when they are least obvious. How does this colour my philosophy of the IB Diploma Programme? It means two things to me in particular. First, I support non-selective access to the programme. Second, whilst I am extremely competitive and aspirational in so far as I want schools to give all their students the best possible chance of the highest possible academic grades, I also recognise that, as argued by Dr Aurelia Curtis in McRae (2010), 'The prize is not the Diploma, it is the shaping of the person' (p. 240). But in a world where success for schools is measured largely by the grades students achieve in examinations, who can be surprised when other measurements, such as commitment to service, or a capacity for creativity, compassion and ethical behaviour, appear to be less important – especially when teachers' careers depend just as much on a narrow interpretation of 'success'. Thus another batch of young people are consigned to the mindless rush for a future few can envisage, the subject of popular satire from The Beatles to Blur: 'Running everywhere at such a speed, till they find there's no need' (Lennon & McCartney, 1966).

If we find that young people emerging from secondary education are having to run just to stay still, perhaps we should take the time to stop and smell the roses; to learn to slow down and walk again, remember how to see and listen; in so doing we might explore the places we visit with fresh senses, so that even at the end of our exploring, we might yet 'know the places for the first time' (T. S. Eliot, 1922). In forgetting to hurry we can take in a little bit of the view along the way so that, by some chance, we find that we enjoy where we are and what we are doing. In our school designs we might even come to prioritise the creation of reflective space in architecture and timetable, to reflect the centrality of a Creativity, Action, Service (CAS) programme to whole school well-being. Get CAS right, get the IB Diploma core right, and achievement – academic scores and all – should improve. Moreover, through reflection and meditation, we might better know ourselves and, through conversation, those around us – so that we can nurture the hope that our journey will be one of excitement and camaraderie and that our preferred futures might be based on ideas of shared humanity more than anything else. Perhaps then we might be able to recognise a sense of shared humanity more readily than feelings of conflict, so that such feelings become a learned response; surely Kurt Hahn would have approved. We might come to realise that there is no hurry after all.

And what of our teachers who travel with us?

> If they are indeed wise, they do not bid you enter the house of their wisdom, but rather "lead you to the threshold of your own mind". (Gibran, 1923).

The IB recognises that for a school going through authorisation, it is by no means certain that there will be a shared understanding of what the values espoused by IB philosophy can and do mean; part of the journey involves developing just such a thing, with an open caring heart and a principled mind: "Hard on issues, soft on people" as one principal put it. We need to be ready to work, without prejudice, with the parent who rips anti-Berlusconi propaganda from the 'ToK wall' because he only wants to recognise one side of the story (he leaves that side intact), and to listen without prejudice to the students who are concerned that the IB programmes are a 'totalitarian educational system' (Bocchi, 2009). This is perhaps a time when the true value of IB philosophy and the Diploma programme can be realised. By returning to the IB learner profile and the caring, ethical and aspirational values at the heart of the IB mission statement, we are able to engage in Socratic dialogue with people who are different with a sense not of cultural relativism, but of ethical absolutism. Such dialogue is an essential element in developing opportunities for the delivery of continuity. Confidence and faith in a new way of doing things is built on trust through conversations, not through dogma and confrontation. After all, in the best tradition of ToK, we need also to recognise that we 'might be wrong' (Hazell, 2005).

It seems to me that new schools in particular have a remarkable opportunity to be inventive and creative in thinking about how their chosen curriculum informs their architecture and environment. For instance, for an interdisciplinary programme such as the IB Diploma, why not explore in quite literal and physical terms how mathematics can lead into Visual Arts? In defining and redefining use of space, the question that is equally applicable to existing and new schools is 'where and how can teaching happen?'. Jacobs (2010) points out that Wiggins and McTighe (2005) suggest much the same, reflecting that first we need to know 'what it is we want students, in the end, to be able to do with what they have learned', before 'we start short-sighted activity writing for the classroom' (Jacobs, 2010). Therefore, it seems to me to be absolutely essential that for the sake of establishing a sense of continuity, consideration is given to how the physical environment can best reflect the nature, purpose and potential (and indeed the history) of the place; this is as much a question of ideology as it is of pragmatics. Once again, whilst one should inform the other, the trick as ever is finding the balance between the two. Imaginative solutions I have seen include an amphitheatre just inside the 18th century entrance to the school, providing a multipurpose space ideal for Theory of Knowledge where Socratic dialogue feels very much at home; interactive hubs in and around the campus, so that teaching and learning can happen in a variety of situations; a Visual Arts studio surrounding an atrium which is just about the first thing seen when entering the main building. These are inspiring experiences; in and around this place, the fruits of creativity are visible in a celebration of human ingenuity, invention, innovation and inquiry whilst a sense of wonder and respect for the environment is pervasive. Recently I was fortunate to be involved with the design and development of a group of schools whose purpose was defined by creativity and, of all things, happiness. And why not? The following is one part of what we sought to create (Plommer Watson Associates, 2011):

> In these places, the buzz of industry, empowered by technologies, is audible whilst collaboration and team work happen intuitively. In this place happiness is an epiphenomenon for the disciplined, synthesizing mind and the compassionate, generous heart. In these places you can see the art, hear the music and feel inspired. These are places where young people never cease striving to turn their dreams into reality.

If teaching and learning, the core business of any school, measures success primarily by examination results and equates this with well-being, then how can we expect an educational experience to result in significant feelings of happiness? Well-being, the subject of extensive research (Michalos, 2007; OECD, 2010; Hicks *et al.*, 2011) needs to drive the curriculum, not the other way around. And that brings us back to IB and the Diploma Programme.

iii. What kind of future are we imagining?

We are entering a new age where we will live and work in a world it is currently difficult for us to envisage. Generations starting school now will inherit enormous challenges from ours. Therefore our task is to prepare them for a future we can scarcely begin to imagine. We must develop young people with intelligence, courage and leadership, who are able to manage their own learning and their own lives, and to contribute positively to civil society. Schools must be actively involved at the heart of the local community and their work should be able to resonate regionally and globally in partnership with like-minded organisations.

If schools are to achieve their potential then, through a process of reflection, they must discover what is distinctive about their context; for this will inform their vision. If schools are to move forward with confidence on their journey, then the vision must be an inclusive one, in which the community is able to deal with the idea that 'learning environments, like life itself, are complex, non-linear and open-ended' (Codrington, 2004).

Implementing continuity necessitates building flexibility into structures, so that the institution and those whose lives depend on it can identify, pursue and achieve their preferred futures. In order to give students the best possible chance of achieving their preferred futures, the teaching and learning environment needs to reflect what Pink (2006) calls 'high concepts' which encourage 'the capacity to detect patterns and opportunities, to create artistic and emotional beauty, to craft a satisfying narrative, and to combine seemingly unrelated ideas into something new'. Pink's 'high concepts' should be embedded in coherent, logical and meaningful ways through the 'written' and 'hidden' curricula of schools, where leadership qualities in every individual are nurtured by process-rich opportunities which encourage initiative and develop long term commitment to community involvement; projects requiring student participation as leaders in local community service work and civic leadership. In my experience only one written curriculum already does these things: the transformational IB Diploma Programme.

Today an increasing number of new schools open as IB Diploma schools, yet the degree to which the interdisciplinary Diploma informs systems thinking and is encouraged to perfuse infrastructure design, operations and marketing suggests that the potential in becoming an IB World School is not always particularly well understood. So why might a school aspire to deliver the Diploma Programme? Is it, primarily, to be used as a barometer, a safeguard, protecting the intellectual integrity of the learning in the institution? Is it simply seen as a kite-mark for quality? Or is there really a transformational educational magic within, which is irresistible and irrepressible?

Case studies: Understanding context – the essential elements of continuity in action

Case Study 1: Reflecting on the moral purpose of a school meeting the needs of its population in a situation of conflict

A journey to the heart of the IB mission statement through the experience of living and working at a time of political upheaval and terrible violence, this personal history explores what might be required to retain a sense of shared humanity in such a context. It is also a story about how the IB mission statement can inspire lives of dedication to making the world a better place.

It is my privilege to serve on the Board of the United World College in Mostar (UWCiM), Bosnia and Herzegovina. The UWCiM mandate extends to providing teacher training and curriculum development across the cantons of the country; it is a real force for positive change. When I see a college such as Mostar in action, I am profoundly moved by the capacity of education to heal wounds and, just as importantly, to create hope for a better, more peaceful and sustainable world. Though the following personal narrative is not from Mostar, it is an example of how education in general and the IB Diploma in particular can be an antidote to conflict in the manner envisaged by Kurt Hahn and others.

The school was in the Middle East and the context was, shall we say, 'complicated'. Here was an ostensibly faith-based school, situated adjacent to a local population of another religion, neighbours who actively demonstrated their resentment of the school's presence and were not shy of making their feelings known (and felt). This was a time of political maelstrom. Outside the school walls, bombs blared and violence raged. But, inside, peace and reconciliation reigned. From an educational perspective it seemed there was only one logical way to move forwards: to recognise and celebrate what Sacks (2002) calls 'The Dignity of Difference' which had always been an inherent part of the city's magic and appeal and, in so doing, to make a stand against the purveyors of hatred and division who saw difference as something to be reviled. Both the geographical location and demographic of the school population demanded a pluralistic and inclusive vision, whilst the school's interpretation of its own faith reflected the same. The school comprised 80 nationalities among only 40 staff and 350 students K-12, many of whom were living the phenomenon of the 'Third Culture Kid' (Pollock and Van Reken, 1999), drawn as the student population was from the international population of the city: journalists, diplomats, the United Nations and any number of international aid organisations. Becoming an IB World School seemed to be an obvious notion.

When I arrived, this newly authorised IB World School had begun to use the IB Diploma as a means to drive whole school improvement and reshape its hybrid UK/American curriculum. Hitherto, the primary school followed the national curriculum of England and Wales, and then moved gradually across the Atlantic towards the Advanced Placement (AP) programme and a U.S. High School Diploma. Continuity was compromised because a) there was neither logical progression in the curriculum nor vertical articulation of it, and b) the curriculum did not reflect the international context. I observed that, perhaps inevitably, much of the good work of teachers and students seemed to happen in isolated and disconnected ways, which contributed to a general lack of shared understanding of what students might expect from their educational experience. This operational disconnect was reflected in the lack of attention to continuity inside and outside the classrooms. It is noteworthy that, in this place where 'the world went to school', the history textbook for the AP programme at the time was entitled 'Triumph of the West'. Academically the school could not be regarded as outstanding, in so far as teaching and learning did not always give students the best chance of achieving their potential. However, what was truly remarkable about the school was the tangible sense of companionship between linguistically and culturally fluent and emotionally mature young people, who hugged each other 'hello' in the morning and 'goodbye' in the evening – with good reason: there was a much less certain world waiting for them outside the school gates. The attributes of the IB learner profile were already implicit. What the school required was a better way of reflecting this extraordinary sense of companionship in teaching and learning. Further, the school needed to find ways to better reflect the inherently international nature of its stakeholders and the city, simultaneously creating a sense of natural progression in both experience and curriculum for the students, teachers and parents and, crucially, generating a sense of aspiration and challenge. In short, the school needed to better understand its context and create a new vision to reflect it. But what price, what possibility, continuity in this context, where conflict raged outside and disconnection reigned in the classroom? In order to realise its potential, what the school also required was a visionary to lead it. For, as Collins (2001) points out, 'Great vision without great people is irrelevant.' By fortune as much as by design (and how many of us have had cause to say the same?) the school got both, just at the right time.

The leader created a 'moving culture' (Law & Glover, 2000) that was learning enriched, where goals were collaborative and approaches shared. This resulted in positive mental attitudes among teachers which rendered apparently previously insurmountable organisational obstacles, such as collaborative planning, at the very least negotiable. Collaboration extended to burgeoning relationships with other schools and sharing best practice nationally and internationally. The school developed a holistic focus and began looking out and beyond as well as within, 'acting locally, thinking globally' (Allen, 2000). The cumulative effect of the impact of the new leader was that structurally, symbolically and culturally the school had begun to operate as an organic whole. The catalyst, quite strategically, was the IB Diploma Programme and the authorisation process which led to it, whilst the IB standards and practice created a framework for whole school improvement.

The school community was challenged to consider whether 'other people, with their differences, can also be right' (IB, 2013b). The students were not only encouraged to imagine a better world through intercultural understanding and respect, but were also able to explore and define their preferred futures through the curriculum. Education came to be seen as the bridge between contemplation and action; Theory of Knowledge a means by which students and teachers could better understand the history, the perceptions and emotions behind their own and each other's reality; the Creativity, Action, Service (CAS) programme presented opportunities through reflection to better know oneself and others whom one had hitherto only known as 'the other'; Extended Essays offered a chance to examine real-world evidence and to plan and pursue a research project with intellectual initiative and insight from their real lives, such as water use and misuse in the Middle East. Whether they liked it or not, students were at the centre of an issue of global importance and they were encouraged to respond by dealing with humanitarian issues related to human rights. Yet they were not overtly political; rather they were objective and academic, so that Theory of Knowledge presentations would regularly examine ideas through the eyes of a traditional 'enemy', in order better to understand their perceptions, reason and emotion, and the role language was playing in reinforcing existing prejudice.

In Visual Arts, some of the images were disturbing. Students travelling to and from areas where violence sometimes seemed to be spiralling out of control were encouraged to record and document their personal narratives and reflect upon them with their peers. One student brought to school photographs of the city taken through a shell hole in his bedroom. I remember picking up a senior member of the IB Visual Arts examining team from the airport, slightly anxious that there were some very challenging political pieces of work in the Visual Arts exhibition. "I'd be very disappointed of there weren't", she reassured me.

The leader successfully bridged the gap between cultural relativism and ethical universalist principles (Shaw and Welton, 1996). His consistency was in demonstrating sensitivity with a global perspective and flexibility with a broad range of transferable, interpersonal skills requiring multiple intelligences (Gardner, 2005) including, I submit, what Gill and Frost (2000) refer to as 'Emotional Intelligence'. But the vehicle to drive this transformation was IB philosophy; fortunately for the school, the right person happened to be behind the wheel and he knew where he wanted to go with it.

Case Study 2: Adapt to your environment – don't attempt to adapt the environment to suit you

This case study raises questions related to transplanted British education systems around the world, wider ideas such as international education as a form of western hegemonic benevolence and the dangers of misreading context. It also points to a situation which the new IB authorisation and evaluation processes seek to address before a school begins teaching the Diploma Programme.

Out of the frying pan into the wok of South East Asia, the antithesis of the Middle East and a school just five years young; determinedly, even mono-culturally insistently British, but equally unsure what this might mean – except that it became apparent that the majority of staff understood 'British' to mean 'not foreign'. This is an example of a transplanted British system school mired in cross-cultural confusion (Shaw and Welton, 1998), which actively resists what people including Hill (1994, in Hayden & Thompson, 2000: 51) regard as an essential aspect of international schools – namely 'the ethos is one of internationalism as distinct from nationalism'.

Metaphorically, the school was just out of nappies and teething problems remained. This young school was not particularly selective; their priority was getting enough students into the school to break even financially – a common phenomenon with many new international schools but one which brings its own set of educational, ethical and financial challenges. With a non-selective intake, many of whom on arrival had little or no English (the language of instruction), the school needed to be able to demonstrate that it was capable of significant success, but was struggling to do so when it measured success by academic results alone. It was an IB Diploma school too, from the outset, with tiny numbers the symbol of a 'loss-leading', financially sapping programme. The Board were remote and were not 'educationalists'. Geographically, it was set in an idyllic rural community on the coast, and was blessed with extensive recreational facilities. Nonetheless, the extent to which anybody had ever considered what was particular or distinctive about the school remained unclear; such an essential element of understanding context, promoting continuity and unleashing the potential of the school had been hidden away, not least from the idea of a logical progression in the curriculum. The IB Diploma Programme was promoted by senior leadership as a problem confined largely to the last two years of school and consequently, unsurprisingly, was widely perceived as such within the school community; question marks remained about its academic and financial viability, contributing to an unstable and anomic environment. Recruiting students and staff was becoming difficult; no member of staff had been IB trained for three years. The school leadership had misread a fundamental tenet of IB philosophy, that 'The IB is not just for IB students; it is for the whole school' (Curtis in McRae, 2010: 241) as reflected in IB's Standard A4 (Philosophy): 'The school develops and promotes international mindedness and all attributes of the IB learner profile across the school community.'

Cynics unkindly suggested that here was a case of the blind leading the deaf. A sense of 'can't do' culture was pervasive. However, reflecting on its geographical context finally allowed the sunshine in. Ostensibly, this school delivered the national curriculum of England and Wales until Year 11 and the IB Diploma in Years 12 and 13. But crucially, instead of exploring ways of adapting to its environment, it attempted to adapt its environment to suit its narrow, parochial outlook. The cure for its wilful myopia lay in the Diploma core and the key to continuity in this context was right in front of their eyes, but the leadership team were not blessed with vision of the leader in the first case study. The answer lay in CAS – the Creativity, Action, Service programme, the "heartbeat" of the IB Diploma – and in recognising that:

> Education does not begin or end in the classroom or examination hall and the most essential elements of education may exist outside of both (IB, 1996).

Led by the Diploma Coordinator (who had to overcome significant resistance), the school leadership team reluctantly agreed to place CAS at the centre of how teaching and learning happened throughout the school. Suddenly, students and teachers worked together from primary school upwards to think about what Creativity, Action, Service could mean for them. Creative ideas and possibilities proliferated and were unleashed on a rejuvenated school community; soon a different and cohesive dimension unified the formal curriculum by a focus on what happened outside the classroom as well as inside. I suppose an artist would call it 'drawing the negative space'. Hitherto unseen links between primary and secondary school were revealed, explored and evinced, and 'vertical' articulation of the written curriculum soon followed. Every student in the secondary school, not only IB Diploma students, kept a CAS diary and reflective learning became a natural part of the school day. In this beautiful setting it seemed perfectly natural and appropriate to embrace the environment and its possibilities. CAS provided the showcase to advertise its success to the local and regional communities. At the same time, it set the standard for aspiration in the classroom.

When I listen to the current education debate in the UK, I hear many comments related to a perceived lack of values (as well as 'skills for the 21st century') in young people leaving secondary school, and I wonder why the CAS programme is rarely, if ever, mentioned. Whilst the vocabulary of IB has begun to permeate mainstream education in the UK (still the IB's second biggest market) the idea that CAS is extra-curricular and therefore less important than 'traditional academic subjects' is still pervasive; left to a Wednesday afternoon, for instance, a modern version of 'games'. Even McRae (2010) only arrives at CAS at the end of his chapter on the IB Diploma in *What Works: Success in Stressful Times*. It should have come first! And whilst I might agree with him that as part of their education we should seek to embed the notion in young people that 'the concept of service is central to the survival of human beings' (McRae, 2010), I would suggest that altruism is not a natural inclination and that it needs to be learned, just like 'traditional academic subjects', and that the best way to learn it is by embedding experiential service learning at the heart of a school's operations. The curriculum design of the IB Diploma is perfectly deliberate: CAS (and the other central components ToK and the Extended Essay) are intended to enthuse, inform and inspire what happens on a daily basis inside and outside the classroom. Returning to the heart of Europe, we shall see how the core of the Diploma did just that in the third and final case study.

Case Study 3: Fusing the values and traditions of the school with the philosophy of the IB

The third case study is based in the heart of Europe and reflects on how becoming an IB World School can drive whole school improvement if the values and traditions of the school can be successfully fused with the philosophy of the IB. It considers how the IB Diploma core can reshape attitudes and aspirations towards whole school teaching and learning.

To the heart of Europe. Another school which identified itself as British, without having ever reflected in any significant depth on what this might mean until, that is, the school embarked on its IB journey and parents came up with some interesting responses when asked to consider the 'Britishness' of the place. Was it the uniform? The sense of discipline in the place? Or perhaps the fact that students knew their place to the extent that they moved with military precision on the proper side of the staircase? There were certainly very strong historical and commercial reasons for maintaining a British identity; it was what the parents wanted – whatever it was. Moreover, the city already had plenty of IB Diploma options for prospective parents, including a transplanted American school and a well established IB continuum international school, so they had to be careful to retain and develop an already distinctive brand.

A visionary principal had realised that the school was in danger of 'coasting' and needed to reinvent itself. The IB authorisation process provided the perfect opportunity to revisit the mission, identity and purpose of the school and to provide, through professional development, opportunities for staff to contribute directly to the vision and direction. The principal's vision was very clear; he wanted to move from 'good to great' (Collins, 2001). In such circumstances, inevitably, there are inherent tensions to be managed.

The principal did a great job of convincing the parent-only board that becoming an IB World School was the best way to generate a process of continuous whole school improvement, looking beyond authorisation to the regular process of five-year programme evaluations. He did this through inclusive and reflective self-study and in so doing he reinvigorated the teaching staff, some of whom had drifted into the arena of complacency.

Observe once more the transformational power of the IB Diploma programme! With a little bit of imagination and creativity, but most of all an acute appreciation of context, the seed of continuity was sown. The new school mission statement sought to blend the best of 'British educational tradition with the values, practices and beliefs of the IB'. Revising the philosophy was an important first step in generating understanding and momentum. There was a balance to be struck between moving forwards and looking back in conceiving what continuity might mean, the trick being that, like learning to ride a bicycle, after a while you hope that the team is focusing so hard on pedalling themselves forwards that they forget to look around at who is holding the saddle – so that by the end of the process, those who have travelled the journey might say of their leaders 'we did it ourselves' (Lao Tse, 2013).

One of the ways in which the Diploma Programme drove whole school transformation was through the school's Personal Social Health Education (PSHE) programme, a pastoral component of the national curriculum of England and Wales which, as it was prescribed and without contextualisation, had questionable relevance in a setting in the heart of Europe. Hitherto, PSHE had not offered teachers enough choice to make the course locally relevant and grounded in a way consistent with IB principles (IB, 2009), and it was in danger of becoming moribund. Yet it took up two periods of 40 minutes every week for every year group in the school. Here was an opportunity. Enter the Diploma Foundation Programme (DFP), a school-based whole-school programme designed by the Diploma Coordinator, affirmed in his role as pedagogical and philosophical leader. Mirroring the revised school mission, the DFP sought to unite the best of pastoral British education with a modified IB Diploma core by examining areas of PSHE such as drugs and alcohol, and cultural differences, through the critical thinking inherent to ToK, characterised by 'student-centred learning' and internationalism, the rigours of research-based essay writing in the Extended Essay (EE) and local, regional and global responsibility through the CAS programme (as with the school in South East Asia). All students in Years 7-13 kept a CAS diary, a place where all reflective PSHE work could be stored, developed and celebrated. The DFP also did something else; by encouraging vertical articulation it became a unifying force between primary and secondary, two sections of the school which had seemed intent on going their separate ways. A new whole school PSHE programme was underpinned by the articulation of a natural synthesis between the attributes of the IB learner profile and the values of the primary school. Gradually, primary school teachers delivering the national curriculum of England and Wales began to take advantage of the opportunities which came with working in an IB World School; even if the formal IB curriculum was the Diploma Programme. Primary staff became interested in becoming Extended Essay supervisors and attending ToK presentations. Simultaneously, the DFP breathed new life into the PSHE programme and raised the profile of the IB Diploma. The potential of context was being evinced.

Conclusion

We have seen three case studies of IB philosophy – the mission – in action, brought alive through the IB Diploma Programme. The Diploma core, through the IB learner profile, CAS, ToK and Extended Essay, is a means of driving transformation. To some extent all three case studies can be seen through the prism of leadership; in each of these situations to varying degrees, transformational leadership was necessary for the Diploma Programme to flourish. There are two things to be said about this. First, over-dependence on a single person is a dangerous thing for continuity, potentially leaving a vacuum following an inevitable departure. So facilitating and planning leadership throughout the school is an important component for implementing continuity; although whilst I might agree in essence with Morrison's (1998) suggestion that leaders need not be heroes or geniuses, sometimes (and certainly in the case study in a conflict situation) it seems to help. Second, the nature, purpose and potential of the IB Diploma Programme seems to me to invite transformational leadership, as well as actors who are driven by a great shared passion for teaching and learning and making the world a more peaceful, more sustainable place. The Diploma Programme is a potentially transformational educational experience which can and should inspire a school community. This is asking a lot, especially if a prevailing culture inside and outside the organisation is not familiar with what can appear to be quite radical ideas; there are plenty of examples of cultures around the world for whom 'questioning authority', for example, is a problematic concept.

The IB understands the dilemmas it faces and has taken significant steps in the past few years to address quality assurance and the concerns of the 'IB world', which are inevitable companions to exponential growth, and its ungainly cousin, potential overstretch. Two of these steps in particular are relevant to implementing continuity and understanding context. The first is the IB's global programme of professional development, designed to provide high quality (and mandatory) training for all IB teachers in all subject areas, including differentiation by experience, wherever in the world they might be. This extraordinary undertaking and provision includes new workshops for new courses following the continuous cycle of research and development that informs curriculum development. It also includes the possibility for regional associations to organise in-school workshops for local IB world schools thus alleviating, at least to some extent, one of the key pressures on schools; the cost of ongoing professional development. It also shows that the IB is listening and responding to the concerns of its constituents.

The other key development, which I alluded to earlier, is the new IB authorisation process (2011) and, in particular, the mandatory appointment of an experienced and IB authorised consultant to a candidate school. From the outset, this helps aspiring IB world schools to develop the relationship between the philosophy of the International Baccalaureate and local values, traditions and their environment, and to understand fully the potential of the curriculum and the integrative role of the IB Diploma core. In short, the IB understands that, when it comes to implementing continuity, context really is everything.

If, as Wright (2008) suggests, 'the future of humanity lies in the hands of those who are able to pass to future generations reasons for living and hoping' then the IB seems ideally placed to meet this, the greatest challenge. I have been fortunate enough to see the magic at work. And if is to continue to work, then we must embrace the notion that teaching for the 21st century carries with it a serious responsibility: to remain inclusive and compassionate on the one hand, yet resolute, critical and firm on the other. Because education and those who work in it have to make the choice whether they want to be the mirror of society, as Hechinger (1985) suggested they are, or the change agents of society. Or to paraphrase Dumbledore in the Harry Potter novel The Goblet of Fire (Rowling, 2005), education has to make a choice between 'what is easy and what is right'. Nobody promised the journey would be easy. But that doesn't mean it can't be fun.

References

Allen, K. (2000) *The international school and its community: think globally, interact locally.* In: Hayden, M. and Thompson, J. eds. International Schools and International Education. London: Kogan Page.

Bocchi, A. (2009) Personal Communication.

Bronowski, Dr J., (1973) *The Ascent of Man*, Complete BBC Series. DVD, 2005.

Chesterton, G. K. (1924) "The soul of society" Illustrated London News, July 5, 1924. Selected Quotes from G.K. Chesterton. 2013. *Selected Quotes from G.K. Chesterton.* Available online at: http://www.cse.dmu.ac.uk/~mward/gkc/books/quotes.html (last accessed January 4, 2013).

Codrington, S. (2004) Applying the concept of 'best practice' to international schools. *Journal of Research in International Education*, 3 (2), p. 173–188.

Collins, J. (2001) *Good to Great*, London: Random House.

Davidson, M. (2009) English schools abroad: Forever England, *The Telegraph*. Available online at: www.telegraph.co.uk/education/6202622/English-schools-abroad-Forever-England.html# (last accessed January 4, 2013).

Eliot, T. S. (1922) *The Waste Land*. Available online at: http://www.bartleby.com/201/1.html. (last accessed January 7, 2013).

Gardner, H. (2005) *Multiple lenses on the mind*. Paper presented at the ExpoGestion conference, Bogota, 25 May.

Gibran, K. (1923) *The Prophet*. New ed. 1999. London: Jaico Publishing House.

Gill, R. and Frost. J. (2000) *Emotional Intelligence: the 'Heart' of Leadership*. Paper presented at the Third Annual Conference: The Head and Heart of Leadership, Ross-on-Wye, 6-7 September.

Hazell, N. (2005) *Learn to Live to Learn*. Pattaya Mail, XIII, 33, 19-25 August 2005.

Hechinger, F. M. (1985) About Education: Students are Mirrors of Society, *New York Times*. Available online at: www.nytimes.com/1985/01/22/science/about-education-students-are-mirrors-of-society.html (last accessed July 29, 2013)

Hicks, S., Newton J., Haynes, J. and Evans, J. (2011) *Measuring Children's and Young People's Well-being*, Office for National Statistics and BRASS, Cardiff University.

Hill, I. (1994) in Hayden, M. and Thompson, J. eds. (2000) International education: Flying flags or raising standards? *International Schools Journal*, XIX (2), p. 48–53.

Hofstede, G. (1997) *Cultures and Organizations, Software of the Mind*. London: McGraw-Hill.

IB (1996) *CAS Guide*. Cardiff: International Baccalaureate.

IB (2002) *A continuum of international education*. Cardiff: International Baccalaureate.

IB (2009) *IB Learner Profile Booklet*. Cardiff: International Baccalaureate.

IB (2009a) *The Diploma Programme*: From principles into practice. Cardiff: International Baccalaureate.

IB (2010) *Primary Years Programme, Middle Years Programme and Diploma Programme standards and practices*. Cardiff: International Baccalaureate.

IB (2012) *Theory of Knowledge draft guide*. Cardiff: International Baccalaureate.

IB (2013a) *Access and Advancement*. Available online at www.ibo.org/accessandavancement/ (last accessed 4 May 2013).

IB (2013b) *Mission and strategy*, Available online at www.ibo.org/mission/ (last accessed 4 May 2013).

Jacobs, H. H. (2010) *Curriculum 21: Essential Education for a Changing World*. Alexandria, VA, USA.

Lao-Tse (2013) *Winston Churchill Leadership principles and their relevance today*. Available online at: www.winston-churchill-leadership.com (last accessed 7 January 2013).

Law, S. and Glover, D. (2000) *Educational Leadership and Learning; Practice, Policy & Research*. Buckingham: Open University Press.

Lennon, J. and McCartney P. (1966) "*Running everywhere at such a speed, till they find there's no need*" from 'I'm Only Sleeping'. From the Album 'Revolver' (1966), Northern Songs Ltd/ EMI Records.

McRae, H. (2010) *What Works, Success in Stressful Times*, London: Harper Press.

Menand, L. (2011) *Why we have college, Debating the Value of College in America*: A Critic at

Large, Live and Learn, The New Yorker. 2013 Available online at: http://www.newyorker.com/arts/critics/atlarge/2011/06/06/110606crat_atlarge_menand#ixzz2HOofnraH (last accessed 4 January 2013).

Michalos, A. C. (2007) *Education, Happiness and Wellbeing.* Institute for Social Research and Evaluation, University of Northern British Columbia, Canada.

Middleton, J. (2007) *Beyond Authority; Leadership in a Changing World.* New York: Palgrave Macmillan.

Morrison, K. (1998) *Management Theories for Educational Change.* London: Paul Chapman Publishing Ltd, Sage Publications.

OECD (2010) *Learning to Learn – Student Engagement, Strategies and Practices (Volume III).* PISA 2009 Books - OECD iLibrary, 2012, Available online at: http://dx.doi.org/10.1787/9789264083943-en (last accessed 18 December 2012).

Perkins, D. (2010) Are You Teaching for Real Life? *IB World,* 59.

Pink, D.H. (2006) *A whole new mind: Why right-brainers will rule the world.* New York: Riverhead Books.

Plommer Watson Associates (2011) Available online via http://plommerwatson.com/ (last accessed 9 May 2013).

Pollock, D. and Van Reken, R. (1999) *The Third Culture Kid Experience: Growing Up Among Worlds.* London: Nicholas Brealey Publishing.

Rowling, J.K. (2005) *The Goblet of Fire,* London: Bloomsbury Publishing.

Sacks, Rabbi Jonathan (2002) *The Dignity of Difference,* London: Continuum.

Shaw, M. and Welton, J. (1996) *The application of education management models and theories to the processes of education policy making and management: A case of compound cross-cultural confusion.* Paper presented at conference: Indigenous Perspectives of Education Management, Kuala Lumpur.

Thomas, P. (1998) *Education for Peace, The Cornerstone of International Education.* In: Hayden, M. and Thompson, J. eds. International Education, Principles and Practices. London: Kogan Page.

Tsolidis, G. (2004) How do we teach and learn in times when the notion of 'global citizenship' sounds like a cliché? *Journal of Research in International Education,* 1 (2), p. 213–226.

Uys, J. (1980) The Gods Must be Crazy, Ster Kinekor, 20th Century Fox (US).

Walker, G. (2004) *To Educate the Nations 2: Reflections on an International Education.* Woodbridge: John Catt Educational.

Walker, G. (2011) *The Changing Face of International Education: Challenges for the IB.* Cardiff: International Baccalaureate.

Wiggins, G., and McTighe, J. (2005). *Understanding by Design.* Expanded 2nd ed. Alexandria, VA: ASCDUNESCO (1996) Learning: The Treasure Within, International Commission on Education for the 21st Century. Paris: UNESCO.

Wright, C. (2008) Personal Communication.

Younge, G. (2006) Silence in Class, *Guardian Weekly,* 14-20 April 2006.

Chapter 7

Connecting theory to practice: continuity in teacher development

Beverly Shaklee and April Mattix

Introduction

The International Baccalaureate (IB) maintains that fundamental to ensuring rigor and consistency within its three programmes is continuity between teacher practice and learner goals (IB, 2013a). Key to success in this endeavor is creating a terrain in which teachers can develop their pedagogical skills while at the same time nurturing the development of their learner attitudes. To help meet this end, in 2005 the International Baccalaureate established university-IB preparation partnerships. The purpose of these partnerships is two-fold: first, they provide additional opportunities for teachers to become prepared to teach in IB schools, and second, they offer current IB teachers further opportunities for advanced preparation. The partnership programmes envisioned were designed to offer teachers a deeper understanding of the principles and practices of the three IB school-based programmes, while simultaneously allowing participants to demonstrate a commitment to their own professional learning by incorporating significant elements of critical reflection and research within their areas of study. To achieve these goals, two visions of university-level coursework were created, named initially as the IB Teacher Awards but now described as follows:

1. The **IB certificate in teaching and learning** offers teachers the opportunity to examine the principles and practices associated with each of the three IB programmes (Primary Years, Middle Years, and Diploma Programmes). The courses that lead to this certificate shape pre-service, new, and experienced educators into reflective practitioners.

2. The **IB advanced certificate in teaching and learning research** offers teachers the opportunity to supplement their existing IB experience with rigorous, systematic investigative work to further their knowledge and experience. Participants delve deeper into curriculum development, pedagogy, and assessment through exploring relevant literature and their own IB practices (IB, 2013a).

The intent of this chapter is to explore the critical elements that provide continuity between the practices of IB teachers worldwide and the postgraduate programmes offered by universities. This exploration will be situated in the research terrain of effective teacher education programmes and will examine characteristics of effective international teacher preparation. The structural components that serve as the foundational pillars of university-IB preparation programmes will be presented, and an exemplar of practice will be provided as a tangible illustration of the partnership in practice. Finally, future considerations for maintaining continuity within university-IB partnerships will be addressed.

Effective teacher education

The current landscape of educational research is laden with investigations into teacher preparation and training. Ranging from examinations into the knowledge, skills, experiences, and dispositions necessary to do the work of teaching (Ball & Forzani, 2009; Ball, Thames & Phelps, 2008; Shulman, 1987) to inquiries into how teachers can best develop the capacities to enact the work of teaching (Feiman-Nemser, 2001; Putnam & Borko, 2000; Hammerness *et al.*, 2005), the wide swath of research aimed at improving and developing the ways in which teachers are prepared reflects the consensus that teachers should be given rich preparation to navigate the dynamic classrooms of today. There is no doubt that highly powerful teaching is increasingly important in contemporary society (Darling-Hammond, 2006: 300). What is not clearly established are the elements of a teacher education programme that provide connections to the pre-kindergarten–Grade 12 (PK–12) classrooms in such a way that the teachers being prepared are able to negotiate complex classrooms with highly diverse and linguistically rich populations of learners.

In order to create viable preparation programmes, the university-IB partnerships had to consider what elements should be included in such an endeavor and how the programmes should be constructed. To tackle this undertaking, consideration had to be given to what good teacher preparation programmes do and how they articulate to the field of practice. A number of authors have addressed salient issues related to the development of pre-service and in-service teachers for international schools including, for instance, contributors to *The SAGE Handbook of Research in International Education* (Hayden *et al.*, 2007). Among the elements that appear most often in teacher preparation for international schools are teachers' ability to: understand global perspectives; understand student characteristics and the relationship to learning; develop intercultural and multicultural understandings; demonstrate effective pedagogy; employ appropriate assessment strategies to enhance learning; practice skills and understandings in an international context; and develop a professional disposition toward reflective practice (Levy, 2007; Hayden, 2006, 2007; Snowball, 2007). Shaklee and Baily (2012: 6) contend that all teachers – domestic as well as those prepared for international schools – should be prepared as 'internationally-minded educators focusing the preparation programme on a coherent philosophy of teacher development throughout the program'. Cushner (2011) argues that the development of intercultural competency is increasingly important for all educators 'where teachers must effectively teach students and interact with families from a wide range of backgrounds' (2011: 41).

Helping to contextualize the field of teacher education programmes and practices from a larger stage, Korthagen, Loughran and Russell (2006) take a cross-cultural approach to identifying fundamental principles to which teacher preparation programmes should attend in order to connect theory to practice in teacher education. Among these principles of practice are a focus on understanding the demands of teaching, shifting the focus from curriculum to the learner, teacher research, collaboration with peers, modeling of approaches, and meaningful relationships between schools, universities, and student teachers. Coupled with these essential elements, Darling-Hammond has identified three critical components of effective teacher education programmes for both pre-service and in-service teacher preparation in the 21st Century: 'tight coherence and integration among courses and between coursework and clinical work in schools; extensive and intensively supervised clinical practice; and close proactive relationships with schools that serve diverse learners effectively and develop and model good teaching' (2006: 300). Taking these and like considerations into account, the university-IB partners collaborated to create practical, applicable, and meaningful criteria for the IB certification programmes.

Structure of IB university programmes

Each programme of the IB promotes the education of the whole person, emphasizing intellectual, personal, emotional, and social growth, through all domains of knowledge. This emphasis is embodied within the elements of the IB learner profile, which calls for learners to be: inquirers, knowledgeable, thinkers, communicators, principled, open-minded, caring, risk-takers, balanced, and reflective (IB, 2008). The goal of the teacher awards, beyond developing teacher understanding of effective learning and instruction, lies in bolstering a teacher's ability to foster the elements of the learner profile within his or her instruction, pedagogical approach, and general methodologies of practice. Inherent in the university preparation programmes, therefore, is the implicit goal of facilitating the development of these skills through an in-depth programme of studies.

To address the issues of what a teacher should know and be able to demonstrate, IB teams created a series of elements, or areas of inquiry, for prospective and practicing teachers in IB schools. Within each area of inquiry, domains of understanding were identified and, for each of the three programmes, an 'essential question' was established which guided the domain with particular areas of emphasis. The system was designed around four areas of inquiry, each one 'derived from essential common components associated with the implementation and operation of the IB programmes' (2005: 3) and includes: curriculum processes; teaching and learning; assessment and learning; and professional learning. Each of the domains includes additional frameworks for planning postgraduate programmes that guide the curriculum developers, ensuring continuity with the critical elements of the PK-12 IB programmes.

Area of Inquiry 1: Curriculum processes

The first inquiry strand focuses upon the actual curriculum processes within the IB continuum. The IB recognizes that to develop knowledge and understanding as well as skills and attitudes in students, the focus must be on the learner and learning. To achieve this, demonstrating an understanding of the curriculum frameworks of the IB's programmes and the processes that underpin them is an integral part of the knowledge that an IB teacher should possess. Therefore, the teacher certificate programmes focus on developing practical knowledge about the design and structure of the IB programmes. This in turn provides a foundation for understanding how the programmes are implemented and how student learning developed within them is assessed (see Table 1).

Domain	Primary Years Programme	Middle Years Programme	Diploma Programme
A. International education and the role and philosophy of the IB programmes	What is international education and how does the IB's mission and PYP philosophy promote it?	What is international education and how does the IB's mission and the MYP philosophy promote it?	What is international education and how does the IB's mission and the aims of the Diploma Programme (DP) support it?
B. Curriculum frameworks (principles, structures, and practices)	How is the PYP curriculum framework structured and what principles of learning underpin it?	How is the MYP curriculum framework structured and what are the principles that underpin it?	How is the DP curriculum framework structured and what are the educational principles that underpin it?
C. Curriculum and instructional design	What is a programme of inquiry and how are they constructed?	What are the essential elements when developing a programme of learning within the MYP and how is it constructed?	What processes are involved in designing effective programmes of learning within the context of the DP programme? How are they combined to create authentic learning activities?
D. Curriculum articulation	What are the essential features of the IB programme continuum and what features of the PYP conform to or differ from the other two IB programmes?	What are the essential features of the IB programme continuum and how does the MYP conform to or differ from the PYP and Diploma programme?	What are the essential features of the IB programme continuum and how does the DP conform to or differ from the PYP and MYP programmes?

Table 1: Area of Inquiry 1 (IB, 2013a)

Area of Inquiry 2: Teaching and learning

The second area of inquiry focuses upon the fundamental skills of teaching and learning for IB practitioners. The purpose of the second line of inquiry is to acknowledge the professional craft and expertise of the IB educator. While knowledge of curriculum processes is certainly essential, the capacity to interpret the curriculum and adopt appropriate teaching strategies and techniques stands instrumental in ensuring that learning outcomes are achieved. To accommodate this need, the teacher certification programmes focus on developing understanding of the relationship between teaching and learning, as well as the various teaching strategies that can be demonstrated to be effective in enacting the programmes (see Table 2).

Domain	Primary Years Programme targeted understandings	Middle Years Programme targeted understandings	Diploma Programme targeted understandings
E. Learning theories, strategies and styles	What is constructivist learning and how is this exemplified in PYP practice?	What learning strategies are appropriate in supporting effective implementation of the MYP?	What learning strategies are appropriate in supporting effective implementation of the DP?
F. Teaching methodologies and the support of learning	What learning activities and teaching strategies support PYP learning outcomes?	What teaching strategies and learning activities support MYP learning outcomes?	What teaching strategies and learning activities support the achievement of DP learning outcomes?
G. Differentiated teaching strategies	How does the PYP enable the learning needs of all students to be supported?	How can students with additional learning needs be supported within the context of the MYP?	How can students with additional learning needs be supported within the context of the DP?
H. Selection and evaluation of teaching and learning materials	What learning resources support PYP practice and how are they selected?	What learning resources support MYP practice and how are these selected?	How are learning resources that support the achievement of learning objectives associated with subject disciplines and/or core elements selected?

Table 2: Area of Inquiry 2 (IB, 2013)

Area of Inquiry 3: Assessment and learning

The third area of inquiry examines assessment and learning in the IB. As student understanding and performance is central to the learning process, the IB places considerable emphasis on practitioners being able to demonstrate knowledge and understanding of assessment practices in terms of both formative and summative processes. The need for assessment to be an integral part of the curriculum and continual part of the learning process is essential if learning and understanding are to be effectively supported. Therefore, the teacher certification programmes are concerned with developing understanding of the assessment practices required and recommended by the IB programmes (see Table 3).

Domain	Primary Years Programme targeted understandings	Middle Years Programme targeted understandings	Diploma Programme targeted understandings
I. The principles of assessment	What is the role of assessment in PYP practice?	What is the role of assessment in MYP practice?	What is the role of assessment in DP practice?
J. Developing assessment strategies	How are assessment strategies designed and implemented to support PYP practice?	How are assessment strategies designed and implemented to support MYP practice?	How are classroom-based assessment strategies designed and implemented to support the achievement of subject and core element learning objectives?
K. Designing assessment tasks and rubrics	How are authentic PYP assessment tasks and rubrics designed and applied?	How are authentic MYP assessment tasks, criteria and rubrics designed and applied?	How are authentic subject specific and/or core elements assessment tasks, criteria and rubrics designed and applied?
L. Differentiation of assessment	How does PYP assessment practice acknowledge the learning needs of all students?	How does MYP assessment practice support the learning needs of all students?	How can assessment practice be differentiated to support the learning needs of all DP students?
M. Effective feedback	How is student learning progress effectively communicated to students and parents?	How is student learning progress effectively communicated to students and parents?	How is progress in student learning effectively communicated to students and parents?

Table 3: Area of Inquiry 3 (IB, 2013a)

Area of Inquiry 4: Professional learning

The fourth and final area of inquiry centers on professional learning. The IB asserts that a central tenet of teacher professionalism is the need to engage in critical self-reflection and improvement. In the area of international education where effecting attitudinal and behavioral change is valued as highly as developing knowledge and skills, the need to review practice and to evaluate its success in achieving appropriate student learning outcomes is particularly salient. Teachers reflecting, individually and collaboratively, not only model good learning strategies to their students, but also enhance their own understanding of the practices of the IB programmes and their role in promoting international education. The IB further asserts that it is through the process of self and collegial reflection that teachers are able to develop and articulate a personal, independent and critical stance in relation to contrasting perspectives on issues, policies and developments in the IB programmes and thus are able to contribute to a lasting impact on learning. Based on these principles, the teacher certification programmes call for teachers to demonstrate a commitment to review their practice, identify where improvements can be made, and engage in collaborative learning and collegial activity in support of the aims and objectives of the IB programmes (see Table 4).

Domain	Primary Years Programme targeted understandings	Middle Years Programme targeted understandings	Diploma Programme targeted understandings
N. The principles and processes of reflective practice	What is reflective practice and how does it support programme implementation and enhance PYP practice?	What is reflective practice and how does it support MYP implementation and enhance MYP practice?	How can teachers' reflective practice effectively support student learning in the DP?
O. Collaborative working: planning, implementation and evaluation	What is the role of collaborative working practice in supporting the PYP learning outcomes?	What is the role of collaborative working practice in supporting the MYP learning outcomes?	What is the role of collaborative working practice in supporting the DP learning objectives?
P. The use of ICT to support the building of communities of practice	How does the online curriculum centre and other similar information and communication technologies enable PYP practitioners to professionally engage with each other?	How does the online curriculum centre and other similar information and communication technologies enable MYP practitioners to professionally engage with each other?	How does the online curriculum centre and other similar information and communication technologies enable DP practitioners to professionally engage with each other?

Table 4: Area of Inquiry 4 (IB, 2013a)

In addition to the four areas of inquiry that serve as core to the creation of a university-IB certification programme, domains of knowledge and associated essential questions, intended learning outcomes, and documented target understandings are provided to institutions seeking authorization to design and deliver either of the two certificates. In addition, an authorization visit and review is conducted by the IB for each of the approved programmes to ensure that the areas of inquiry are being met at a standard deemed necessary for the IB.

The ultimate goal of the university-IB preparation programmes rests in providing teachers with experiences, skills, and tools that will not only allow for a rich understanding of the IB, its principles, and its practices, but will also simultaneously enable teachers to develop deeper understandings of their own practice and strengthen themselves as both teachers and learners. In essence, the university-IB preparation programmes develop a teacher's understanding and skills to teach within the international mindedness paradigm that serves as the IB's cornerstone. To meet this need, the IB certification programmes require coursework designed to mirror the IB classroom: the principles and ideas that create supportive and rich environments that generate a space for the learner to develop the attributes of the IB learner profile. While the IB offers workshops that likewise aim to develop teacher understanding and practice, the university-IB partnerships allow for deeper and more robust engagement. Furthermore, the programme design gives IB teachers and learners an opportunity to engage in in-depth research and development of theoretical understandings that undergird practice.

Programme development

A number of prestigious universities including the University of Bath, University of Melbourne, and George Mason University were among the first to be authorized by the IB to deliver the certificate and/or the advanced certificate. Since the advent of the university-IB preparation partnerships, a growing number of universities and organizations have been authorized to offer IB preparation programmes that culminate in a certificate or advanced certificate. Details of the institutions accredited by the IB to offer International Baccalaureate certification programmes may be accessed via the IB website (IB, 2013b).

While the university programmes differ from country to country, linked to national teacher preparation and university constructs, a number of salient components emerge as constants: developing a mastery of the philosophy, practices, curriculum process, learning, and assessment within the IB. The various certification courses provide ample variety in course delivery structures (online, face-to-face, or hybrid), sequencing of courses, assessment formats, and time requirements for completion. However, all programmes provide consistent opportunities for teachers to develop essential understandings about the IB programmes and a richer proficiency in terms of enacting the key values of the IB in the classroom.

The Mason example: Creating a University-IB programme

From a university perspective, it is essential to explore how to address the goal of the IB certification process and attend to the areas of inquiry that provide the basis of the programme. In other words, if we are to assist IB teachers in the development of the skills and dispositions deemed necessary, the question must be how then do we create a teacher preparation programme that provides continuity between what teachers see in practice and what they learn through postgraduate programmes at university? Beginning in 2004, George Mason University's College of Education and Human Development began to tackle this issue when it initiated the process to become authorized by IB for the elementary teacher education programme under the auspices of the IB certificate in teaching and learning with a focus on the Primary Years Programme (PYP) (authorized in 2006). Mason followed the initial authorization by creating two additional programmes, the advanced certificate in teaching and learning IB, and the master's degree programme in conjunction with the programme advanced studies in teaching and learning (ASTL), authorized in 2008 as qualifying teachers for the IB advanced certificate in teaching and learning research. While the first programme focuses solely on the PYP and is deeply embedded in the elementary programme, the remaining two independent programmes focus on an integrated approach to studying the PYP, Middle Years Programme (MYP) and Diploma Programme (DP).

The College of Education and Human Development (CEHD) at Mason has five core values that inform the development of programmes and strategic decision-making. The core values are: research-based practice, ethical leadership, social justice, innovation and collaboration. We use the core values along with the IB areas of inquiry as a framework for our design of the new IB programmes for teachers. Long known for its innovative work in the preparation of international teachers, the faculty in CEHD turned their attention to the creation of a new model of education for IB practitioners.

With a focus on collaboration, teams of IB practitioners and university faculty began the process of determining the scope and sequence of the IB certificates (all processes used for each programme were similar, so only one example will be used here). The integration of field-based knowledge and experience from IB practitioners was connected with the understandings and experiences of the university faculty to develop a plan of action for programme development. Using the IB Teacher Award Programme Requirements as a guide, the team laid out a series of courses from introductory to advanced action research that embodied the IB requirements and could be supported by research-based practice. The scope and sequence of the programme was designed to be strongly coherent and connected each course to the next, building upon dispositions, knowledge and skills used in the IB curriculum. Further, each course requires a minimum of 20 hours of fieldwork within an IB school to complete performance-based assessments and assignments linked to the coursework and to the IB programme level: PYP, MYP or DP. Further, the capstone for each series involves IB teachers in action research within their own classrooms. Finally, a critical element throughout the teachers programme was that of critical reflection. Using a model of critical reflection developed by Biggs (1999), we developed activities and experiences that would help teachers move from 'making meaning' to 'transformative reflection'. Reflective practice was not only based on personal growth but also based on deeply understanding issues of ethical practice as well as social justice and access in IB school settings, such as addressing the needs of multilingual learners or students with special learning needs.

Several decisions were made that provided IB practitioners and those seeking an IB position the opportunity to examine their practices in-depth and through the lens of the IB PK-12 curriculum. Each course is taught by a highly qualified IB instructor who meets the standards of the university and has demonstrated leadership capacity in IB. Our current faculty comprise IB level 3 workshop leaders, curriculum developers, assessment coordinators and former principals of IB schools. In addition, the instructors meet university requirements for advanced degrees primarily at the PhD level. We believe these qualifications help to maintain continuity with the university expectations for student performance and also expand the university level coursework with authentic IB experiences. A second decision was to include a minimum of 20 hours of documented fieldwork in an IB school. This was primarily designed for those seeking an IB position, but we have found that it affords IB practitioners an opportunity to visit classrooms across the IB continuum of programmes and helps to develop a deeper understanding of the continuum. Finally, in each of our courses we designed a performance-based assessment to provide evidence of candidates' acquisition of the essential skills, dispositions and abilities documented in the framework. Arends notes that 'performance assessments are designed around the principles considered to be most essential for the profession and are designed around what teachers actually do' (2006: 20-21). Rubrics aligned with the performance are scored by the instructor. We can review an individual candidate but we can also review by cohort or longitudinally across cohorts to gain insight and feedback for programme improvement.

The performances for each course are reviewed annually by the faculty and also by teams of IB practitioners to determine authenticity (*eg* is this something that an IB teacher would do?) as well as relevance (*eg* is the information derived going to enhance teaching and learning in the IB classroom?). Sample performances range from planner assignments at the onset of the programme, to videotaping analyzing and reflecting on inquiry teaching episodes at midpoint, to action research in the IB classroom as a capstone.

Our annual evaluations of the programme(s) have revealed some interesting information in several areas. First, the integration of programmes in the plan of study has been cited by students as providing a rich and robust understanding not only of their specific IB programme, but also of how the IB continuum functions as a whole. As one student elaborates: 'It is especially helpful to me to hear about what is going on in both the primary grades and upper grades because it gives me a good idea of what my students should already have a grasp on and also where I should be aiming for my students to go.' Understanding the continuity inherent within the three programmes of the IB adds to the practitioner understanding in the Mason model, and allows not only for increased horizontal articulation of programatic understanding, but also for vertical articulation.

The annual evaluations also drew two other salient themes that reaffirmed the importance of continuity. The first of these is the significance of utilizing IB-qualified faculty. As one student commented: 'Too often in professional development activities we are 'taught' best practices in the classroom via lecture and other didactic and mimetic methods. In this course our learning environment comprised various instructional strategies and techniques both modeled and experienced by us as learners. The method in which the course was conducted demonstrated effective instructional practices that should be present in an IB classroom.' The second additional theme was providing time and attention to genuine classroom practices, principles, and strategies. As one student noted, 'I believe that our immersion in the IB process [through the advanced certificate programme] holds the key to coping with the demands of constricted time. By using the inquiry-based approach wisely, much more student involvement will be guaranteed, and much of the work that we previously believed depended entirely on us will be happily accomplished by our eager, open, and wonderfully inquiring students.'

We continue to examine feedback from students and instructors in order to ascertain the degree to which we implement the IB Teacher Award programme requirements for postgraduate coursework with fidelity. There will continue to be a series of large and small adjustments to the programme over time to ensure the continuity between what is practiced in the IB PK-12 classroom and what is taught, practiced and researched in the university setting.

Moving forward

There has been remarkable development in the past decade of university-IB partnerships. Nevertheless, as the IB-university partnerships move forward, considerations of continuity must remain a focal point. Additionally, attention and consideration of the field of educative research and the new understandings it provides us about teaching and learning should be incorporated into the advanced degree work. Equally as important are communication and collaboration between the IB and the authorized university programmes, and continuing to focus on the partnerships as a cycle of development is paramount. IB has recently established the university partnership group which is designed to facilitate sharing and inquiry into the advanced degree work. This is a good step in sustaining the continuity between university programmes and IB practice.

References

Arends, R. (2006) Performance Assessment in Perspective: History, Opportunities and Perspectives. In: Castle, S. & Shaklee, B. eds. *Assessing Teacher Performance: Performance Based Assessment in Teacher Education,* 3 (22). Lanham, MD: Rowman & Littlefield.

Ball, D. L., Thames, M. H. and Phelps, G. C. (2008) Content Knowledge for Teaching: what makes it special? *Journal of Teacher Education,* 59 (5), p. 389-407.

Ball, D. L. and Forzani, F. M. (2009) The work of teaching and the challenge for teacher education. *Journal of Teacher Education,* 60(5), p. 497-511.

Biggs, J. (1999) *Teaching for Quality Learning at University.* Buckingham: SRHE and Open University Press, p. 165-203.

Cushner, K. (2011) Intercultural Research in Teacher Education: An Essential Intersection in the Preparation of Globally Competent Teachers. *Action in Teacher Education*, 33 (5-6), p. 601-614.

Darling-Hammond, L. (2006) Constructing 21st Century Teacher Education. *Journal of Teacher Education*. May/June, 57 (3), p. 300-314.

Feiman-Nemser, S. (2001) From preparation to practice: Designing a continuum to strengthen and sustain teaching. *Teachers College Record*, 103(6), p. 1013-1055.

Hammerness, K., Darling-Hammond, L., Bransford, J., Berliner, D., Cochran-Smith, M., McDonald, M. & Zeichner, K. (2005) How teachers learn and develop. In: Darling-Hammond, L. & Bransford, J. eds., *Preparing teachers for a changing world: What teachers should learn and be able to do*. San Francisco: Jossey-Bass, p. 358-389.

Hayden, M. (2006) *Introduction to international education*. Thousand Oaks, CA: SAGE.

Hayden, M., Levy J. & Thompson J. J. (2007) eds. *The SAGE Handbook of Research in International Education*. Thousand Oaks: SAGE.

Hayden, M. (2007) Professional Development of Educators: the International Context. In: Hayden, M. Levy, J. & Thompson, J. eds. *The SAGE Handbook of Research in International Education*. Thousand Oaks: SAGE, p. 223-232.

IB (2005) *Programme Standards and Practices*. Cardiff: International Baccalaureate.

IB (2008) *IB Learner Profile booklet*, Cardiff: International Baccalaureate. Available online at www.ibo.org/programmes/profile/documents/Learnerprofileguide.pdf. (last accessed 4 May 2013).

IB (2013a) Available online via www.ibo.org (last accessed 4 May 2013).

IB (2013b) Find a Course of Study. Available online at http://www.ibo.org/programmes/pd/university-certificates/ (last accessed 5 May 2013).

Korthagen, F., Loughran, J. & Russell, T. (2006) Developing fundamental principles for teacher education programs and practice. *Teaching and Teacher Education*, 22(8), p. 1020-1041.

Levy, J. (2007) Pre-service teacher preparation for international settings. In: Hayden, M., Levy, J. & Thompson, J. eds. *The SAGE Handbook of Research in International Education*. Thousand Oaks: SAGE, p. 213-222.

Putnam, R. T. & Borko, H. (2000) What do new views of knowledge and thinking have to say about research on teacher learning? *Educational Researcher*, 29(1), p. 4-15.

Shaklee, B. & Baily, S. (2012) Introduction: A Framework for Internationalizing Teacher Preparation. In Shaklee, B. & Baily, S. eds. *Internationalizing Teacher Education in the United States*. 1-13. Lanham, MD: Rowman & Littlefield.

Shulman, L. S. (1987) Knowledge and teaching: Foundations of the new reform. *Harvard Educational Review*, 57(1), p. 1-22.

Snowball, L. (2007) Becoming More Internationally Minded: International Teacher Certification and Professional Development. In: Hayden, M., Levy, J. & Thompson, J. eds. *The SAGE Handbook of Research in International Education*. Thousand Oaks: SAGE, p. 247-254.

Chapter 8

Continuity, school leadership and the IB continuum

Darlene Fisher

Successfully implementing the IB continuum in order to achieve the best experience for the students is one of the most important challenges for leadership in IB schools. It is not enough to have been authorised to offer the IB programmes, or to have curriculum plans in place. It is essential that the continuum be implemented well so that students can achieve the learning objectives outlined by the IB. The issue for leaders is, of course, how is this to be done? The situation is complicated by the fact that the context of every school is different, and what might work for the implementation of a good programme in one school does not necessarily work in any other school in exactly the same way – in spite of some clear expectations on structures and style from the IB. The challenge is further complicated by the need to provide continuity in the programme offering, as many schools have significant turnover of staff and leadership. How can these challenges be dealt with in order to provide the best programme?

In this chapter I will discuss what the IB considers the appropriate structures and procedures for schools, and consider the implications of these expectations. The elements of leadership that might be considered most effective in the implementation of the continuum in IB schools will be explored, while acknowledging that some aspects of leadership will differ from school to school. Reference will be made to IB recommendations, as well as to research and experience in a variety of examples of leadership. How continuity can be encouraged will also be explored throughout.

IB programmes and cultures

In a variety of documents, the IB clearly indicates what sort of leadership is expected in schools and how this leadership should be implementing the continuum:

> Implementing the IB continuum of international education means bringing about institutional change in order to improve teaching and learning and to strengthen the school community and culture. An IB World School that implements the continuum is committed to reflection, improving practice and to long-term sustained change. (IB 2008: 7).

This provides an expectation that school leaders will implement the continuum in a school culture committed to on-going development and constant improvement, as the IB goes on to point out:

> Given that IB World Schools are communities of learners, school leaders should be mindful of ways to motivate, challenge and empower teachers to accept and enjoy leadership roles and to support them on that path. The 'distributed leadership model', whereby 'deeper and wider pools of leadership talent' are developed within the school (Hargreaves and Fink 2006) is the most effective and practical model for the implementation of the three IB programmes individually, and the implementation of the continuum. (IB 2008: 22).

This appears very clear. Leaders are to work through a 'distributed leadership model', encouraging teachers to reflect on improving practice and implementing long-term sustained change. Information provided on subsequent pages (22-23) makes further suggestions for membership of the leadership team and roles of the coordinator.

However, the concept of 'distributed leadership' – what it involves and how it can be implemented – is not given detailed consideration, nor is it so clear when one delves deeper into research on this topic. The majority of the remainder of this chapter is a discussion of the term 'distributed leadership' and how related practices might be considered to support the best implementation of the continuum and continuity in the school.

The clear support by the IB for the concept of 'distributed leadership' (DL) is a reflection of what has been discussed in educational leadership and research circles for some time; the concept has considerable support as an example of good leadership practice, particularly in the West. Hallinger and Heck (2010) provide an excellent overview of the field, including empirical research which strongly supports the assertion that a collaborative style of leadership supports school improvement and student achievement. However, in spite of the depth and breadth of this discussion, I believe there are two significant issues that leaders in IB schools, and all schools in international settings perhaps, should take into consideration. One is that, in spite of considerable discussion, DL cannot be easily 'defined' – a point that will be further explored later in this chapter. The second issue is much more ephemeral. Are the IB recommendations for leadership the only practical and best options? The IB continuum has been developed with roots firmly in a western educational philosophical and cultural setting using western concepts of knowledge, and good learning and teaching practice. All the IB requirements and expectations of implementation are in line with this, and while the IB is designed to be used internationally and to encourage international understanding, the western educational values underpinning it are clear and valued. George Walker's 'East is East and West is West' position paper (2010) explores this theme briefly.

Yet in many schools in international settings a variety of cultures can be found, in their leadership, staffing, students and parent community (see Hallinger and Leithwood, 1998 for an introductory discussion of this issue). Kai-Ming Cheng (1998) explores differences in educational values, asking if western values can be borrowed and concluding that they are not easily transferred. Dimmock and Walker (2005) explore issues of culture and leadership in some depth, while Walker (2007) explores the problems when reforms arising from one culture are implemented in another. These and other readings highlight the differences in values related to education in different cultures, differences which must be considered when planning the implementation of any educational programme in a setting where more than one set of values is present.

The question therefore arises as to whether or not the IB recommended methods of leadership are the most effective under all circumstances. I would argue that this is not necessarily the case, though they may be the best policies for most schools in most cases. Yet I believe strongly that it is not necessarily the best idea to implement DL totally in all schools, especially if done without consideration of how it might impact the local community. As leaders, we must ask ourselves how we know when DL is or is not an efficient practice, and what alternatives might work better.

Schools can vary considerably in their socio-economic and political environments, and there must be some consideration given to the influence of the various cultures and their values within the school community, in order to enable the most effective leadership to implement the continuum. Developing a positive school culture is not so simple. Deal and Peterson in *Shaping School Culture* (2009) explore, through a focus on schools in the USA, many issues of implementing a positive school culture. They focus on different cultural values within the local communities and on how positive communication between the school and community may be developed. Schools in international contexts face these issues to an even greater extent, partly because of the large number of cultures present and also because of frequent changes of leadership and staff.

In addition, organisational culture is not the only aspect of culture that needs to be considered. Lumby (2012) discusses four cultural areas that need to be taken into consideration and this more broad perspective includes the impact of national culture on a school community. The cultural areas are firstly the global context, secondly the local community impacting how learners and their families engage with the organisation and with learning, thirdly the organizational (school) culture and, finally, the sub/counter cultures of staff and learner groups who may be aligned or in opposition to the organisation's culture (p. 581). All these need to be considered when leaders make policy and develop procedures for implementing an educational programme. Examples will be explored below when discussing particular practices.

How these areas of culture might affect leadership needs to be planned for. Lumby (2012) suggests:

> There are no easy prescriptions for how to relate internal and external cultures, but developing staff's cultural competency to question the socialized assumptions of the teaching profession and to develop trustful dialogue with the external community members may be productive. (p. 583)

I would add that it is not just the staff who need cultural competency training, which is needed especially by the leadership team of a school. In addition, it must be acknowledged in these circumstances that a western concept of school leadership is not the only possibility for implementation of the continuum. This is especially the case as many schools that implement the IB programmes are not run by western-trained educators, and many schools are local national schools with national students of non-western cultures with different values relating to education, learning, knowledge and communication – to name only a few pertinent areas.

It could be argued that any school accepting the IB programmes should be expected to adopt the values that underpin the IB. An excerpt from George Walker's discussion paper on the learner profile highlights this point:

> There is little doubt that, with its strong emphasis on individual inquiry, personal responsibility and independent critical thinking, the learner profile is embedded in a Western humanist tradition of learning. However, since the IB offers evidently successful programmes of education and continues to expand rapidly, particularly in its Asia-Pacific region, there is little incentive to change. Besides, how should it respond to Indian cultures and to the huge variety of different cultures in Africa? The IB cannot be everything to everyone (2010: 8).

While this discussion paper was focused on the learner profile, some might see this quote as suggesting it is unnecessary or inappropriate to take into consideration the values of Walker's 'local cultures' in leadership practices because the IB is successful as it is. However, I believe that is not a valid interpretation of the intent of the paper, and that such an approach would be a very fast road to ineffective and confrontational leadership in many situations. We should look for guidance on this to the philosophy of the IB programmes themselves and their focus on international understanding, as well as to the final words of Walker's paper which indicate development of understanding between east and west is the best outcome:

> Over the years a slow process of osmosis might occur across the cultural East–West divide until the point is reached where a student submits an extended essay entitled The Cultural Other: A Study of Western Humanism (2010: 9).

I believe that international understanding must be our motivation in creating a programme and structure, rather than an unthinking acceptance of the western philosophy of education and management styles. We must see things in a broader context, and be more flexible in considering leadership in many cultures and how leadership might be adapted to support the implementation of western culturally-based programmes in western, non-western or mixed cultural contexts. This is the big challenge for leaders in schools in international settings.

Not all staff, students or parents believe that western educational values are all good, and there needs to be a considerable amount of effort put into learning how to blend the needs of all values present in the community into a fusion for any particular school in order to take the implementation of the continuum to the highest level. School leaders having a measure of 'cultural competency' is a starting point, and experience in different cultures can support flexible understanding, decision-making and structures. Open mindedness and a flexibility of approach are essential to start with, but the process of developing a fusion of cultures for the school is a discussion for another chapter, or perhaps another book! Here we can but mention it in each area that will be explored with respect to school leadership.

Distributed leadership: what is it?

We now focus on the concepts that the IB's preference for distributed leadership imply are the most important for leaders to implement, and will consider some issues in different contexts and how they might be addressed and developed to support continuity of the programmes. While focusing on these associated concepts, examples will be given of where they might not be the best option. It must be the school leaders who decide what is best within each school in each different context.

Gronn (2008) wrote an overview of where the concept of distributed leadership (DL) came from (it is not new), where it is now, and what might happen in the future. The fact that it is often equated with other leadership models such as 'democratic leadership' or 'teacher-leadership' only serves to complicate any understanding. Spillane (2005), while outlining DL's concepts, exhorts readers to treat the term not as a model or prescription for leadership but rather as a diagnostic tool to discuss practice.

Bolden (2011) in a review of DL in theory and practice writes of the emerging themes of DL, which include that leadership is emergent and can be found in varying degrees in different places within the structure of an organisation. An important point noted by Pearce (2004: 55, cited by Bolden 2011: 263) is that the issue is not whether horizontal or vertical leadership is better, but how shared leadership can be developed, and how one can utilize both to improve practice. These are questions that face all leaders in schools aiming to improve practice, and are further complicated by local educational cultures.

Some studies confirm the importance of DL in teacher commitment to schools (Hulpia and Devos, 2010), and the positive impact of DL on teacher optimism and student achievement of learning outcomes (Chang, 2011: 508).

In a significant longitudinal study of the impact of DL on school improvement and student achievement, Heck and Hallinger (2010) similarly argue that DL's focus on improvement and engaging all in the education process, alongside high academic expectations of staff and students, appears to have significant positive effect on student achievement.

Heck and Hallinger acknowledge four assumptions about DL which can help us to understand what is generally accepted as being involved in this style of leadership and organisation. Distributed leadership includes, they say:

1. a clear vision of direction for the school and the ability to enact that vision

2. distributed leadership among more than just the head of school or leadership team

3. a commitment to capacity building and on-going professional development for staff

4. increasing capacity which builds higher student achievement

(2010: 870)

In addition to these assumptions about DL, Heck and Hallinger explore school improvement capacity which allows for the full support and enactment of DL principles for improved student achievement. They consider school improvement capacity is determined by the quality of:

- the school's implementation of the state curriculum
- the academic expectations of students
- the sustained focus on academic improvement
- resource support provided to enact the above
- continuous professional development
- open communication
- parental support for student learning.

(2010: 871)

These concepts provide school leaders with some guidelines as to what areas to focus on to implement distributed leadership in order to achieve increasing academic success for students and achievement of learning objectives. In brief, both the IB and the arguments above suggest that DL should:

a. engage a wide spectrum of participants in school leadership;

b. be focused on high academic achievement for staff as well as students; and

c. engage in sustained and on-going improvement of the academic programme.

It is believed by the IB that these points enacted together enable very successful student achievement and a successful implementation of the continuum. Yet none of them is easily put into place, and they require considerable skill to establish securely, especially in schools in international settings with frequently changing community members, a variety of cultures within the community and potentially insecure political and socio-economic environments.

Regardless of the challenges, good leaders will aim at ensuring the school's best possible achievement. Some might ask 'How is this all to be done? And what are the details?' It would be possible to provide a check list of things to do, with some theoretical background thrown in for good measure, implying that if all are completed the results are assured. But even with a 'to do' check list' it is not possible to enact specific practices in the same way in every school. Context and the situation of each school have significant impact on any leader's ability to achieve what they wish. Therefore heads and leaders in schools need to consider the areas of leadership practice that would support the development of DL, school improvement and high student achievement, while always keeping in mind how these will be affected by the particular context of the schools they are in and how much turnover is ever present in the community.

Spillane (2005) insists on the importance of the situation or context to leadership practice. He says, 'my argument is not simply that situation is important to leadership practice, but that it actually constitutes leadership practice – situation defines leadership practice in interactions with leaders and followers' (p. 145). While we discuss DL, it is important to see it in context and in relation to the different members of the community.

Distributed leadership: how might it be enacted?

Bearing in mind the areas of leadership practice noted above, and drawing on my experience as a school leader in five countries with different cultural communities, I consider the following areas need addressing in order to implement what might be considered DL and achieve the outcomes desired by the IB:

1. A leadership team and shared/distributed leadership with teacher involvement and developing leadership potential

2. Developing teacher involvement in and ownership of the educational programme

3. Establishing a stable teaching population focused on the school's improvement and their students' highest achievement

4. Budgets supporting the resources required for the maintenance of the staff, and the implementation of the curriculum

5. Curriculum mapping: development, review and improvement of the curriculum

6. Clear, frequent and open communication

These areas will now be explored with some context included as a way of assessing potential issues in implementation.

1. A leadership team and shared/distributed leadership with teacher involvement and developing leadership potential

Establishing the areas that can be shared and/or distributed among the leadership team and the teachers in general could be the starting point for consideration. The school head might start this discussion and involve potential leaders in order to clarify areas of potential shared responsibility.

In some countries and cultures such sharing might be considered inappropriate. Local context and teacher expectations will need to be taken into account. Most western-educated teachers and parents will expect to be involved to some degree in decision-making, and this is clearly confirmed in research as a positive influence on teacher commitment (Hulpia and Devos, 2010; Heck and Hallinger: 2010, 2011; and Chang, 2011). Contrary findings (Walker and Dimmock, 2005) suggest that authority is not so easily shared in some cultures, so a head needs to consider the expectation of members of the community and how the community can be brought around to accept increasing proportions of shared responsibility.

My own experience in three different cultures showed that some teacher leaders did not want to be held accountable for making decisions, but preferred to follow instructions. This was an attitude slow to change. While giving incremental small areas of responsibility, and encouraging trust that decisions and any mistakes would not be used as the basis for dismissal (making sure the responsibilities are small to start with), a democratisation of values among the staff grew. It might be possible to use this model to help develop teacher leader involvement in other schools.

A school leader or head will in some instances have to work and decide things 'solo', teacher evaluation being one such area. In Goldstein's (2004) research of DL and peer assistance and review, it became clear that teachers were very capable of conducting peer evaluation and could make and justify decisions on teachers' contracts. In fact more teachers were dismissed and more teachers improved under this system, though the teachers did not wish to have this responsibility and eventually disempowered themselves and shared the responsibility again with the principal (or other senior leader). Some areas will clearly be more easily shared in some schools, and some areas may perhaps never be a shared responsibility.

The development of a leadership team in schools is not something new, as in many schools principals and business managers will meet with the head on a regular basis. What research into DL incorporates though is widening the groups involved in responsibilities, and engaging more of the community in decision-making. Subject departments or grade level teams are communities of practice that can be given shared responsibility for curriculum decisions, and this can be a single very powerful way of obtaining more involvement from teachers.

It is also an extremely useful way of building leadership capacity as leaders in these teams can try out leadership skills in a limited way prior to seeking or achieving more significant responsibility. These leaders have to be given significant responsibility though, if they are to grow. If they are only paper pushers in charge of examinations, or distributing texts, there is nothing shared about any responsibility. Decisions on courses, content, resources, responsibility for budgets, mentoring new/young teachers, communication with parents, review and goal setting for the curriculum and staff development, are but a few of the possible areas of shared and/or distributed responsibility.

2. Developing teacher involvement in and ownership of the educational programme

The IB offers suggestions (and indeed requirements in the PYP and MYP) for collaborative meetings, and time allocation so teachers can meet to work on the curriculum and its implementation. This should be given time and importance by the school leadership, so that it is clear that this area of teacher involvement is significant and considered important. Teams may be held accountable to goals that are discussed and agreed at the end of the preceding year or beginning of the academic year. Either way, if there is to be a shared vision of where the department/team is going and specific goals for them to achieve, then more teachers need to be involved in the process of development of the programme, as well as its daily implementation and on-going review.

Hulpia and Devos (2010) found that a combination of frequent personal interaction with leaders helped build teachers' connection to the school. In addition, participation in decision-making was a positive aspect, but only if ideas were respected and valued. Therefore, to ensure teachers are involved in developing the educational programme, there should be no token involvement; only real respect for their input will have the desired results.

Enabling and expecting teacher involvement might be time-consuming, along with the time required to create and maintain frequent interpersonal interactions with leaders. However, with this input, teachers are likely to support the school and research shows that, as noted above, the school improvement supports higher student achievement (Heck and Hallinger, 2011). With greater commitment to the school a teacher will also be more likely to remain employed there, which will clearly support continuity of the programme and is thus to be encouraged.

3. Establishing a stable teaching population focused on the school's improvement and their students' highest achievement

A stable teaching population is probably one of the most important goals of school leadership. With the increasing numbers of new schools being set up internationally and the pressure to recruit teachers for them as well as for the schools already in place, it is not a problem that is going to go away. Therefore school leadership teams need to focus a considerable amount of effort on ensuring stability where possible. With this in mind, it is good to note that change is not necessarily a problem in high achieving schools. If the changes are communicated to all staff and measures put in place to ensure a smooth handover, then change does not need to have a negative impact on staff engagement, according to research by Hulpia and Devos (2010: 572). Their research does not indicate, however, just how much change was being measured so, in schools with a 25–30%+ turnover at the end of each school year (as is found in a number of schools in international settings), a more stable teaching staff would clearly be considered a significant advantage.

Odland and Ruzicka (2009) investigated teacher turnover in international schools and it is sobering to read their conclusion that administrative support and faculty involvement in decision-making (or lack thereof) is most significantly correlated to teacher turnover. Meanwhile teacher involvement in decision-making and positive relationships between leadership and staff, with strong support for teachers, have been indicated as reasons for teachers to commit to a school by Hulpia, Devos and Van Keer (2010) and Heck and Hallinger (2011). The importance of good relationships cannot therefore be over-emphasised.

The issue with good relationships as a simple criterion for staff continuity is that relationships and how we communicate differ significantly from person to person, school to school and national culture to national culture. Direct, to the point, and honest communication is considered appropriate and in fact required in some cultures, but would be nothing less than offensive in others. The complication for school leaders is that there might be both perspectives represented in one staff room, so how do they develop positive relationships? I believe there is no simple answer and this can only be worked out by the leader(s) through conversations, through having knowledge and understanding of the cultures present in the school, and through a determination to develop trust and respect, however they are understood within that community.

One other significant reason for teachers leaving, according to the research by Odland and Ruzicka (2009), was the inconsistency between what was said by administrators in recruiting interviews and what eventuated on the ground when the teacher arrived. A lack of honesty on the part of the recruiter is clearly not going to encourage teacher commitment to the school, yet it is high on the list of reasons for teachers leaving. If the findings also hold for schools beyond Odland and Ruzicka's research sample, this means that too many school leaders are misleading potential staff – which is certainly not consistent with the long-term view of school improvement or continuity and student achievement. Good relationships must be developed between the administrative team and staff if there is to be two way respect and commitment.

If the school encourages continuing professional development which supports the implementation of the educational programme, this too encourages staff support and enables continuous school improvement. Professional development can also be a shared responsibility, and allowing staff and teacher leaders some say in the distribution of funds and the direction of professional development can encourage engagement with the school programme. Care must be taken, though, with the distribution of funds and the expectations of staff. One school I know had a clause in teachers' contracts indicating that all funds spent on their professional development during the period of their contract (3-5 years) would need to be paid back if they left early. The end result was a refusal to participate in professional development. In another school a teacher resigned in the week after attending an IB PYP workshop in another country, when school leaders had trusted teachers to treat the school with the same respect as the school did them. These are examples of problems in both directions. School leaders will have to find ways of balancing and compromising with respect to the issues that work in their community.

The IB offers many professional development workshops in line with their programme requirements, but on their own these are not sufficient for teacher development. Many areas of professional development are subject-specific or grade level-specific, which can enhance teaching methodologies and impact student achievement. Lifelong learning is a concept not only relevant for students, but an attitude to life that should be embraced by the entire school community. If the leaders are not learning, then why should teachers? It is important that leaders are always engaged in professional conversations about how to improve teaching and learning, and that they engage teachers in these discussions so as to ensure the educational programme is being implemented as best it can be.

An open, clear evaluation system, combined with high expectations and a great deal of support for teachers, provides a very strong basis for the high achievement of teachers and students. However, evaluation can be affected by culture as is seen very clearly in Dimmock and Walker's work (2002, 2005). Examples are discussed of how western-educated leaders, or national leaders trying to implement a western type of evaluation, struggled significantly in cultures where no direct criticism was expected. Calmness and diplomacy were always expected, so evaluation was not possible in the same way as is expected by western-trained teachers. Local culture needs to be taken into account when developing fair means of evaluation and teacher support.

Criterion-referenced teaching skills, such as those in Charlotte Danielson's framework for teaching (2007), are an excellent source for developing guidelines for teaching skills and evaluation, but would need to be implemented with care to ensure the procedures are not automatically considered acceptable. In cultures where criticism is difficult to take, especially face-to-face, it may be that procedures have to be adapted to enable good communication and teacher development. If a system causes confrontation or gives the appearance of acceptance but actually results in non-compliance, then it is ineffective and time is wasted.

Schools' professional development budgets can differ considerably with respect to what is available, but there are also very many ways of ensuring staff can develop themselves professionally. Differentiated professional development can include many offerings including online short or long courses, training and mentoring from other schools or specialists online, groups within the school sharing teaching methodologies, potential communities developed through the IB, contacts with other schools providing focus questions to discuss issues and best practice, or supporting staff with further studies with an expectation that they feed back information and learning to the community.

These are but a few of the possibilities and staff can suggest many themselves. If they believe that growth is an expectation and is supported where possible by the school, then they will find ways of developing. It is the leaders' responsibility to ensure their staff clearly understand the expectations, and that they have the support required to achieve what is expected. Some reward or celebration of success is also an effective way of encouraging a positive attitude. This can all combine to support teacher continuity and thus support the strong implementation of the educational programme, in this case the IB continuum.

4. Budgets supporting the resources required for the maintenance of the staff, and the implementation of the curriculum

School leadership need to allow sufficient funds for resources to support the learning and methodologies that are in place to underpin ongoing improvement. Schools that require a profit margin may have more difficulty ensuring that budgets are generous enough in the right areas for intangibles such as professional development or time to plan and collaborate, but it is a requirement of the IB that they do so. Privately-owned schools do not necessarily present a problem in this area: I know of two such schools, one of which was much more profit motivated than the other. It is for the school leaders to plead their case as they see fit with the owners. Individual heads of school will need to consider their options using the whole staff's input if possible, and take requirements to the board or individual with responsibility for deciding the final budget.

Not-for-profit schools that struggle financially might also have difficulty in providing excellent support for teacher development. However, if teachers are involved in planning, have the situation explained to them (though not necessarily in detail) and are then asked to contribute ideas for less costly means of professional development, the school can still have a very positive attitude to on-going development, both for the school and personally for all individuals. This can only help with staff continuity and the developing of a very positive school culture.

5. Curriculum mapping: development, review and improvement of the curriculum

With a requirement for regular review and development of curriculum as part of implementing the IB programmes, it is important that schools put in place curriculum mapping of some description so that regular reviews can be efficient and effective in improving the education programme provided. This will also mitigate some of the negative effects of high teacher turnover. Some schools have online curriculum management systems, which enhance the process of review and ensure that there is a possibility of viewing the whole curriculum both horizontally and vertically. With potentially large numbers of staff moving each year, some of whom are involved in administration, it is essential that schools have a permanent record of what plans and resources are in place for teaching and learning in the school.

At present, I know of schools that do not have any system for curriculum management, other than the teacher's own notes and curriculum folders in cabinets, classrooms or offices, with perhaps a yearly plan held by the head of department. While this might be effective enough for classes when the teacher is there, if the teacher leaves and takes it all, or destroys it all, or the head of department or coordinator is not organised and leaves the documents in disarray or 'trashed' (all of which have happened in schools I know), there will be a huge gap in the school plan. It is also the case that the absence of a curriculum management system does not facilitate any overall review of the curriculum content, methodology or success even when all the paperwork is available. In addition, some schools have long-standing teachers who are content with their curriculum and not interested in what anyone else is doing. This is clearly not acceptable practice for the implementation of the continuum as it creates many problems when trying to enact curriculum improvement.

Schools that do not have a published version of the curriculum are most in danger of having shortfalls or gaps in their offering to students. It is in the interests of students to have a clear understanding of the horizontal and vertical alignment for curriculum at all levels of the school, and is a requirement of the IB continuum. It is an essential part of an improving school attaining high student achievement – though how it is achieved, with what programmes, and how and when it might be reviewed, is for the leadership team to decide.

6. Clear, frequent and open communication

In 'western culture', good relationships are built on clear and open communication. Keeping the community appraised of the school, its development, activities and challenges can enhance commitment to the school and the community, wherever it is based. Once again the local context of the school can significantly impact the methods used and the style of communication required to keep communication open, but communication is required wherever the school is located.

The importance of good relationships between the school and its constituencies has been mentioned above and is included here again. An important aspect of good relationships is good communication. Keeping parents informed of the challenges experienced by, and success of, their children helps encourage group responsibility for a student's achievement, although the content and method of communicating might be different in different schools. Some parent communities expect to be heavily involved and asking questions about their children. Other parent communities expect the school to do the job while they keep their distance. It is for the school to communicate the rationale for why, how, when and what will be communicated to ensure all are content with the level and content of the communication.

Ensuring that teachers are appraised of the economic, social and political situation can keep their confidence that leadership has their interests at heart. Encouraging teacher input into decision-making where possible, and communicating the challenges with reference to the decisions being made, can help to encourage engagement and commitment to the school which again enhances continuity. Communication enables leaders to share their vision for school improvement and to engage all in the process. It is at the heart of good leadership.

Conclusion

Following the characteristics most often agreed as being central to distributed leadership will involve a wide variety of skills and practices from school leaders. The challenge is that the context for each school is different, and schools therefore face different types of values related to leadership, relationship behaviours, and communication. Leaders need to understand the values present in their community in order to lead the school effectively and provide the best environment to support continuity of staff and programme. By using the most effective leadership practices, adapted to the local context, leaders have the strongest chance of providing the best programme and implementing the continuum to the highest level of achievement.

References

Bolden, R. (2011) Distributed Leadership in Organizations: A review of Theory and Research. *International Journal of Management Reviews*, 13 (3), p. 251-269.

Cheng, K.-m. (1998) Can education values be borrowed? Looking into cultural differences. *Peabody Journal of Education*, 73(2), p. 11-30.

Danielson, C. (2007) *A Framework for Teaching.* 2nd Edition. The Association for Supervision and Curriculum Development.

Deal, T. & Peterson, K. (2009) *Shaping School Culture: Pitfalls, Paradoxes and Promises,* San Francisco: Jossey Bass.

Dimmock, C. & Walker, A. eds. (2005) *Educational Leadership: Culture and Diversity.* London: SAGE.

Goldstein, J. (2004) Making Sense of Distributed Leadership: The Case of Peer Assistance and review. *Educational Evaluation and Policy Analysis,* 26(2), p. 173-197.

Gronn, P. (2008) The Future of Distributed Leadership. *Journal of Educational Administration,* 46(2), p. 141-158.

Hayden, M. (2006) *Introduction to international education: international schools and their communities.* London: SAGE.

Hallinger, P. & Heck, R. (2010) Collaborative leadership and school improvement: understanding the impact on school capacity and student learning. *School Leadership & Management,* 30(2), p. 95-110.

Hallinger, P. & Leithwood, K. (1998) Unseen forces: The impact of social culture on school leadership. *Peabody Journal of Education,* 73(2), p. 126-151.

Heck, R. & Hallinger, P. (2010) Testing a longitudinal model of Distributed Leadership effects on school improvement. *Leadership Quarterly,* 21(5), p. 867-885.

Hofstede, G. (2005) *Cultures and Organizations: Software of the Mind,* New York: McGraw Hill.

Hulpia, H. & Devos, G. (2010) How Distributed Leadership can make a difference in teachers' organizational commitment. A qualitative study. *Teaching and Teacher Education,* 26 (3), p. 565-575.

Hulpia, H., Devos, G. & Van Keer, H. (2010) Influence of Distributed Leadership on teacher organizational commitment: A multilevel Approach. *Journal of Educational Research,* 103(1), p. 4-52.

I-Hua-Chang (2011) A study of the relationship between Distributed Leadership, teacher academic optimism and student achievement in Taiwanese elementary schools. *School Leadership & Management,* 31(5), p. 491-515.

IB (2008) Towards a continuum of international education. Cardiff: International Baccalaureate.

Lumby, J. (2012) Leading Organisational Culture: Issues of Power and Equity. *Educational Management Administration and Leadership,* 40(5), p. 576-591.

Odland, G. & Ruzicka, M. (2009) An investigation into teacher turnover in international schools. *Journal of Research in International Education,* 8(1), p. 5-29.

Spillane, J. (2005) Distributed Leadership. *The Educational Forum,* 69, p. 143-150.

Walker, A. (2007) Leading authentically at the cross-roads of culture and context. *Journal of Educational Change,* 8(3), p. 257-273.

Walker, A. & Dimmock, C. (2002) *Development of a Cross-Cultural Framework and Accompanying Instrumentation for Comparative Analysis in Educational Administration.* The Hong Kong Research Grants Council, Chinese University of Hong Kong.

Walker, G. (2010) *East is East and West is West.* IB Position paper, Available online via http://blogs.ibo.org/positionpapers/files/2010/09/East-and-West_George-Walker.pdf (last accessed 5 May 2013).

Part C

Programme Transitions in the IB

Chapter 9

Constructing values in a plural world ... others with their differences can also be right

Roger Marshman

The challenge

In 2002, I was challenged by an International Baccalaureate (IB) Middle Years Programme (MYP) workshop participant with a question asked in a slightly belligerent tone: "What does the MYP have to say about values?". Perhaps I had always naively assumed that all education was suffused with values, and that the MYP at least offered a framework with an overt values perspective as reflected in the IB mission statement and the MYP fundamental concept of intercultural awareness. The MYP embraced the need to understand multicultural and ethical perspectives and gave encouragement to do so, especially through the Areas of Interaction. Answers along this line were insufficient for my questioner, and it was quickly apparent in the subsequent discussion that he was coming from the perspective of a committed Christian, perhaps even with fundamentalist leanings. What he seemed to mean was rather: How does the MYP instil a set of values of which I would approve? Reflecting subsequently about values education, my conviction has grown that people learn their values and learn about values in the same way that they construct other behaviours and knowledge. I believe that this was always the implicit view of the developers of IB programmes. In practice the perspective can be hijacked, albeit with the best of intentions.

It was not difficult to understand how someone with a commitment to a sincerely held and specific set of values (derived quite possibly from religious conviction) might be puzzled by the lack of specificity about values in IB parlance and might, at worst, see that as embracing a relativist and uncritical acceptance of otherness. At best they might accept a possible statement of universal values – for example peace, justice, fairness, compassion (Gellar, 2002) – as positive but insufficiently explicit. Readers might reflect that this conversation occurred before the adoption across the IB continuum of the IB learner profile which, in my view, accommodates and promotes a pluralist perspective; that is, it promotes desirable values-related objectives while being neither fundamentalist nor absolutist nor relativist.

Alfie Kohn's entertaining *How not to teach values* (1997) begins with a provocative quotation from John Holt:

> Teachers and schools tend to mistake good behavior for good character. What they prize is docility, suggestibility; the child who will do what he is told; or even better, the child who will do what is wanted without even having to be told. They value most in children what children least value in themselves. Small wonder that their effort to build character is such a failure; they don't know it when they see it. (Holt, 1964)

Kohn rejects several programmed approaches to 'character education' – based on behaviourism, religion or traditionalism – and while one might not accept all his dismissals as pernicious, they are reminders that schools must consider closely what they really mean by such 'virtues' as 'citizenship', 'cooperation' or 'obedience', or what is rewarded in the 'student of the month' selections or schemes involving extrinsic rewards.

It is seductive to indoctrinate for conscientiously held 'right' reasons and I can sympathise with my interlocutor's wish to instil his doubtless decent values in his pupils, the more so as the excesses of relativism are perhaps more visible now than a decade ago. It is easy to empathise with the view of American social critic and professor of humanities and media studies, Camille Paglia:

> [Lady] Gaga's fans are marooned in a global technocracy of fancy gadgets but emotional poverty. Everything is refracted for them through the media. They have been raised in a relativistic cultural vacuum where chronology and sequence as well as distinctions of value have been lost or jettisoned by politically correct educators ...

> Borderlines have been blurred between public and private: reality TV shows multiply, cell phone conversations blare everywhere; secrets are heedlessly blabbed on Facebook and Twitter. Hence, Gaga gratuitously natters on about her vagina ... (Paglia, 2010)

As educators wanting to help our students to become decent, compassionate adults, we may well feel compelled to counteract the values implicit in the cult of popular celebrity, the trivial narcissism of social networking, soundbite advertising culture or the facile opinions of shock jocks and tabloid journalists, opinions frequently without justification and argument, and masquerading as fact. If we do not, we will not achieve the reasonable goal of helping children become thoughtful and reflective participants in a democratic society in a changing world. We must not be apathetic about these problems, but there are many challenges for educators wishing to support students to construct a defensible, personal values system. The process must, I think, begin in helping children achieve understanding of their own values systems. It seems reasonable to assert that there is little chance of understanding, and engaging with, the values systems of others if one does not explicitly understand the nature and origins of one's own.

I consider that four aspects are needed for growth and learning:

- The identification, articulation and clarification of the position held
- Increasingly clear understanding and analysis of the origins of that position
- The capacity to challenge or defend the position
- The capacity to reflect deeply on beliefs and actions and their implications

My fundamental assumption in this chapter is that learning values is a matter of constructing meaning from a multitude of experiences and in a non-linear way, as in any other area of learning. Values education should be less a matter of the deliberate inculcation of a set of values, a kind of indoctrination, than a matter of clarifying the nature and origin of the values one holds. This position is intrinsically recognised in the non-absolutist stance expressed in the IB mission statement and learner profile.

In debunking many practices of what he calls the narrow definition of 'character education' – training mechanisms to promote compliance, Kohn asserts that:

> Ironically, some people who accept character education without a second thought are quite articulate about the bankruptcy of this model when it comes to teaching academic subjects;

and poses the pertinent question:

> Why would all these people, who know that the "transmission" model fails to facilitate intellectual development, uncritically accept the very same model to promote ethical development? (Kohn, 1997: 10)

Kohn's answer is essentially that such thinking rejects children's critical construction of social and ethical understanding for reasons relating to religion, politics or tradition, or to a view of human nature that children are fundamentally in need of reformation. Such views may well be held subconsciously. Schools should, therefore, be alert to the potential for subliminal and uncritical inculcation of values systems. The IB philosophy embraces the need in a plural world not merely to understand otherness but truly to engage with it – the opposite of a fundamentalist world view, but not mindless or apathetic relativism. It is not intended to be about indoctrination, but about deep, critical understanding and, beyond understanding, action.

My intention in this chapter is to suggest at least some elements for a constructivist framework through which schools might address the challenges that come with a desire to develop 'global citizenship' or 'international mindedness', or to meet the expectation of service activities. At the least, such elements require schools to develop some conceptual understanding of the issues and, I believe, a meta-language to assist engagement in this and other partly affective, values-laden, ethically problematic aspects of learning. Terminology to mediate learning in these areas is emerging in ways analogous to learning in more defined subject disciplines. The discussion to follow is framed in the context of IB programmes, including their expectations of service, the IB learner profile and its implications for school leadership in promoting self-regulated, autonomous learning.

Pluralism: *others with their differences can also be right*

During meetings at the IB's Cardiff office in 2005 about the IB continuum and the possible adoption of the learner profile by the Middle Years Programme (MYP) and Diploma Programme (DP), an intriguing spectre was raised: the potential for an IB Diplomate with the highest possible 45-point score to be also a 'card-carrying, head-kicking Nazi'. This led to some thankfully short-lived debate about assessing values outcomes as a graduating requirement. I believe it is important to accept that affective outcomes – which, at least in part, I take values perspectives to be – are amenable to neither legislation, which seeks to mandate particular outcomes, nor assessment in any objective form; they are, of course, the source of constant subjective evaluation, which is also why schools should be cautious about judging, or reporting on, attributes like the IB learner profile in any way which suggests objectivity. Teachers and schools believe in helping children to become 'better' people. Few any longer think that there can be values-free education, so the questions become: Which values? And how do we promote them? In rejecting educative processes of indoctrination – the slippery slope to fundamentalism or absolutism – I want also to reject cultural and moral relativism. The IB mission statement includes the statement that 'Others with their differences can also be right'. *But others with their differences can also be wrong!* There are people who hold abhorrent values and do abhorrent deeds. Mere acceptance of difference – extreme cultural relativism – is an insufficient ethical position, regrettably both apathetic and common.

In his final essay, Isaiah Berlin (1998) argues that human beings can and do pursue a range of differing values while retaining their essentially human character, and that it is possible to understand the values of the 'other' and the circumstances that gave rise to them:

> If I am a man or a woman with sufficient imagination (and this I do need), I can enter into a value system which is not my own, but which is nevertheless something I can conceive of men pursuing while remaining human, while remaining creatures with whom I can communicate, with whom I have some common values – for all human beings must have some common values or they cease to be human, and also some different values else they cease to differ, as in fact they do.

> That is why pluralism is not relativism – the multiple values are objective, part of the essence of humanity rather than arbitrary creations of men's subjective fancies. Nevertheless, of course, if I pursue one set of values I may

detest another, and may think it is damaging to the only form of life that I am able to live or tolerate, for myself and others; in which case I may attack it, I may even – in extreme cases – have to go to war against it. But I still recognize it as a human pursuit. (Berlin, 1998: 1)

Berlin illustrates his point with the example of Nazism being an understandably human behaviour, given enough misinformation or false belief about reality, concluding:

If ... respect between systems of values which are not necessarily hostile to each other is possible, then toleration and liberal consequences follow, as they do not either from monism (only one set of values is true, all the others are false) or from relativism (my values are mine, yours are yours, and if we clash, too bad, neither of us can claim to be right). (Berlin, 1998: 2)

Pluralism must consequently be seen as an encounter of commitments, something more than just the recognition of common humanity as mentioned in the preamble to the learner profile; it must be an engagement with otherness.

Kapuscinski (2008) embraces a complementary perspective relating to an individual's construction of identity and values, arguing that it is only by reflecting 'otherness' in the mirror of self that one's own cultural identity grows; there is no identity without the 'other'. Following the philosophers of dialogue, Kapuscinski stresses the importance of the process at the level of the single person:

I the Self can exist as a defined being only in relation to ... the Other when he appears on the horizon of my existence, giving me meaning and establishing my role. (p. 67)

Walker (2010) considers the criticism that the IB is too restrictively associated with Western values; he summarizes a range of attitudes to understanding supposed differences between 'Western' and 'Eastern' cultures. Avoidance of stereotypes and superficiality are clear dangers, as is the assumption that key words, 'compassionate' for example, may carry the same meaning in different cultures. Following Nussbaum (1997), Walker notes other significant dangers: chauvinistic over-accommodation and romantic views of the non-comparable alien:

One way of avoiding these difficulties, suggests Nussbaum, is to focus on common human problems. All human beings have to cope with the fear of death, regulate their bodily appetites, take a view on property and the distribution of resources, and plan their own lives. This focus will enable the learner to construct a sense of shared humanity while accepting that the responses to these problems may be culturally very different. (2010: 5).

Walker also points to the work of Hofstede (2001, 2005), who discerned some social challenges, found universally, which can provoke very different cultural reactions:

- Social inequality
- Relationships between the individual and the group
- Concepts of masculinity and femininity
- Attitudes to risk
- Long-term versus short-term orientation

Pluralist attitudes can thus elucidate a values perspective for the service aspects within IB and other programmes, for learning about communities and cultures, both historically and contemporaneously, and for making concrete the attributes of the learner profile. Nevertheless, I consider that schools may all too easily fall into the danger of Nussbaum's chauvinism in the context of service activities, especially those organized by schools rather than by individual students. Charity can be condescending towards the Other and may reflect a false altruism. 'Fly-in, fly-out' expeditions to the developing world or a disadvantaged community are potentially cases in point, yet such activities may serve a worthwhile educational and sensitising function while offering scant or even dubious benefit to recipients. They come at significant cost, the funds for which might more usefully contribute, for example, towards the provision of expert services in recipient communities.

Values and the IB learner profile

The IB learner profile (IB, 2006) began in the Primary Years Programme (PYP) and, despite some opposition during discussions held between 2002 and 2005, was eventually adopted, with minor modifications, to describe attributes desirable in learners in all three IB programmes. Supporting the concept of the hidden curriculum, the learner profile booklet reinforces the relevance of the profile to the actions of all members of IB learning communities, parents and governors included. The learner profile attributes are often considered in two groups. Some: 'inquirers, knowledgeable, thinkers, communicators and reflective, imply the development of cognitive competencies ... [T]he other attributes—principled, open-minded, caring, balanced and risk takers—emphasize dispositions and attitudes' (IB, 2008), or what may be considered the more obviously values-laden aspects. While this is a useful division, it is nonetheless highly permeable, especially when one accepts the values-laden nature of all educational experience.

The point reinforced here is that values are constructed in ways analogous to the construction of other knowledge. The real-world contexts in which learning should or does occur are multifaceted, and require insights from a range of disciplined understandings for a rich capacity to understand and engage intelligently with complex issues. The learner profile implicitly presupposes that children have a propensity for 'right' action (for example being helpful, fair, just or compassionate) just as much as they may be capable of mean, selfish, cruel and unjust acts. There is no presupposition either of fundamental sinfulness that needs fixing, or that tradition is necessarily good or bad. Kohn argues that:

> Character education, or any kind of education, would look very different if we began with other objectives – if, for example, we were principally concerned with helping children become active participants in a democratic society (or agents for transforming a society into one that is authentically democratic). It would look different if our top priority were to help students develop into principled and caring members of a community or advocates for social justice. To be sure, these objectives are not inconsistent with the desire to preserve certain traditions, but the point would then be to help children decide which traditions are worth preserving and why, based on these other considerations. (Kohn, 1997: 6)

The learner profile is intended to inform a school's practice amongst its whole community, to underscore a broader consciousness of character education: everything a school does to help children grow into good people, rather than a narrow and particular style of moral training.

One danger for teachers and schools is in treating the most heavily values-laden attributes of the profile, or any similar set of characteristics, as a programmable type of instruction, divorced from context and at worst exemplified by, for instance, lessons on being 'principled' or a scheduled 'risk-taking week'. Another is the way rewards are used:

> The lesson a child learns from Skinnerian tactics is that the point of being good is to get rewards. No wonder researchers have found that children who are frequently rewarded – or, in another study, children who receive positive reinforcement for caring, sharing, and helping – are less likely than other children to keep doing those things. In short, it makes no sense to dangle goodies in front of children for being virtuous. But even worse than rewards are awards – certificates, plaques, trophies, and other tokens of recognition whose numbers have been artificially limited so only a few can get them. When some children are singled out as 'winners', the central message that every child learns is this: 'Other people are potential obstacles to my success.' (Kohn, 1997: 4)

Kohn argues that those picked competitively as most virtuous are likely to have less intrinsic commitment to being good, and to have poorer relationships and sense of community. Mitigation of these dangers can lie in criteria to assist children (and teachers) with seriously analytical, rather than superficial, reflective practice.

Reflection for better or for worse

Schools and teachers must, in this view, structure opportunities for students to be consciously aware of their own construction of understanding in values-related areas. We must aim for metacognition with respect to values. At its best, this is what reflection means. 'Reflection' has had some deservedly bad press because much of what passes for reflection is barely more than facile opinion, expression of feeling or hopeful assertion of better quality work in the future. Structured thinking sometimes does not enter into the processes.

In a quite amusing article (albeit one that seems unjust to Donald Schön) Samuel Freedman notes that:

> Dewey viewed 'reflective thinking' in such classic works as 'How We Think' as a 'triumph of reason and science over instinct and impulse'. Seventy years later, reflection has largely become the very thing Dewey wanted to rebel against — the consecration of emotion and feeling.

> By making every teacher and student the unchallenged arbiter of his or her own achievement, reflection dovetails neatly with progressive education's preference for process over content and with the confessional, therapeutic strain of American culture. (Freedman 2006)

All IB programmes provide opportunities for serious and beneficial reflection, indeed they demand it, but it is regrettably still possible to find superficial, time wasting reflection activities in some IB World Schools. Aspects of purposeful reflection and productive habits of mind are developed in later sections of this chapter.

The IB Diploma Programme (IBDP)

One place where demanding reflection on values is expected in the IB Diploma is in the Theory of Knowledge (ToK) course. When values positions are metacognitively clarified, constructed and reflectively analysed, they become propositional knowledge claims which fit the context of ToK as seen in the objectives:

Having followed the ToK course, students should be able to:

1. analyse critically knowledge claims, their underlying assumptions and their implications

2. generate questions, explanations, conjectures, hypotheses, alternative ideas and possible solutions in response to knowledge issues concerning areas of knowledge, ways of knowing and students' own experience as learners

3. demonstrate an understanding of different perspectives on knowledge issues

4. draw links and make effective comparisons between different approaches to knowledge issues that derive from areas of knowledge, ways of knowing, theoretical positions and cultural values

5. demonstrate an ability to give a personal, self-aware response to a knowledge issue

6. formulate and communicate ideas clearly with due regard for accuracy and academic honesty. (IB, 2006b: 5)

From a practical perspective, and even more so from a philosophical perspective, this approach should inform schooling practice from the earliest years and not just in the young adults engaged in the IBDP. It is important to note the emphatic expectation of DP subjects and teachers to incorporate knowledge claim issues – the epistemology or 'ToK-ness' of their disciplines – within their subject-based teaching and learning. ToK should not be seen as an add-on or something different from the construction of subject learning. ToK poses questions such as:

> What counts as knowledge? How does it grow? What are its limits? Who owns knowledge? What is the value of knowledge? What are the implications of having, or not having, knowledge?

> What makes ToK unique, and distinctively different from standard academic disciplines, is its process. At the centre of the course is the student as knower ... In ToK they have the opportunity to step back from the relentless acquisition of new knowledge, in order to consider knowledge issues. (IB, 2006b: 3)

Such issues include knowledge claims of ethical, emotional, religious and aesthetic kinds, all values laden, and often require starting with basic questions:

> What do I claim to know [about X]? Am I justified in doing so [how?]? Such questions may initially seem abstract or theoretical, but ToK teachers bring them into closer focus by taking into account their students' interests, circumstances and outlooks in planning the course. (IB, 2006b: 3)

A constructivist approach is inescapable in a properly demanding inquiry-based ToK experience. Amongst other characteristics, the learning will almost always be non-linear and heavily dependent on prior learning.

The Primary Years Programme (IBPYP)

Unequivocally, the PYP is similarly committed to structured inquiry:

> Students should be invited to investigate significant issues by formulating their own questions, designing their own inquiries, assessing the various means available to support their inquiries, and proceeding with research, experimentation, observation and analysis that will help them in finding their own responses to the issue. The starting point is students' current understanding, and the goal is the active construction of meaning by

building connections between that understanding and new information and experience, derived from the inquiry into new content. (IB, 2007)

The PYP framework is implemented through its five essential elements:

- concepts
- knowledge (both transdisciplinary and disciplinary)
- skills
- attitudes
- action

The last two of these, especially, have a strong values-related aspect. The elements inform two related requirements in unit planning:

- a curriculum planned to develop disciplinary knowledge and skills within a framework of eight structural or organizing concepts; and
- a process or programme of inquiry based around six transdisciplinary themes which subsume the contributing disciplines but develop discipline-based understanding and skills for those contributing disciplines.

The eight structural concepts and related key questions are as shown in Figure 1.

Concept	Key question
Form	What is it like?
Function	How does it work?
Causation	Why is it like it is?
Change	How is it changing?
Connection	How is it connected to other things?
Perspective	What are the points of view?
Responsibility	What is our responsibility?
Reflection	How do we know?

Figure 1: PYP structural concepts and related key questions (IB, 2007)

Some of these concepts are epistemological in nature, one (Responsibility) is heavily values-oriented, but so also can be Causation, Change, Connection and Reflection. Through this mindset, links to the concerns of ToK in the Diploma Programme and the Areas of Interaction (soon to be replaced by significantly redeveloped 'Global Contexts' (IB, 2012) in the Middle Years Programme can be readily discerned and are outlined later. They reflect a holistic focus on the experienced world, a key aspect of constructivist learning theory.

Similarly the six transdisciplinary themes (see Figure 2), around which units of inquiry are based, are reflective of the same desire for authentic, real-world contextualization of learning which underpins the MYP Areas of Interaction/

Global Contexts, and which should include cultural, ethical and values contextualization. Traditional subject disciplines inform and are developed within these units of inquiry.

PYP Transdisciplinary Themes
Who we are
Where we are in place and time
How we express ourselves
How the world works
How we organize ourselves
Sharing the planet

Figure 2: PYP Transdisciplinary themes (IB, 2007)

The PYP uses the Think-Act-Reflect sequence (What am I aiming for? How will I do it? How successful have I been and by what measure?) as a daily classroom tool, and this is a potentially powerful approach to learning good (*ie* reflective as distinct from unreflective or conformist) habits of mind that could usefully transfer to more senior classrooms, and indeed are reflected in the changes to the MYP currently under development.

The IB Middle Years Programme (IBMYP)

Through the Areas of Interaction/Global Contexts, values clarification seems more directly required in the MYP than in the other two IB programmes; in an earlier paper (Marshman, 2006) I suggested some guiding questions to sharpen and help make explicit the values perspectives implicit in the Areas of Interaction. In Figure 3, I have added exploitable links between the Areas of Interaction and Theory of Knowledge in the Diploma Programme, together with some suggestions regarding consistency with the concepts and key questions of the PYP programme model.

As the MYP has recently undergone significant review, culminating in the launch of a new *MYP: from Principles into Practice* in 2014, some of what follows has a changing relevance. The new documents will emphasise the use of key concepts, several somewhat similar to those in the PYP, as a basis for unit planning with an increased focus on inquiry. The Areas of Interaction are to be replaced by Global Contexts; these also bear similarity to the PYP transdisciplinary themes. Although the contexts are worded as inquiries into potentially transdisciplinary questions, MYP schools have been assured that the Areas of Interaction 'can transition smoothly to the use of global contexts' (p. 2). The process will derive from that aspect of the Areas of Interaction which gives meaning to learning through the exploration of real-world issues. The links between old and new approaches will, I believe, require deep transitional thinking by teachers, but the potential for values-clarification as a constructivist tool is clear in the draft new wordings.

MYP Areas of Interaction (AOI)	Characterizing Questions taken from the AOI Guide	Further suggestions for focussing on values	Related to DP Theory of Knowledge: Ways of Knowing (plain type) and *Areas of Knowledge (italics)*	Related PYP concepts and key questions
Approaches to Learning	How do I learn best? How do I know? How do I communicate my understanding?	What values do I bring to this task? Where do my values come from? How do they colour my learning? Is there another view?	Language, Reason, Emotion, Perception (sensory and cultural)	Reflection (How do we know?)
Community and Service*	How do we live in relation to each other? How can I contribute to the community? How can I help others?	What are my values? How have they been formed? What action can I take? What power do I have?	Perception (Cultural), *History, Ethics*	Responsibility (What is our responsibility?) Connection (How is it connected to other things?) Perspective (What are the points of view?)
Environment	Where do we live? What are my responsibilities?	What are my values? How have they been formed? What action can I take?	*Natural Sciences, Ethics*	Responsibility (What is our responsibility?) Perspective (What are the points of view? Causation (Why is it like it is?)
Health and Social Education	How do I think and act? How am I changing? How can I look after myself and others?	What are my values about personal relationships? What action can I take? How should I act?	*Ethics, Human Science, Natural Sciences*	Responsibility (What is our responsibility?) Change
Human Ingenuity	Why and how do we create? What are the consequences?	Where does the power lie? By what values were famous thinkers motivated? What might the future hold? What is the truth? How do I know what is right?	Language, Reason, Emotion, Perception *History, Sciences (Natural and Human) Ethics, Arts, Mathematics*	Reflection (How do we know?) Responsibility (What is our responsibility?) Causation (Why is it like it is?) Perspective (What are the points of view?

*The Service expectation within CAS in the DP and the place of Action as an essential element in the PYP come readily to mind as values-related perspectives in this cross-programme articulation.

Figure 3: Seeking values-laden relationships between IB Programmes

MYP unit planning within and across subjects will require a Global Contexts focus just as it has hitherto for an Area of Interaction. It may be a useful transition exercise to ask colleagues (or indeed students and parents) to identify in a further column where the wordings of new Global Contexts best fit the former Areas of Interaction; another useful task might be to map where aspects of the learner profile seem most likely to be reinforced or developed. In a values-related context, it is also interesting to note that revisions of the MYP seem likely to involve an increased emphasis on action and a better-developed, more conceptual, focus on service.

The questioning and reflective habits of mind demonstrated here imply perseverance as a value in metacognition and it is worth reflecting further on 'effort'.

Effort grades and a school's social values

Under a variety of names, many schools include in student reports an 'effort' grade, regrettably sometimes seen as a generic approaches to learning (ATL) grade in the MYP. It is frequently undefined as though effort is a single, universally understood virtue. In practice such grading is often highly subjective, open to favouritism, begging and grade creep, especially when associated with rewards. I have even seen an example where some attempt at definition conflated the idea with academic progress which should be fully addressed through criterion-based academic achievement levels. The conflation was obvious in this case, but I suspect is more often insidiously present in high correlations between achievement and 'effort' grades.

One school set out to overcome these issues in a reform context of an increased focus on student autonomy and self-determination within broad and positive learning community expectations rather than a set of rules. Its approach was to try to define more carefully what might be meant by the preferred term 'engagement'. Criteria were developed to aid student reflection and, slightly adapted, are set out in Figure 4. The approach recognizes that students can choose their actions within the classroom context and that they are not in competition with each other; there was a strong attempt to help all members of the school community to see the mutual and collective benefit to student learning in a collaborative environment in which all students benefit with potential for the growth of empathy and a more pluralistic outlook.

Readers may rightly object that only some items in this list fully imply the cultivation of autonomy, and that other terms are quite conservative and could sit equally well in a highly teacher-directed and conformist environment. The totality of the school culture will see such elements variously interpreted, of course. Readers will also note that some extrinsic motivation remains in the idea of reportable grades and certificates; however, an important point is that the possibility of such recognition is open to all students. The essential motivation is for a mutually beneficial classroom environment rather than a

---

Engagement Grades

These grades are intended to reflect a student's effort and engagement with classroom learning as an active, responsible learner. Three aspects are considered to be of prime importance.

Sustained Effort and Commitment
The student
  • is punctual in attendance at class
  • meets deadlines for presentation of work
  • completes homework regularly and thoroughly
  • takes care in the presentation of work and keeps organised notes and files
  • maintains diary to the expected requirements

Positive Attitude
The student
  • is courteous and cooperative, supporting other students when appropriate
  • works diligently at all times
  • makes a positive contribution in class
  • shows perseverance in the face of difficulty

Independence and Personal Responsibility
The student
  • shows initiative when appropriate
  • seeks to develop the skills of active listening and collaboration
  • works responsibly when not directly supervised
  • is properly organised and prepared for class
  • manages time effectively
  • is reflective about her or his own actions and tries to learn from mistakes
  • uses diary effectively as an organisational tool

The descriptors for levels of engagement are:
  5: conscientious in all three areas at all times
  4: conscientious in all areas at most times
  3: generally conscientious: noticeable lapses in one area
  2: noticeable lapses in more than one area
  1: not conscientious in these areas

Following the completion of each assessment period a special assembly will be arranged for the formal presentation of certificates to students receiving 5s for effort in every subject or a combination of 4s and 5s.
These awards are designed to recognise meritorious and sustained attitude and commitment, irrespective of a student's natural flair or ability.

Figure 4: Engagement Grades (adapted from student handbook 2007: St Dominic's International School, Portugal)

fundamentally competitive one. Some slippery terms do indeed remain, but some of the most dangerous ('obedient', 'patriotic', 'respectful') are avoided; the desirable capacities to negotiate, challenge and be sceptical are not as apparent as they might be but can be sought in other aspects of school culture. The value lies in the attempt to do away with masquerading monism: mistaking good behaviour for good character, prizing docility and suggestibility, demanding conformity in the name of respect; these are the slippery slopes to absolutism, not pluralistic engagement. The concept reflects the school's desire for a process less negative and restrictive than a long list of rules. It recognizes that schools are social systems within social systems, an important constructivist perspective. All children's concepts and understandings, intellectual and affective, are constructed within these systems, which exhibit varying models of authority and the locus of responsibility.

Matters of leadership

I believe that leadership values are a most important element in a school's social system and a vital aspect of values embedded in the hidden curriculum. It has been my privilege to visit many IB World Schools and to respond to many progress reports from schools on their *matters to be addressed* arising from IB authorization or evaluation visits. Many issues have arisen from evaluation standard B:

> The school demonstrates ongoing commitment to, and provides support for, the programme through appropriate administrative structures and systems, staffing and resources. (IB, 2005)

The relevant point in the context of this chapter is that so many problems, and even proposed solutions, illustrate inappropriate models of leadership; in particular I have noted the prevalence of top-down rather than bottom-up models of authority at work. Top-down (pyramidal) models tend to show processes of management rather than leadership. At worst, such models impose authority and solutions to problems from above. They can:

- discourage initiative in an atmosphere of what might be viewed as 'residual fascism'
- lead to reorganisation which can give the appearance rather than the reality of progress
- misplace the locus of responsibility for leading change
- 'solve' problems by adding layers of management or imposing directives instead of empowering teachers, programme coordinators and heads of departments to be autonomous leaders
- involve job descriptions that list a host of administrative specifics without indicating the broad sense of a curriculum and pedagogical leadership position
- tend to have inspectorial appraisal processes

Bottom up (inverse pyramid) models, by comparison:

- assume that authority is accorded upwards from those led to the leader, because of the leader's demonstrated competence
- consider carefully the locus of responsibility for change
- empower change in practice at the lowest level possible

- have job descriptions emphasising leadership and autonomous responsibility in terms of curriculum and pedagogy
- promote collegiality in the best sense of shared vision, productive teams and collaborative change
- tend to have reflective accountability/appraisal processes

By way of illustration of inappropriate management values in operation, I include reference to one school where the MYP Coordinator was viewed, as shown by her job description, as responsible for every facet of the implementation of the programme, without any suggestion of the importance of the individual and collective responsibilities of heads of departments and other teachers. Another school responded to a recommendation that the MYP Coordinator and heads of departments work on a certain curriculum reform, by adding another curriculum supervisory layer of management, thus potentially removing autonomy and disempowering the essential leaders. Yet another school had a recommendation that the school leaders should gain a more complete understanding of the philosophies and requirements of the MYP. Their solution was, in a strangely ironic reversal, to send junior colleagues to acquire that understanding!

It is interesting to note, in this context, the wording adopted in the new Standard B1: 3, which should generate a great deal of reflection:

> The head of school/school principal and programme coordinator demonstrate pedagogical leadership aligned with the philosophy of the programme(s). (IB, 2010)

Another standard relevant to the construction of values is C3:

> Teaching and learning at the school empowers and encourages students to become lifelong learners, to be responsible towards themselves, their learning, other people and the environment, and to take appropriate action. (IB, 2005)

It is interesting that this standard has quite often led to recommendations regarding academic honesty issues and policies. A clear corollary of autonomy and self-determination is the acceptance of responsibility for one's actions.

Positive current developments in some schools are leadership training programs to replace mechanisms such as prefectship, which have sometimes legitimised top-down authority of students over other students. Elsewhere constructive peer mediation programmes involve quite sophisticated training for volunteers.

I conclude that teachers led with an inverse pyramid model of leadership and treated as autonomous beings will have greater skill in adopting a classroom leadership strategy which treats children as autonomous. Regrettably there are still classrooms in IB World Schools where the management remains at odds with the learner profile and IB philosophy as interpreted in this chapter. One still encounters 'rules in disguise', including banners with homilies such as: 'Respect your teachers'! Lest I be misinterpreted, I should stress that in distinguishing between inverse-pyramidal *leadership* and pyramidal *management*, I am not advocating consultative or democratic decision-making in a leadership vacuum. Leaders must lead in a process which itself is empowering of others in their locus of responsibility; lack of leadership is itself disempowering. In both more and less hierarchical school or national cultures, knowledgeable and philosophically committed leaders are essential. In cultures which work in a more hierarchical way an enlightened leader can, for example, encourage collaboration in situations where teachers are not used to it, even if the structure remains in principle top-down.

Conversely, in more consultative cultures dangers abound where the leadership does not properly understand the programme. It is disheartening to find schools with competent coordinators or teachers who are working in a vacuum because they cannot convince the leadership of what is really needed for the programme, or good MYP schools which do not succeed in maintaining a strong programme when a new head of school is appointed who has no experience with the programme. Moreover, consensus decision-making without informed and authoritative leadership can lead to mere stagnation.

Service activities and reflective constructivist practice

The action/service expectations of students in IB programmes provide a superb opportunity to demonstrate a theory of learning in practice that sees students as learners to be engaged; it can thus avoid the pitfall of manipulating children into the mere rehearsal of preconceived right answers – and teachers 'fishing' for them. Not that service is a magic bullet. One still sees examples of teacher-managed activities – sometimes more like humanities field trips – with little room for students to show initiative or autonomy in their social growth and values development within learner profile attributes such as *principled, open-minded, caring, balanced* and *risk takers.*

Branksome Hall in Toronto, Canada, set out to help students be autonomous, compassionate and reflective in their Diploma Programme Creativity Action Service (CAS) programme. They devised rubrics around a series of desirable characteristics of worthwhile student engagement in service activities. At St Dominic's in Lisbon we considered this work a great step forward and adapted the rubrics to give students guidance in their MYP years also, as shown in Figure 5.

Community and Service Rubric				
This Area of Interaction supports the fundamental concept of intercultural awareness, which aims to encourage tolerance and respect, leading to empathy and understanding. Students engage in interactive situations that will enrich them emotionally, socially, morally and culturally through involvement in positive action and contact with other social and cultural environments. Service may take place on campus or off.				
Criterion		Expectations not met	Approaching Expectations	Expectations met	Exceeds Expectations
A	Challenge	No opportunity for the student to extend herself	Provides some opportunity for the student to extend himself	Overall experience presents a challenging opportunity	Overall experience pushes the student beyond previous limits
B	Benefit to others	Benefits only the student	Has some benefit to others	There is an identifiable benefit to others	There is an identifiable, substantial benefit to others
C	Acquisition of skills	Little skill required	Requires skills that student would be expected to have mastered	Enhances existing skills	Develops new skills
D	Initiation and planning by student	Student participates in but does not organize a school-sponsored activity	Student participates but does not organize an activity sponsored by an outside agency	Activity is organized by a student group with an adult leader and student actively participates	Activity is planned, organized and run by the student. Activity requires active participation and input from the student. Plans reflect the needs of the community.
E	Establishing links with the community	Does not involve working with others	Involves working within the school community only	Involves working within the school and the wider community	Involves working with and within the local community and/or the international community. The student demonstrates exceptional interpersonal skills.
F	Commitment	The activities are one-off. There is little evidence of sustained commitment	There is a mixture of one-off and short duration activities. There is insufficient evidence of sustained commitment	The overall programme requires sustained commitment. The student shows evidence of self-direction	The overall programme requires a high degree of commitment. The student shows perseverance and a high degree of self direction.
G	Reflection	The reflection and other documentation of the experience are incomplete	The reflection and other documentation of the experience have some omissions	The reflection and other documentation of the experience are complete. The reflection demonstrates awareness of successes and failures.	The reflections demonstrate empathy, respect and self-awareness.

Figure 5: Community and service rubric: St Dominic's International School, Portugal (2007), with grateful acknowledgement of permission from Rosemary Evans, Director of Academic Studies, to use developmental work carried out at Branksome Hall, Toronto.

I would personally be more rigorous in places, for example with respect to criterion E in the context of promoting genuine engagement with the Other, but the approach seems entirely defensible in constructivist terms; it leaves a great deal of room for initiative and autonomy and it gives guidance, as good rubrics do, as to how to proceed to intrinsically valuable experiences. The criteria are totally consistent with the IB learner profile, although I would wish to see greater cognizance of the dangers, outlined earlier in the *pluralism* section of this chapter, arising from insufficiently considered ethical perspectives for such activities. This example is at least more effective in guiding both the development of worthwhile activities and constructive reflection on them, than the standard approach still often seen, as in this example of typical reflection sheet questions:

What did this activity involve? How did it help others?
What aspects of this project suited my personality/strengths?
What did I do well? What could I have done better?
What did I learn about myself? What did I learn about others?

though, of course, the usefulness of such an approach will depend on the guidance offered to students.

Another school has a fairly typical Community and Service Self Evaluation Report, which asks students to rate themselves on a seven-point scale (regrettably, to my mind, given its use in the context of IB academic assessment) on the parameters:

I was punctual
I completed my work/task on time
I was reliable
I assumed responsibilities
I used my time well
I listened to and encouraged others
I enjoyed what I did

While this self-evaluation report is clearly not all pointless in values-construction terms, it offers students little in terms of guidance towards rigorous critical thinking. Most importantly, these approaches do not touch on moving beyond personal comfort in engagement with others and 'otherness'. Improvements in the choice of service activities, and in the learning which may arise from them, will I think require the use of appropriate terminology – a meta-language – for discussing the ethics of obligation within the concepts of global citizenship, international mindedness and service. The IB appears to have recognised such a need in its recent initiation (November 2012) of studies to define and track relevant terminology in its documents as a precursor to research to underpin future delineation of desirable learning in these areas.

IB Programme Standards and Practices

Current Standards and Practices (IB, 2010) address the matter of values and constructivism most relevantly in Philosophy standard A4:

> The school develops and promotes international mindedness and all attributes of the IB learner profile across the school community.

This is supported in the PYP specific standards, rather more than in those for the MYP and DP, in standard 3 (c):

> The school is committed to a constructivist, inquiry-based approach to curriculum development.

I would like to see these matters specifically linked in future developments, and in some respects regret the disappearance of the former standard A2.4 (IB, 2005):

> The school encourages student learning that strengthens the student's own cultural identity, and celebrates and fosters understanding of different cultures.

While, from a pluralist perspective, mere understanding of otherness is not as desirable as engagement with it, the older wording seems better to open the door of the critical clarification of one's own values as a precursor to the critical appreciation of the values of others. It is clear that future developments must grapple with dimensions coming from political and ethical philosophy. Students will need to form sophisticated concepts of highly problematic areas such as human rights, political and economic relationships, reciprocal obligations locally and internationally, and the value of such injunctions as 'think globally, act locally'.

This chapter reflects a position that self-regulated learning and the capacity for autonomous decision-making are desirable educational goals, yet these concepts are themselves problematic and culturally dependent, perhaps especially in terms of the values made palpable and urgent in a globalised world. As difficult as it may be for schools and organisations such as the IB, however, there is an obligation to expand students' critical thinking abilities into the areas of ethics and moral cognition if they are to grapple conceptually with the issues of 'global citizenship' and 'international mindedness'. To meet the expectations of the learner profile for learners and their school communities, values education as discussed in this chapter is a vital component in supporting children's critical thinking as they grow towards full and decent humanity. It is the capacity to understand their own values and the capacity to articulate, challenge and defend their own values. That critical capacity will, it is to be hoped, counteract the narcissistic excesses of the culture of celebrity, soundbites, cyber bullying and sometimes meretricious gadgetry.

Furthermore, and in particular, schools must develop a meta-language to support conceptual understanding of global citizenship in a plural world. These are the tools for engagement with the Other and a critical capacity to challenge bigotry and monism.

References

Berlin, I. (1998) The first and the last (extract). *New York Review of Books*, XLV, 8.

Freedman, S. J. (2006) Upon Further Reflection, a Few Random Thoughts, *New York Times*, 30 August 2006.

Gellar, C. A. (2002) International education: a commitment to universal values. In: Hayden, M., Thompson, J. and Walker, G. eds. *International education in practice*. London. Kogan Page, p. 30-35.

Hofstede, G. (2001) *Culture's Consequences*. London. Sage Publications.

Hofstede, G. (2005) *Cultures and Organizations*. New York. Sage Publications.

Holt, J. (1964) *How Children Fail (Classics in Child Development)*. New York: Perseus Books.

IB (2005) *Programme standards and practices*. Cardiff: International Baccalaureate.

IB (2006a) *IB learner profile booklet*. Cardiff: International Baccalaureate.

IB (2006b) *Theory of Knowledge Guide*. Cardiff: International Baccalaureate.

IB (2007) *Making the PYP happen: A curriculum framework for international primary education*. Cardiff: International Baccalaureate.

IB (2008) *Towards a continuum of international education*. Cardiff: International Baccalaureate.

IB (2010) *Programme standards and practices*. Cardiff: International Baccalaureate.

IB (2012) *MYP: The Next Chapter*. The Hague: International Baccalaureate.

Kapuscinski, R. (2008) *The Other*. London. Verso.

Kohn, A. (1997) How not to teach values, *Phi Delta Kappan*. February, p. 429–439.

Marshman, R. (2006) *Constructivism, values and the IB continuum*. Paper delivered at IBAEM Regional Conference, Athens, October, 2006. Accessed 14 April 2010. www.ibo.org/ibaem/conferences/documents/ValuespaperRMarshman.pdf.

Marshman, R. (2010) *Concurrency of learning in the IB Diploma Programme and Middle Years Programme*. Cardiff: International Baccalaureate.

Nussbaum, M. (1997) *Cultivating Humanity*. Cambridge, MA. Harvard University Press.

Paglia, C. (2010) Gaga and the death of sex, *Sunday Times Magazine*. 12 September 2010.

Walker, G. (2010) *East is East and West is West*. Cardiff: International Baccalaureate

Bibliography (suggestions for further reading on pluralism)

Boix-Mansilla, V. & Gardner, H. (2007) From teaching globalization to nurturing global consciousness. In M. Suarez-Orozco (ed.), *Learning in the global era*. Berkeley: University of California Press.

Eck, D. (2006) *What is pluralism?* Harvard Project on Pluralism www.pluralism.org (last accessed 15 April 2007).

Khan, A. J. (2008) *Global education and the developing world.* International Baccalaureate Peterson Lecture, April 2008.

Sacks, J. (2003) *The dignity of difference.* London: Continuum International Publishing Group.

Chapter 10

Brain research: some implications for the transition from the IB Primary Years Programme to the Middle Years Programme

Richard Parker

Introduction

Transition from primary to secondary school is a period in any child's education that deserves serious attention, but is often neglected. A study by Fouracre, for example, concludes that secondary teachers in the UK underestimate the abilities of students joining their school, and there is a real mismatch between students' expectations of life in these schools on the one hand, and the reality on the other (Fouracre, 1993). Increasingly educators are looking to neuroscience to inform their practice, and it is of particular relevance in this transition phase because the brain goes through a time of tremendous change in early adolescence. In this chapter I will explore some of the implications of this research for the International Baccalaureate Primary Years Programme (PYP)/Middle Years Programme (MYP) continuum, in terms of practice in schools and the overall development of the programmes. As the PYP covers the age range 3-12, and the MYP ages 11-16, the transition period from PYP to MYP coincides with the transition between primary and secondary phases of education. I will refer to my own experience in my current school, a three-programme school in Hong Kong, and places in which I have worked previously.

I will begin with a caveat. Neuroscience is still in its infancy. In my view, there is a tendency for educators to over-interpret findings related to the brain and come to conclusions that do not necessarily have the research to back them up. There are many examples. One is the oversimplification of the left/right divide, when both sides are massively interconnected. Another is the idea that every child has a visual, auditory or kinaesthetic learning style, when in reality we use all our senses to learn. Gardner's theory of multiple intelligences has also been misinterpreted in many classroom settings and used to limit the idea of intelligence, rather than seeing the different functions of the brain as working together. John Geake talks about the blossoming of neuromythologies in schools (Geake, 2009: 1). Although brain research has serious implications for teaching and learning, it does not mean that those implications are proven. Educators should be wary of jumping on the latest brain-based bandwagon. It is important to approach all findings on brain-based learning (as one would the findings of any other research) with a spirit of healthy scepticism.

Neuroscience should not be seen as one-way traffic, with scientists dictating practice to schools. Rather there is a need for a conversation between educational psychologists, educators and neuroscientists, with each informing the others. That is not to deny that neuroscience is bringing important new perspectives to the educational debate. As a corollary effect, neuroscience could well help teachers in the never-ending battle to be valued as professionally independent pedagogues and not to be seen as pawns in various political agendas.

The brain in transition

The last years of primary school and the first years of secondary school are a time of significant change in the brain's anatomy and neurochemistry, particularly in the frontal lobes. Typically the frontal lobes experience rapid growth between the ages of 9 and 10, and then a period of massive pruning of connections begins at around 11 (Wolfe, 2010: 84-87). The period of rapid growth in connections is known as synaptogenesis (synapses connect neurons), and is followed by synaptic pruning (Blakemore and Frith, 2011: 112-117). In addition, the frontal lobes go though a process of slow myelination throughout adolescence and into early adulthood (Wolfe, 2010: 84-87). Myelin insulates the connecting parts of neurons, and those connections are far more efficient when myelinated (Sousa, 2011: 21-22).

The frontal lobes, or more particularly the pre-frontal cortex (the area right behind the forehead, at the front of the brain: see Figure 1) is sometimes described as the executive centre of the brain: the section that deals with emotional inhibition, empathy, goal setting, various organization skills and judgment; in other words those very characteristics that many adolescents struggle to master (Wolfe, 2010: 84-87). There are implications here for both the design and implementation of the curriculum at transition, and I will explore them in the section on creative inquiry. Researchers have also found that the emotional centre (the amygdala) matures before the frontal lobes, meaning that adolescents are likely to have highly emotional reactions without having fully developed the inhibition controls necessary to properly channel them (Wolfe, 2010: 84-87). Schools therefore need to consider how they motivate and care for students in transition. Lifestyle also has implications for cognition at this age, a point which I will discuss in the final section of this chapter.

Recent research suggests these changes in the brain have a greater impact on learning at the age of transition than was previously understood. Evidence comes from a study by Robert McGiven in San Diego State University, where children of various ages were asked to match faces to emotional conditions (a function associated with the frontal lobes). At the age of 11-12 they were less able to match a face to certain emotional conditions than were younger children: in fact they were about 15% slower (Blakemore and Frith 2011: 119). It might be the case that there is such a proliferation of synapses at this age, and such huge reorganization in the frontal lobes, that cognition is actually poorer

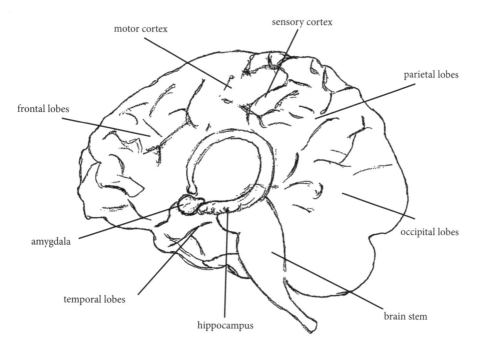

Figure 1: structure of the brain

for a period of time. If so, this is a problematic time in which to be facing a change of schools and/or curriculum.

With such massive change occurring it is important that educators recognize this period as crucial time for cognitive development, creating a learning environment that allows the mind in transition to blossom.

Creative inquiry

There is substantial evidence to suggest that secondary teachers often underestimate the ability of students when they first arrive at secondary school, and consequently many students under-perform in their first year (Department for Children Schools and Families, 2008). The International Baccalaureate (IB) recognises the importance of the continuum but, in curriculum terms, what should be happening in transition to ensure students do not lose their way?

The IB is working to improve the transition from PYP to MYP by identifying key concepts in the two programmes, and linking them (International Baccalaureate, 2012a), with a focus on inquiry. Brain research does, to a degree, support the notion of exploring concepts in depth. One of the most widely accepted models of the brain and cognition is that put forward by the Canadian teacher-turned-neuroscientist Donald Hebb, who focused on the importance of synaptic connections and the plasticity of the brain (Geake, 2009: 48-58). Hebb defined learning in terms of these synaptic connections. One of the key implications of Hebb's model of synaptic plasticity is that working memory can only focus properly on a certain amount of information, so it is depth in learning that matters more than quantity (Geake, 2009: 48-58). The neuroscientist Edward Vogel uses the metaphor of the bouncer, deciding what can come in and what cannot, to describe neural plasticity (Geake, 2009: p 71). Vogel is trying to show that we should envisage the brain as choosing which information it stores, as opposed to the commonly used metaphor of the sponge, which invokes the idea of the brain simply soaking up information. When the brain is pruning neural connection some connections are made strong, and others are lost. An oft-used catchphrase for the brain's plasticity is 'neurons that fire together, wire together' (Geake, 2009: 48). The time of the primary/secondary transition is one where there is a burst of neural activity. When they experience this change, young adolescents need time to properly explore concepts and understand them.

Strong connections are also dependent upon repetition and elaborate rehearsal. It is therefore crucial that any concepts explored at the end of the PYP be revisited in a more sophisticated manner in the early years of the MYP – that is the nature of a spiral curriculum, and central to inquiry. In my experience schools do not always identify when particular concepts are explored in a PYP unit of inquiry and ensure they are then integrated into designated units in different subject areas in the MYP. So, for example, a PYP unit looking at the transdisciplinary theme of 'where we are in place and time' might well focus on the central idea of migration. Migration is of course a significant concept in humanities. It is simple to explore the concept in an increasingly sophisticated manner in the MYP, by beginning with more personal experiences with the younger students, then looking at more global and complex issues later on as they progress. At one school in which I worked the entire humanities curriculum was planned in this vein. The younger students explored concepts through personal and local experience. The curriculum gradually expanded to consider national and regional perspectives, and in the latter years of the MYP there was an increasing emphasis on more abstract global issues.

At the moment, the situation is made complicated because the IB moves from a clearly concept-driven curriculum in the form of the PYP in the primary years (International Baccalaureate, 2007: 15), to a discipline-centred curriculum in the middle years (International Baccalaureate, 2008). In my view the PYP can be more rigorous by being less discipline-dependent, because it expects that a concept is properly understood in a context. As an example: in a school in which I have worked, students focused their final year exhibition on the theme of how we organize ourselves, then looked at the economics of an organization, and then the PYP concept of function. At a higher level this is exactly the kind of activity that would engage a real economist.

The IB is planning to provide better continuity in conceptual thinking, but is still staying with the disciplinary-led model in the MYP (International Baccalaureate, 2012b). An over-emphasis on traditional subjects can result in schools adopting rigid structures, with timetables divided into small blocks of time where students do not have space to explore complex ideas. If depth is key, as brain research suggests, then this kind of traditional school structure is very unhelpful. A young adolescent with a hyperactive amygdala and a rapidly changing pre-frontal cortex needs authentic and challenging problems to solve, and time to explore key concepts. Although this can be achieved within each of the disciplines, I would argue it is at its most effective, in the MYP, when approached through well-constructed interdisciplinary units. They do not have to be complicated. A recent IB guide for interdisciplinary planning describes a number of multi-faceted questions, but it also gives examples of interdisciplinary units that simply follow the design cycle or link two subjects (Boix-Mansilla, 2010). Recently our year sixes designed and built kites. They explored aerodynamics in science, context in humanities (kites have a particular cultural history in China) and worked on design in technology and art.

Such units must be rigorous and avoid the pitfalls identified by Howard Gardner, who points out that projects are often described as interdisciplinary when there is actually no evidence of thinking that could be meaningfully described as disciplinary (Gardner 2008: 55). He cites an example where students study 'water' but simply explore their common experience with no real academic expectations (Gardner 2008: 55). There is, of course, no contradiction between academic rigour on the one hand and a dynamic and flexible curriculum on the other; it is a question of ensuring that the ideas explored are substantial and lead to greater understanding of discipline-specific concepts, even if they are not studied in single subject classes.

Another implication of the changes in the pre–frontal cortex is that many students will be struggling with basic organisation and planning skills in the transition years. The IB is sensibly moving to make the language of ATL (approaches to learning) common across the three programmes (International Baccalaureate, 2012b). A large study by the Department for Children Schools and Families in 2008 suggests that this is an important area to focus on in transition (DCSF, 2008). In the last years of the PYP and the first years of the MYP, students need to be given explicit strategies to help them navigate the many organizational demands faced in school each day.

In terms of curriculum design there are also implications relating to creativity. Some brain-based learning specialists make strong assertions about creativity. Geake, for example, makes a sound case for the importance of analogies in the brain's connecting mechanisms, with particular focus on the frontal and parietal lobes (2009: 94-106). Patricia Wolfe demonstrates how brain research points to the importance of story telling and metaphor (Wolfe, 2010: 107-109).

Certainly there is evidence to suggest that creativity helps the brain to build connections, and it is important in the transition years, because the developing prefrontal cortex has a key role in building connections.

The importance of creativity and the interconnectivity of the brain has led many commentators to argue that we should be giving greater prominence to the arts (drama, music, visual art) in the curriculum. In my experience many schools undervalue the arts, missing crucial learning opportunities in the MYP. The culmination of any inquiry study should be some kind of demonstration of understanding, and the arts provide the perfect tool to develop interesting performance models. As an example, our school recently planned for an interdisciplinary unit to culminate with a festival of wearable arts, based on a very popular New Zealand concept. Students had to design clothes to illustrate a story on stage, then choreograph and retell the story through dance.

Connecting brain research and creativity is not without its problems. The first is that there are no agreed definitions for creativity. Ken Robinson uses the term to talk about various aspects of artistic endeavor (Robinson 2006). Geake, on the other hand, discusses creativity in terms of making analogical links (Geake, 2009: 94-107). Gardner explains that there is no sharp line separating what he calls synthesis from creativity, but the impulse is different. Synthesisers wish to illuminate what has already been established, while the creator tries to find new directions (Gardner, 2008: 98).

Many commentators, like Geake, are actually talking about an idea that fits well with Howard Gardner's model of the synthesizing mind. Gardner describes this as the ability to select key information from abundant material and make sense of it (Gardner, 2008: 155). In his RSA lecture on his 'Five Minds for the Future', Gardner claims that the synthesizing mind is perhaps the most important for our time, because the modern learner has to deal with overwhelming amounts of information, often from the internet, and make sense of it (Gardner, 2006). Brain research does suggest that this type of synthesizing is important, and it is particularly pertinent to the transition years, because the necessary skills for synthesis are developed in the frontal lobes. One could argue that this again supports an emphasis on interdisciplinary units, which, by their very nature, encourage students to synthesise material. It also suggests that there should be a focus at transition on teaching students strategies to select and organise information across subject areas.

Any discussion on brain-based learning is necessarily limited by the range of study in neuroscience, which can only be instructive in those aspects of the brain that can be easily measured, and some aspects of creativity are not easy to measure. A perfect example is imagination. Many neurological studies have regarded a subject's imagination as experimental noise, or off-task thinking (Geake, 2009: 104). That is not to say that neuroscience cannot be instructive on certain aspects of imagination (such as empathy or prediction), but there are other more elusive qualities that are harder to identify. Education already has a tendency to over-value that which can be easily measured, and it would be a pity if something as impenetrable as imagination were marginalised because educators were to become too reliant on the findings of brain research.

Motivation and care

The report on transition undertaken for the Department for Children, Schools and Families demonstrates that for many students this is a very worrying and emotional time, and the emotional side of transition needs careful attention (DCSF, 2008). In 2007, a group of psychologists from Stanford and Columbia ran an experiment in a junior high school to look at the power of what was described as a growth mindset (Heath and Heath, 2010: 165-168). One group of students were taught that the brain is like a muscle that can be developed with appropriate exercise (meaning that with work they could get smarter). The other group were taught generic study skills. At the end of one term, the growth mindset group significantly outperformed the generic skills group. Motivation and self-confidence matter, especially with young adolescents (Heath and Heath, 2010: 165-168). However, as Geake rightly points out, self esteem is not raised in pupils by their being constantly told that every remark they make is wonderful (Geake, 2009: 121). Rather success breeds success. Students need to know they can achieve and be shown how. When this happens, success will become self-perpetuating.

One area that is brought into question by research on motivation and learning is the MYP grading system. The IB's new directions for MYP assessment are, in my view, not doing enough to address this. Currently, in transition, a student moves from a PYP assessment structure that tries to assess a range of learning outcomes to one where a student finishes with a grade in each subject, which can therefore be seen as a label. Students can identify a grade three or below with failing, since achievement of the final MYP certificate is dependent on achieving an average grade of four. There are surely serious questions to be asked about the wisdom of moving from a generic assessment system to a rigid grading system in this sensitive period.

Emotion in general has a far greater effect on cognitive development than was previously understood, and it is particularly important for young adolescents. The centre of the brain, the amygdala, has fully matured, while the emotional inhibitor in the pre-frontal cortex is in a state of huge flux. I have seen two talks by Dr Joann Deak, a well-known commentator on brain-based learning, in which she identifies the optimal emotional zone for cognitive development of the young adolescent, where the learner is excited and engaged without being over-anxious. When students are challenged and excited the brain produces greater amounts of dopamine, a neurotransmitter that aids learning, because it mediates synaptic plasticity (Geake, 2009: 118). This is particularly important in the period of transition, because early in adolescent development dopamine levels are relatively low (Wolfe, 2010: 86). Conversely, boredom has a highly negative effect on cognition in a young mind. As Wolfe rightly argues, the worst thing we can do with this age group is make them sit still and listen (Wolfe, 2010: 91). Lessons should be active and engaging, where the teacher is the meddler in the middle of an exciting inquiry-based classroom, rather than simply the voice at the front.

Equally important, too much stress actually damages the young brain. When a person is under high stress, the hormone cortisol is released into the blood stream (Sousa, 2011: 89-91). Cortisol is designed to alert the brain to danger. This is because the brain still has a primitive 'flight or fight' response to threats. When a brain is stressed the heart rate increases, blood pressure goes up and senses become alert, because the body is preparing to run away from danger (Wolfe, 2010: 137-140). At the same time the cognitive functions are shut down. High concentrations of cortisol over time can provoke hippocampal deterioration (the hippocampus is possibly the key component of working memory) and cognitive decline (Wolfe, 2010: 141-142). Because the young adolescent brain is in a state of emotional flux, it has not developed the proper inhibition controls to limit stress. Stress at school, whether it is social or classroom-related, needs to be managed. This means taking the social side of schooling, both in and out of the classroom, very seriously. It also means that an overly packed curriculum, with too much emphasis on traditional tests, is likely to be detrimental to long term cognition. An IB position paper on Concurrency of Learning recognizes the importance of the 'less is more' principle (Marshman, 2010) and this is particularly true in transition, when the brain is undergoing such a sensitive period of development.

The importance of appropriate care in transition cannot be emphasised enough. A lack of care has a detrimental effect on both the frontal lobes and the development of memory (Geake, 2009: 113-125). When students feel positive about their learning experiences the brain releases endorphins, which makes the students feel good and stimulates activity in the frontal lobes (Sousa, 2011: 89). Schools need supportive and effective pastoral structures, and it should be made explicit that caring, or the appearance of caring (meaning students believing the teacher cares), is a core expectation in the classroom. Recently scientists have discovered mirror neurons which, as the name suggests, are used to mimic others' behaviour. Their development is essential in our capacity to empathise (Geake, 2009: 108-113). Not only do teachers need to be caring; they should also model appropriate behaviour in all aspects of learning.

Broadly speaking the IB is, at least philosophically, supportive of the approach outlined in this section, and it is probably most evident in the learner profile, where a number of attributes (caring, balanced, principled) are self evidently in the same vein (International Baccalaureate, 2006). A question in IB schools is the degree to which these attributes are treated in a tokenistic manner, or are central to the school's culture.

It is important to add a note of caution at the end of this section. Not all scientists agree with the claims made by certain neurologists about adolescent emotions and the brain. The roots of behaviour are complex, and brain-based commentaries can sometimes appear reductionist, linking certain behaviors with a single cause. Although research supports the assertions made in this section, it is important to see them in the context of wider educational debates.

Balance

Brain research has much to say on the importance of a balanced life style, and by extension the IB commitment to developing the whole child. Sleep, exercise and diet all affect cognition. A major study on sleep was conducted by Mary Carskadon of Brown University, who found that teenagers need more sleep than they did as children (Wolfe, 2010: 88-90). To fully function and stay alert, the optimum they need nightly is about nine-and-a-half hours. Sleep is important in terms of brain function, because it is the time information is encoded in long-term memory, specifically during the rapid eye movement (REM) stage (Sousa, 2011: 107-110). It is the biological revision time, when the information learned in a day is reviewed and sorted. Studies suggest that long term retentions and high order thinking can both be adversely affected by lack of sleep (Blakemore and Frith, 2011: 171-175), but sleep deprivation is clearly a common problem. Carskadon's research suggests that, in a survey of 3,000 teenagers, the majority slept only seven hours per night (Wolfe, 2010: 89). In my school in Hong Kong, where there is a very strong culture of extra tutorial classes and out-of-school activities, the amount of sleep is a lot less. It has become an emerging priority to educate both students and parents on its importance. Often, in my experience, many parents need more convincing than students and do not always easily accept the importance of a balanced lifestyle.

Sleep cycles are dictated by circadian rhythms, which act as a biological clock. Another of Carskadon's findings is that it is wholly natural and healthy for teenagers to wake up late (Wolfe, 2010: 89-90). Many teenagers are not naturally ready to wake until 8 or 9 in the morning. Some schools are dealing with this by starting the school day later.

The importance of good nutrition for human health has long been understood, but it is only recently that scientists have begun to look at its impact on the brain. In 1989, the results of a landmark study on the impact of school breakfast on learning outcomes were published (Wolfe, 2010: 98). Students who received a nutritious breakfast significantly outscored those who did not. More than 80% of the brain is water. Blakemore and Frith claim that increasing the amount of water one drinks can improve concentration and memory, and, conversely, dehydration can seriously impair learning (Blakemore and Frith, 2011: 185). The brain's neurotransmitters (chemicals responsible for sending signals that connect neurons) are mostly composed of amino acids, which we obtain from the food we eat (Wolfe, 2010: 100). An amino acid derived from carbohydrates produces serotonin, a neurotransmitter that creates feelings of well being and calm, while an amino acid derived from proteins is used to make dopamine, which acts as a stimulant (Wolfe, 2010: 99-101). There are also studies suggesting real benefits for the brain in consuming healthy amounts of omega-3 fatty acids (Wolfe, 2010: 99-101). There is still much to be researched on food and the brain, but the simple conclusion is that a healthy diet is as important for the mind as it is for the body. Students in the transition years need to understand this and be encouraged to eat well.

Exercise, meanwhile, increases the oxygen flow to the bloodstream and regular exercise has been shown to pump more blood through the body, including the brain, which in turn increases growth and plasticity in the frontal lobes (Wolfe, 2010: 93-99). This is crucial in the years of transition. Exercise also stimulates the release of proteins which also impacts on neural growth (Wolfe, 2010: 93-99). The work of John Ratey has shown that exercise has a positive effect both on learning and emotional well-being in schools (Wolfe, 2010: 94).

Both the PYP and the MYP promote a balanced curriculum, but schools are still able to allocate a reasonably small amount of time to physical education (PE) (the minimum is 50 hours), and there are no guidelines on recess or play. Wolfe's research implies that too little recess time is damaging. An equally important implication of this research is that movement should be incorporated into lessons. Sousa suggests students need to move every ten to twenty minutes (depending on age) and argues that movement impacts positively on, amongst other things, implicit learning, stress, the ability to self regulate and episodic memory (Sousa, 2011: 37-240). Again, movement may be particularly important for the young adolescent brain. What should not happen, as Patricia Wolfe explains, is that energetic adolescent minds move from one class to another, then simply sit still and listen (Wolfe, 2010: 93-95).

The traditional classroom environment may well not be the best model to adopt at the age of transition, because the structure is by its nature rigid and constricting. We should instead think of schools in terms of a variety of learning spaces. David Thornburg's book *Campfires in Cyberspace* (1999) provides some compelling images to describe how these spaces might be organized, by taking some traditional learning scenarios and imagining them in a modern context. The first space Thornburg explores is the campfire, a traditional gathering point to share knowledge, often through stories or even, occasionally, a traditional lecture. The next space is the watering hole, a gathering point for traditional communities, where creative and collaborative discussions take place – the exploratory part of the learning process. In a modern school, this could be achieved in a highly interactive library-type setting or, more simply, outside. The third space is the cave, where students have time to be on their own and reflect on their learning.

A further implication, again supported by IB philosophy but not necessarily practised in all MYP and PYP schools, is the importance of learning outdoors. The IB supports authentic learning based in the real world, and the transition years are the perfect time to take students outside. Some examples from my current school include one unit where students studied the Central district of Hong Kong and used their research to draw up a business plan. In another unit, they attended a Polaroid workshop and used knowledge from that workshop to take a series of street photos in Hong Kong. They then went on to look at reasons for the cultural shift from Polaroid to digital and the economic issues related to that. Moreover, the IB promotes service learning, and there are endless possibilities for good service projects that link different subject areas and get students out of the classroom.

The PYP and MYP both promote a holistic approach to education. The task of schools is to turn that ideal into everyday reality, where it is understood that movement, play and different types of performance are not in opposition to academic rigour. Rather, they help stimulate a young mind, both emotionally and cognitively.

Conclusion

When students change from a primary school to a secondary school they are, at the same time, going through a huge neurological transition, perhaps greater than at any other time in their schooling. How that change is managed has an enormous effect on cognition. What, then, is the perfect school environment for students in this period? Neuroscience is not yet able to tell us with any certainty, but current research supports a certain type of model, one that is very much in line with IB thinking with its focus on a holistic and balanced education.

Emotions seem to have a particularly potent effect on cognition in early adolescence (there is substantial research to support this assertion) and a nurturing and motivating atmosphere at transition is therefore paramount. Students also need space to move and explore, and that means thinking of schools as a series of different learning spaces rather than a set of classrooms, and providing structured opportunities to learn outside. In more general terms a balanced lifestyle has a significant effect on cognition, with the young adolescent mind requiring a good diet, regular exercise and sufficient sleep.

Lessons should be stimulating and challenging but, at the same time, students need to know they can be successful. In terms of curriculum framework, there is a strong case to be made for an interdisciplinary approach, with a focus on key concepts that students explore in the PYP and again in more depth in the MYP (the spiral curriculum). Students in this age group are going through a period, in brain terms, of significant synaptic pruning, so the 'less is more' principle is also important. The arts have a central role to play, and there should be room for creativity, with students being given a stake in the direction their learning is taking.

The student in transition is living through a time of enormous potential. Schools need to create the conditions that allow active young minds to flourish.

References

Blakemore, S. and Frith, U. (2011) *The Learning Brain: Lessons for Education.* Oxford: Blackwell.

Boix-Mansilla, V. (2010) MYP Guide to Interdisciplinary Teaching and Learning. Cardiff: International Baccalaureate.

Department for Children Schools and Families (2008) *What Makes a Successful Transition from Primary to Secondary School?* Available online via http://webarchive. nationalarchives.gov.uk/20130401151715/https://www.education.gov.uk/publications/RSG/ Pupilsupportwelfareandbehaviour/Page10/DCSF-RB019 (last accessed 6 May 2013).

Fouracre, S. (1993) Pupils' Expectations of the Transition from Primary to Secondary School. *Research in Education* (Scottish Council for Research in Education), 53, p.1-2.

Gardner, H. (2008) *Five Minds For The Future.* Boston: Harvard Business Press.

Gardner, H. (2006) RSA Lecture. Retrieved 20 June 2012, from Teachers TV: http://www. teachers.tv/video/5452.

Geake, J. (2009) *The Brain at School: Educational Neuroscience in the Classroom.* Glasgow: Open University Press.

Heath, C. and Heath, D. (2010) *Switch: How to Change Things When Change is Hard.* London. Random House.

International Baccalaureate (2006) *IB Learner Profile Booklet.* Cardiff: International Baccalaureate.

International Baccalaureate (2007) *Making the PYP Happen. A Curriculum Framework for International Primary Education.* Cardiff: International Baccalaureate.

International Baccalaureate (2008) *MYP: From Principles into Practice.* Cardiff: International Baccalaureate.

International Baccalaureate (2012a) *MYP: Excerpts from Principles into Practice for Pilot Purposes.* Cardiff: International Baccalaureate.

International Baccalaureate (2012b) *MYP Coordinators Notes for May.* Cardiff: International Baccalaureate.

Marshman, R. (2010) *Concurrency of Learning in the IB Diploma Programme and Middle Years Programme.* Cardiff: International Baccalaureate.

Robinson, K. (2006) Do Schools Kill Creativity: TED, Ideas Worth Spreading. Retrieved 2 July, 2012, from TED, Ideas Worth Spreading http://www.ted.com/talks/ken_robinson_says_ schools_kill_creativity.html.

Sousa, D. (2011) *How the Brain Learns.* Thousand Oaks: Corwin.

Thornburg, D. (1999) *Campfires in Cyberspace.* San Carlos: Starsong Publications.

Wolfe, P. (2010) *Brain Matters: Translating Research into Classroom Practice.* Alexandria: ASCD.

Chapter 11

Articulating the gap: the International Baccalaureate Middle Years and Diploma Programmes

Gillian Ashworth

When Thomas Menino, Mayor of Boston, asserted that 'children need continuity as they grow and learn' he was not, in all probability, holding at the time copies of the International Baccalaureate (IB) Middle Years Programme (MYP) and Diploma Programme (DP) details, musing on the quality of the articulation between them. Just such a pastime has, however, been a source of debate among many an IB teacher since that time, as a quick survey of internet forums venting opinions on the topic suggests:

> As I never tire of telling people, the three programmes were designed by different people at different times for different reasons and subsequent attempts by the IB to stitch them into a seamless whole are, at best, work in progress. (LinkedIn, 2011)

> Many of us teach or have taught both MYP and DP. If you are an MYP true believer, can you be anything other than a reluctant teacher of the DP? (LinkedIn, 2011)

> Any other thoughts on MYP? I have been looking at schools which do this program for next year and am not sure whether to apply or not. A friend told me that the teachers at his MYP school taught the kids a lot of 'fluff' and when the students got to IBDP they have really struggled. (International Schools Review, 2010)

That the two programmes have different stories to tell of their origins is not in dispute. That the IB organisation has focused progressively more on addressing perceived transitional difficulties is increasingly evident. That the programmes may have more similarities in purpose and nature than frequently seem to be realised, and that solutions to a number of issues which may arise in schools over their articulation might be sought closer to home at times, may also be a truism in need of greater emphasis.

Where and how did transitional issues arise? – the differing backgrounds and natures of the programmes

The IB itself acknowledges that 'The continuum, like the growth of a student, is not a smooth trajectory—moving from one programme to the next may necessitate a few leaps' (IB, 2008: 6). As Hallinger *et al.* reported, however, the question has not been so much one of 'a few leaps' as of 'schools adopting multiple IB programs hav[ing] reported a variety of 'transition problems' as students move from one program to the next' (2011: 123). Long-running debates on the likes of LinkedIn and TES Online, meanwhile, demonstrate that this 'perennial topic of debate' (Hayden, 2006: 138) remains just that.

Two not infrequently-cited reasons for transitional difficulties have lain in the different origins of the MYP and DP, which 'were neither designed at the same time nor designed with inter-program linkages in mind' (Hallinger *et al.*, 2011: 124), and in their natures and purposes: 'The Primary Years Programme (PYP) and MYP are curriculum frameworks, whereas the DP is a prescribed curriculum ... Each programme is designed to meet the developmental needs of students of particular ages and at key stages of identity formation' (IB, 2008b: 6).

In terms of origin, older sibling the Diploma Programme emerged in the 1960s in response to a perceived need 'for an international programme that could be taken by all students and accepted around the world' (Hill, 2002: 24), with the main emphasis being on 'developing an internationally recognized university entry programme' (IB, 2010a: 2). Nonetheless, while university entry requirements necessarily loomed large in the priorities of various stakeholders (and continue of course to do so), Hill makes clear the presence of three underpinnings from the outset, namely ideological (the programme would promote international understanding), utilitarian (it would be recognized for university entrance around the world), and pedagogical (it would promote critical thinking skills, 'rather than an emphasis on encyclopaedic knowledge') (Hill, 2002: 19). He further describes the 'promise' of the newly-introduced IB Diploma Programme to provide 'a common curriculum ... with an international perspective, academic rigour, critical thinking and research skills, and emphasizing the development of the whole person: in sum, the creation of world citizens'.

Younger sibling the Middle Years Programme finally emerged in 1994, after 15 years in the making – and in the debating, for that matter (IB, 2010a: 4-24); wrapped in 'areas of interaction,' 'interdisciplinarity', and schools 'teaching whatever they wished and then sending work for moderation' (Pook, 2009, in IB, 2010a: 29). While claims of the IB programmes having arisen overall in 'relative isolation' (Chapman, 2011: 195) are probably fair, it is worth noting that the MYP's starting point in fact lay in earliest thoughts on a programme 'which would align much more comfortably with the Diploma Programme' (IB, 2010a: 2), as concerns arose in the late 1970s in some schools offering the DP of a 'philosophic and pedagogic disjunction created by using the British O levels as a pre-IB preparation'. Initial discussions were on 'a two-year pilot programme for an examination at Grades 10/11. The term 'pre-IB' had been used, and emphasis had been put on IB concepts of learning how to learn and of educating the whole human being' (ISA 1980a: 13, in IB, 2010a: 3).

The idea of becoming involved in developing such a curriculum at that very early stage was turned down by an IB evidently of the view that there was more than enough to do in continuing to implement the still relatively new DP. One can only wonder how things might have unfolded had a different decision left the development of what would become the MYP under the auspices of the IB from the outset. As it was, the programme embarked from there, largely under the auspices instead of the International Schools' Association (ISA), on a lengthy trajectory through a relentless series of meetings, conferences and the like; all making their own contribution to shaping a programme which would ultimately reunite with the IB in 1994 as the MYP. Its development was chronicled by the ISA, whose 1980 Curriculum Committee meeting records in the earliest stages indicate that initial ideas remained remarkably redolent of the types of concerns which had prompted the DP's emergence:

> Three reasons were advanced and accepted: the need to have a pre-IB programme that leads into the IB; the need to have a credible international school leaving certificate; the need to have an internationally acceptable education for students transferring to and from international and national systems. (ISA, 1980b: 13, in IB, 2010a: 3).

Mention of six subject areas, a project 'along the lines of the IB extended essay' and 'athletic' and 'service' activities represented further nods to the DP, though a focus on 'concepts, thereby allowing some flexibility in content' foreshadowed the later MYP.

On its adoption 14 years later, however, the MYP had been shaped by various key moments and decisions into a five-year programme which would 'correspond to the philosophy of an international system of education' (ISA, 1991: 8–9, in IB, 2010a: 21). Following the ISA conference of 1981, 'interdisciplinarity' began to feature in discussions, after its virtues were extolled in a notable address by Robert Belle-Isle, then director of the United Nations International School (UNIS) in New York: efforts to establish the place of such a concept in the programme were among the factors behind the subsequent emergence of the areas of interaction. A key move in the following couple of years was to expand the parameters of the programme from two years to five, providing scope – particularly in combination with a decreasing focus on a possible terminal examination – for greater focus on educational elements such as interdisciplinarity which were felt to address particular needs of students in the 11-16 age range. In 1987 'there was a clear statement that a formal terminal examination was not envisaged, but that there would be a form of internal assessment based on criteria that the ISA would develop' (IB, 2010a: 14). In 1991 the newly-published *ISAC Programme of International Secondary Education 11–16 years* outlined aspects of the educational philosophy of the programme, a 'philosophy of an international system of education' which was 'appropriate' to the age range at which it was aimed, on the basis that 'the perspective of an examination is remote enough to allow more freedom to schools and teachers'

(ISA, 1991: 8–9, in IB, 2010a: 21). In a further meeting in the same year, focused on assessment, 'the issue of continuity with the Diploma Programme came up but was discounted, as the MYP should have its own integrity and philosophy. The philosophical approach that was decided upon for the programme lent itself more to continuous teacher assessment than to terminal examinations.' (IB, 2010a: 23).

The diverging foci of the MYP and DP over time, evident in the above account, were perhaps encapsulated by Gerard Renaud, a former director general of the IB who took on an increasing curriculum and coordination role in the emerging middle years programme, hence experiencing life in the vanguard of both:

> [the] best niche, the age group where one could truly undertake international education, is the age group broadly from 11–16 because in the Diploma Programme, the examination is too near and demands the full attention of the student ... So I got down to it with great interest, given that I was a little free of the demands of the IB [Diploma Programme] (Renaud 2008, in IB, 2010a: 12).

The programme arrived at its moment of adoption in 1994, therefore, different in nature and purpose in a number of respects to the DP, and a 'curriculum framework, whereas the DP is a prescribed curriculum' (IB, 2008b, p. 6):

> Each programme is designed to meet the developmental needs of students of particular ages and at key stages of identity formation. Schools need room to shape the curriculum according to local requirements and to their cultural realities and priorities. The DP has to provide students with the qualifications to gain entry to universities anywhere in the world, hence the increased level of prescription in the programme. (IB, 2008b: 6)

Efforts to close the gap

Questions arose relating to the MYP's relationship with the DP even before its adoption in 1994, however. In 1991 it seems that 'pressure was growing on the IB leadership owing to the success of the Diploma Programme, with schools asking for a continuum of education. The tensions at that time were around assessment and continuity – should the MYP lead into the Diploma Programme, or should it be a separate programme with its own integrity?' (IB, 2010a: 23).

The decision that 'the MYP should have its own integrity and philosophy' (IB, 2010a: 23) would not delay the question's inevitable return for long; while schools adopting the programme began to experience difficulties at times in getting to grips with 'a set of broad ideas and principles that were cloudy' and which 'needed definition' (Pook, 2009, in IB, 2010a: 29): 'In contrast to the very positive experiences of introducing the Diploma Programme (DP) and the Primary Years Programme (PYP) at Prince Alfred College in Adelaide,

Australia, implementation of the Middle Years Programme (MYP) has been problematic' (Codrington, 2002).

In 2003, 'genuine discussions' on 'what was meant by a continuum of IB education' did take place, with an acknowledgement being made that, at that stage, 'the three programmes were developed separately and were usually stand-alone in schools' (IB, 2010a: 32). Efforts to connect them focused, in the first instance, on philosophical elements such as the learner profile, followed in 2008 by the publication of *Towards a continuum of international education* explaining further connecting elements of the three programmes as a continuum, such as assessment, the language continuum, special educational needs, and the service and action elements of each. Aligning the review cycle for subject guides with those of the DP was also, meanwhile, viewed as 'an important step towards increased articulation between programmes' and one designed 'to help schools in transitioning students between programmes' (IB, 2010a: 32). A more significant initiative directed at MYP–DP transition, however, was announced in 2010 in the form of 'MYP: Avoiding the Gap' (IB, 2010b: 2-4), which sought 'to investigate the MYP as a preparation for the DP' and create 'recommendations that have informed the development of a detailed action plan' (IB, 2010b: 2). Under particular investigation were assessment, curriculum review processes, programme awareness and recognition, and MYP command terms.

Avoiding the gap – before and beyond: assessment

Assessment has always been in the vanguard of debate on MYP–DP articulation and transition, particularly regarding the question of external examinations at the MYP's culmination – a notion which receded during the programme's evolution, and was largely resisted subsequent to its 1994 adoption. Discussion at one point as the ISA's middle years programme was continuing to evolve, on the possibility of its convergence with the equally evolving International General Certificate of Secondary Education (IGCSE) examinations of the University of Cambridge Local Examination Syndicate (UCLES), ended with each continuing 'on their distinctively different pathways', as 'both initiatives were not only too far advanced in their respective developments to really give convergence a fair chance but more fundamentally they were philosophically out of any significant alignment' (IB, 2010a: 16). The 1987 publication *International Curriculum for the Middle Years of Schooling, 11–16 Years*, on which a significant amount of the adopted MYP was based, subsequently contained 'a clear statement that a formal terminal examination was not envisaged, but that there would be a form of internal assessment based on criteria that the ISA would develop' (IB, 2010a: 14). A 1991 meeting, focused on assessment and involving representatives of the IB, contained 'discussion of the most appropriate forms of assessment'. According to Thompson (2010), 'the issue of continuity with the Diploma Programme came up but was discounted, as the MYP should have its own integrity and philosophy. The philosophical approach that was decided upon for the programme lent itself more to continuous teacher assessment than to terminal examinations.' (IB, 2010a: 23)

The decision at adoption in 1994 was for 'the preparation of a model of internal assessment based on external moderation' (IB, 2010a: 24). However, there was 'no assessment model' during the first three years of the programme, 'no criteria of assessment', and schools were 'teaching whatever they wished and then sending work for moderation' (IB, 2010a: 28). An assessment model and criteria created in time for moderation meetings in 1997 'gave a clear indication that schools needed a lot more advice on constructing samples and applying assessment criteria', while a moderator's insight into the meetings themselves provides hints as to reasons for concerns which would persist over validity and reliability in relation to the moderation process: 'There were enormous differences of opinion in how to interpret criteria level descriptors, whether all threads of a criterion needed to be addressed, and how to handle situations when the teacher had chosen some unsuitable tasks' (IB, 2010a: 29).

While the process did develop substantially from there, it remained one in which 'The MYP is assessed internally 'on trust', although schools can submit work in Year 5 for external moderation' (Bunnell, 2011: 262) – most schools do not, however, as Bunnell further points out, do so. Bunnell is among those raising, too, questions of reliability and validity with the moderation process:

> [T]he June 2009 moderation session revealed discrepancies between subjects. For example, only 2 per cent of biology students scored a grade 7, yet 15 per cent achieved that grade in the personal project (2011: 268).

Similar concerns have been voiced via the *TES* forum:

> Another problem is that there is no exam at the end of the MYP (e.g. there is no GCSE equivalent). Samples of work are sent for moderation but I am not convinced that there is consistency between schools and countries. (TES, 2013c).

Anthony Seldon is Headmaster of perhaps the UK's most significant adopter of the MYP so far, Wellington College. For Seldon, speaking at the IBAEM Conference in Liverpool, UK in September 2010, lack of confidence in the final assessment process was the key factor inhibiting wider uptake of MYP in the UK.

Plans for 'Avoiding the Gap' thus sought to address concerns persisting with reliability:

> The MYP assessment model currently demonstrates high validity but low reliability. High validity will continue to be assured by ensuring that prescribed moderation tasks allow students to demonstrate understanding in a wide variety of ways. Although an internally assessed model can never

provide the highest reliability, the aim of the proposed changes to MYP assessment is to increase it as much as possible. (IB, 2010b: 3).

Nor was the internal assessment model immune from concerns over validity, though all has now been quite radically superseded by the forthcoming 'MYP–Next Chapter' project, which at the time of writing proposes the replacement of moderation with 'optional concept-based summative' on-screen e-assessments, from which will derive IB-certificated individual subject and interdisciplinary grades (1–7) for those schools choosing to have them. The move towards e-assessments of this nature is clearly moving the MYP towards formal external assessment, and the perceived greater reliability associated with that, as well as towards a model rather more similar to that found within the DP. At present, in what – it must be noted – are relatively early days and a situation in flux, final certificated grades will be based only on the e-assessments, unlike the use of internal assessment found also in the DP. The initial need for manageable steps in what represents a significant undertaking, however, does not preclude further development of the model, and incorporation of more of the DP's assessment approaches and the arguably greater overall dependability brought by them. Accompanying mandatory moderation of Personal Projects, meanwhile, if not wholly mirroring the requirements of the DP's Extended Essay, represents a move closer to these approaches.

The October 2012 Development Report currently mooting information regarding the 'Next Chapter' project states that 'Most assessment in the MYP is best described as internal, as opposed to external, because the assessment tasks, strategies and tools are designed, developed and applied by teachers working with students in their schools' (IB, 2010b: 10). Much the same is true, though, of any school following a programme which involves external assessment to provide formal certification and grades at its culmination, and the reality is that MYP is about to head down the path of what will be, if the e-assessments prove successful, high stakes end-of-programme formal examinations in all but name, with all that entails. That the move is likely to polarise opinion can already be seen in comments on the IB's Online Curriculum Centre (OCC) forums and elsewhere, and should come as no surprise in view of the manner in which the notion of such terminal assessments in MYP has always done likewise. It certainly represents a bold and radical move in the MYP's continuing evolution, and the consequences which await to be seen will be of very great interest to very many.

Avoiding the gap – before and beyond: curriculum

A second focus of 'MYP: Avoiding the Gap' was 'curriculum review processes', where a set of initiatives was propounded, aimed at establishing more thorough reviews which would 'include staff from each of the three IB programmes', along with the MYP committee and a cross-programme research manager to assist with 'current research and thinking in the subject areas'; and at synchronizing MYP subject reviews with those in the DP to bring about 'greater articulation between the programmes' (IB, 2010b: 3). In addition a document was produced that provides guidance on command terms as used in the MYP and DP.

As with assessment, 'MYP–Next Chapter' has since seen further curriculum developments put in motion which include new guides for all subjects, a switch to 'global contexts' from areas of interaction, and a greater focus on concepts. More guidance on implementation is also mooted, while extensive piloting being carried out in schools should inform the process further. The new developments will hopefully serve to allay some of the ongoing frustrations of teachers in terms of *how* to implement aspects of the programme, and the time taken in trying to do so – two particular issues seemingly in evidence from the outset: '[the staff] thought I was completely crazy talking about a holistic approach, interdisciplinarity, areas of interaction, mini memoires'. But 'after a year and the reading of hundreds of photocopies, we came to an agreement on what we were talking about and how to implement it' (Manzitti 2001, in IB, 2010a: 18). '[O]ur real job at the school was to make it all fly ... a lot of people had put a great effort into thinking about what they wanted in theory ... but we had to make it work day after day' were comments offered by some involved in the initial piloting of the programme. Codrington's account illustrates continuing difficulties and, almost 20 years later, the problem appears to persist: 'The 'what' of the programme had become fairly clear to us, but the 'how' has been taking much longer to figure out' (Field, 2011: 63). Forums such as the *Times Educational Supplement* (TES, 2013a, b, c) continue to provide a home for at times less politely-expressed views on the same theme, while the moniker of 'Many Years of Paperwork' for MYP is long-established in some quarters. Bunnell suggested more recently that 'the MYP seems to have reached the point in its life-time at which educators are beginning to focus more on how to implement the programme, rather than on what it should *look* like' (Bunnell, 2011: 270), though given that 'now' is some 20 years after the MYP's adoption, such a longstanding gap between theory and improvement of practice should be of concern.

Difficulties in implementation contribute to a perception of the MYP lacking rigour, with perceived superficiality in some of the more 'philosophical' aspects of the programme, and less focus on subject content due, as is suggested at times, to misconceptions of its significance in MYP. The pitfalls of both were in fact touched on in Belle-Isle's original speech which first brought the notion of 'interdisciplinarity' to prominence:

> Interdisciplinarity is excellent if it is firmly rooted in disciplinarity. Each subject is not an end in itself but it must be an efficient tool. We must keep its identity and especially its own methodology. Only on that basis will we be able to construct a serious interdisciplinarity. Otherwise we will lead our students to mental confusion and superficial surveys. (ISAC 1991, in IB, 2010a: 20).

Such aspects represent elements of the overall curriculum which must be implemented for MYP, with others lying in subject-related content. More than half of MYP schools now have local requirements, standards and benchmarks to integrate into their MYP offerings, necessitating a framework which allows the flexibility for a variety of such elements to be integrated. Where no such requirements exist, however, schools must populate their programmes themselves with all the complexities that such curriculum-building involves. The issues this may involve were raised in a discussion thread in the MYP Coordinators' forum on the OCC in 2011: 'We are in the process of curriculum review at our school, which requires teachers to develop and write curriculum (content aligned with MYP objectives). A number of our teachers feel that while they are highly skilled in *delivering* curriculum, they are not skilled curriculum writers / designers, and that this should be left to curriculum specialists. Their concern is that they do not have the requisite expertise or judgment about what should or should not be included in the curriculum, and how progression within a subject (from unit to unit, from year to year) should be organized. Is there a rationale put forward by the IB (or indeed elsewhere?!) for teachers as curriculum writers? Why should teachers be writing curriculum (content)? Can anyone point me in the direction of something written by the IB about this? ...... I know that many teachers just want to get on into the classroom and deliver curriculum rather than talk about it – or write it down!' (OCC, 2011)

Opining in response was the faculty member responsible for the forum: 'I have suggested upon a few occasions that IBCA [at that time the IB's Curriculum and Assessment centre in Cardiff] provide training in writing curriculum or at least make an arrangement with folks like Jay McTighe, Grant Wiggins and especially Lynn Erickson, who form the theoretical and practical background to how we are expected to shape our curriculum.' (OCC, 2011)

Hallinger *et al.*, in analysing data from a 2008 survey of IB Coordinators, found it 'indicated a considerable level of agreement among IB Coordinators globally concerning the types of changes needed to improve the MYP-DP transition', with 'publication of MYP vertical and horizontal articulation documents', 'publication of IB cross-programme articulation documents', and 'provision of more teacher support and guidance for the MYP' representing the top three types of change believed to be needed, all with an agreement rating of 78% or more of all coordinators surveyed (Hallinger *et al.*, 2011: 130-1). The collective suggestion, therefore, has been of a gap existing where greater curriculum guidance (in terms of both the mechanics and the content) could and perhaps should be, and of that being a somewhat critical gap at that, in view of the fundamental importance of implementing curriculum in appropriate and meaningful ways. 'Dealing with detailed and prescribed content in the DP' was meanwhile recorded by Hallinger *et al.* as the biggest transition challenge identified in the survey, followed by 'Change in student attitude to learning', referring one presumes to a perceived need for such change once students reach the DP and have to engage in 'proper learning'. Prescribed content is not infrequently cited in the support voiced at times for the IGCSE as a 'better' preparation for DP:

> I have taught in schools teaching either program leading into the IB DP. It seems that the IGCSE can prepare students better for the DP content wise as it is laid out for them. (LinkedIn, 2011)

> MYP ... emphasises communication, problem solving, collaborative working, coursework assessment, integration with other subjects, real-life contexts etc ... It is therefore not an ideal precursor for the academically demanding diploma. Subject content is viewed, at best, as only useful as a conduit for developing generic skills ... My argument is that the essences, and hence the rigour, of individual subject disciplines may be easily lost when generic skills are used to define courses. IGCSE courses have these skills embedded in them too, but the content is foremost. (TESa, 2011)

Respondents do, though, point out the role of a school in the quality of its MYP:

> The MYP is exactly what a school makes of it. If developed and implemented properly it can be whatever you want it to be. Personally I have taught DP to students having been through the GCSE, IGCSE and the MYP and I can tell you that those having been through the MYP are much better prepared for DP in many ways. (TES, 2013a)

> It is possible to use MYP to prepare students well for the DP, but most schools don't do this since it doesn't occur to them that they have to make it happen – the MYP is just a framework that has to be configured to do whatever the school wants. (TES, 2013a)

> [S]ometimes new MYP teachers do not recognise that detailed knowledge is still required, because the MYP framework does not list it. (LinkedIn, 2011)

'Curriculum' has maintained over time a prominent position in the debate on MYP–DP transition, in particular regarding perceptions of a lack of rigour, emanating from inadequately understood requirements for aspects such as interdisciplinary teaching and learning, the areas of interaction, and so on; and/or the nature and amount of the subject-specific content which disciplinary courses should contain. As 'MYP–Next Chapter' moves closer, the curriculum would seem set to remain an area on which debate will be focused.

Where the gap converges ...

Reflection on the respective paths taken by the MYP and DP thus reveals much of interest in considering the question of transition between the two programmes and, perhaps, much of use also in looking at how the paths ahead may be negotiated. This may be a particularly salient moment to do so, meanwhile, as the DP sees as its Head of Development since early 2013 Malcolm Nicolson, former Head of MYP Development and the architect of both 'Avoiding the Gap' and 'MYP–Next Chapter', with the MYP thus welcoming a new Head of Development of its own as it moves towards the launch of 'Next Chapter' in 2014. As has been seen, questions asked of the transition between the MYP and DP since before the former had even been adopted have been looming increasingly large in the development of the programme ever since. While there are clear and valid reasons to ask such questions, there is a need also to acknowledge both where differences are inevitable, and perhaps to be nurtured; and where, conversely, perhaps more articulation already exists than may often be recognised.

For all of the stated ideological and pedagogical aims of the DP, the pragmatic concerns of examinations and university entry wield a heavy influence on much about the programme; and indeed also on much about the MYP at times, judged as it may be on occasion solely in terms of the demands of its sibling – and harshly so if accompanied by angst at its apparent predilection for more philosophical concerns at the expense of 'prescribed content'. The nature of such 'prescribed content' might be queried further, however, particularly in view of sentiments of some involved in shaping the DP, such as then-IB director general Alec Peterson who opined among other things the following, back in 1966: 'What matters is not the absorption and regurgitation either of facts or of predigested interpretations of facts, but the development of powers of the mind or ways of thinking which can be applied to new situations and new presentations of facts as they arise' (Peterson, 2003: 47).

The DP has from its inception included varied learning objectives extending beyond factual knowledge. Hill, when talking of the DP, stated that 'A formal curriculum comprises content (knowledge and concepts), skills and attitudes' (2002: 26), while the DP's version of *From Principles into Practice* talks variously of subject-specific knowledge, understanding, and skills, and declares that 'it is essential that a pre-university education equips students with the depth of discipline-specific knowledge and skills that they will need to follow their chosen university course and for use later in their professional lives' (IB, 2009: 5). Prescribed content in the DP is not therefore, and never has been, knowledge-based to the exclusion of all else, but in fact encompasses the types of learning which should be found in the MYP, whose own *From Principles into Practice* states that 'The objectives of each subject group ... represent the knowledge, understanding, skills and attitudes that must be taught so that students can achieve the aims of the subject group' (IB, 2008a: 34).

Approaches to teaching and learning ...

For this reason, the statement made of DP that 'There are a wide range of teaching strategies and approaches that should be used in the classroom ... What is essential is that each student is actively engaged in classroom activities and that there is a high degree of interaction between students and the teacher, and also between the students themselves ... Teachers should use a variety of different approaches at different times, employing a mixture of whole-class, group and individual activities that are representative of the learner profile.' (IB, 2009: 37) might have equally been written of the MYP, and reflect the need in any teaching and learning context for choosing approaches appropriate and effective at that particular time for the nature of the learning involved. Different subjects meanwhile comprise different proportions of knowledge, conceptual understanding, and skills within their overall parameters, with the task for the teacher being to recognise the type(s) being addressed at any particular time, and to match appropriate teaching approaches to that. Worthy of note too is the constructivist approach of the IB which looks towards the theories of Vygotsky, and at the teacher both facilitating the student to 'work in their 'zone of proximal development'' – 'the range of achievement that lies between what the student can manage on their own and what they can manage with the support of the teacher', and 'engaging and challenging the learner's existing mental models in order to develop a greater depth of understanding and to improve performance' (IB, 2009: 37). Facilitating both aims necessarily involves placing students in a position to engage in independent and collaborative learning, something which may be significantly limited where a predisposition exists to teaching 'from the front'.

The process by which teachers must engage is one of 'creative teacher professionalism' – 'the central responsibility that teachers have in the design and delivery of the programme' (IB, 2009: 9), a concept which is 'critical in understanding the pivotal role played by teachers in designing their own course of study and teaching it in an effective way' (IB, 2009: 35) and which applies equally in the cases of DP and MYP. The picture is a far cry from 'a teacher who lectures, and involves students as passive recipients rather than active participants in the classroom, [who] is likely to be less effective' (DP, 2009: 37). This type of direct instruction is in fact potentially efficient for factual and knowledge-based learning, but cannot be used alone to bring about student understanding of a concept. By the same token, students are unable to learn how to do something simply by being told about it – skills must be learned by doing them.

All such types of learning – knowledge- and skills-based, and conceptual – are very much present in the DP, and creative teacher professionalism must thus be used, as with the MYP, both in designing courses and lessons which address all of those types most effectively, and in considering the roles to be played in delivering each – roles which may alternate a number of times within the same lesson, in accordance with changes in the focus of the learning in that time.

The model shown in Figure 1 provides some possibilities as to what form a teacher's role may take within a classroom, in accordance with the nature of student learning at any given point:

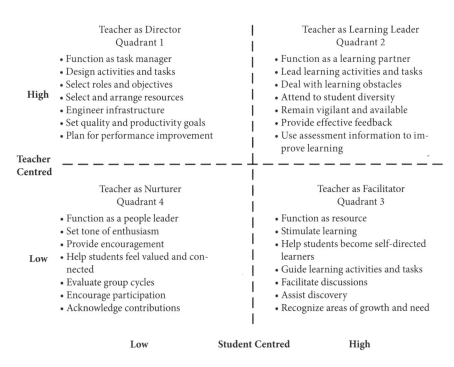

Figure 1: The Four Quadrants of Teacher Directiveness (First Monday, 2002)

Matching teaching and learning, meanwhile, raises the notion of inquiry, which 'interpreted in the broadest sense, is the process initiated by the student or the teacher that moves the student from their current level of understanding to a new and deeper level of understanding', and 'involves synthesis, analysis and manipulation of knowledge' (IB, 2008b: 15). The IB lists a number of types of tasks and activities used in inquiry, which are likely to appear as familiar to DP teachers as they are to teachers of MYP:

- speculating, exploring, questioning
- making connections between previous learning and current learning
- researching
- developing and testing theories
- collecting data, reporting findings and constructing explanations
- clarifying existing ideas and reappraising perceptions of events
- identifying assumptions
- taking and defending a position
- solving problems in a variety of ways
- analysing and evaluating
- considering alternative explanations

(IB, 2008b: 15)

There is, meanwhile, an explicit exhortation to use inquiry-based approaches in addressing the aims and objectives of each DP course, which 'emphasize the importance of students investigating answers for themselves. IB assessments are designed to reward evidence of independent student thinking leading to considered individual responses, so it is important that students practise these skills at every opportunity. Different subjects also provide a number of opportunities for students to design their own inquiry' (IB, 2009: 37). Examples such as an analytical essay in Language A: Literature, or investigations in Biology and Visual Arts, or explorations in Mathematics and so on, could further benefit from the use of inquiry models, of which a wide range exist; a version is already used in Design Technology, for instance, and two further well-known examples are given in Figures 2 and 3. These represent potentially productive tools in providing a structure or framework for such tasks, thus promoting effective and purposeful learning via a 'structured inquiry' approach and teaching strategies which may be associated with each stage.

Such approaches are not, therefore, the preserve of any one programme and such creative teacher professionalism should represent an area where articulation can be clearly discerned between the MYP and DP. Courses in the DP may 'specify a large amount of content, with the area of study often defined in considerable detail', but it is important to identify what that content actually comprises, following which 'it is the way in which content is presented in class that is critical' (IB, 2009: 37). The nature of the learning concerned represents the key consideration, and in this respect, therefore, the expectation for teachers in both programmes is much the same: to consider that learning carefully, along with a possible range of appropriate and effective approaches to support students in acquiring it.

Current IB endeavours are ongoing at the time of writing, aimed at developing the MYP's 'Approaches to Learning' into an articulated scheme encompassing

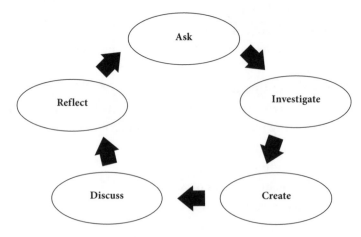

Figure 2: John Dewey's inquiry cycle (Dewey, 1933)

Figure 3: Alberta inquiry model (Alberta Education, 2004: 10)

both teaching and learning approaches and, age-appropriately, the continuum of IB programmes. This should promote further the notion of an already-existing continuum in this area, and may hopefully provide further support in the forms of practical and detailed advice and examples of specifics.

MYP–DP articulation: possible ways forward?
The IB

While creative teacher professionalism is of relevance to both programmes, prescribed content is less so. This leaves MYP schools and teachers to identify such content themselves, and organize and plan this effectively to address all of the learning objectives in a subject, and articulate learning across the programme – and then across to the DP. This requires not insignificant skills in curriculum-building, even where detailed standards, benchmarks, and any other requirements may be involved; it also requires teachers (particularly where such requirements are not involved) with sufficiently wide-ranging subject experience to carry this out as effectively as needed. One wonders where this may leave, for instance, a teacher of lesser experience who does not teach in the DP (nor possibly in a school which offers it), who may be new to MYP and grappling with relatively unfamiliar requirements of areas of interaction/global contexts and interdisciplinary teaching and learning, and could be the sole subject representative – or part of a smaller department where experience in such areas is similarly restricted.

It is perhaps a mistake to assume that all teachers are in a position to be curriculum-builders in the manner needed to put an effective, fully-articulated five-year MYP subject curriculum into place – the demands of which may be partly responsible also for the claims of a time-consuming and paperwork–laden programme. Meanwhile it is not difficult either to see how such a situation may lead to courses which do lack quality, in the absence of mandatory external assessment at their culmination may lack accountability also, and do not thus engender student learning to the levels possible – and perhaps required – at the point of transition into a DP course. The area of curriculum-building, as mentioned earlier, remains an articulation issue which may need greater acknowledgement by the IB, and greater support provided to teachers – perhaps through the 'publication of MYP vertical and horizontal articulation documents' (the most-requested item in the survey of IB coordinators) or through an increased amount of professional development aimed directly at effective curriculum construction in the MYP (including its dovetailing into DP courses), greater detail in subject guides and published teacher support materials as to what is required from courses and processes of planning this, and guidance to schools on how such processes might be supported and overseen within schools through the use of particular expertise, creation of roles of responsibility and so on. Articulation and MYP reputation matters apart, curriculum is fundamental to the quality of student learning, which must surely be the central concern of any school – whatever programme they may offer.

Allied to that may be the need to acknowledge more, and tackle more effectively, concerns and difficulties that some teachers experience relating to meaningful implementation of aspects of the curriculum such as concepts, areas of interaction / global contexts, inquiry, and interdisciplinary teaching and learning. Despite their presence within the programme from its adoption, the gap from theory to practice in respect of these aspects is still, I would argue, to be convincingly plugged. Doing so may perhaps require some reappraisal of approach in terms, for instance, of the provision of more ongoing professional development, perhaps through making greater use of technology for 'guide-along' advice and guidance. The dangers of 'mental confusion and superficial surveys' highlighted from the very start by Belle-Isle (ISA, 1991: 7 in IB, 2010a: 20) serve where they do occur to dilute the curriculum – and, so far as anecdotal evidence suggests, frustrate teachers in the process. Hopefully the 'MYP–Next Chapter' process will see greater clarity and better understanding and implementation, but there may remain scope to develop further understanding in teachers of the rationale behind these elements with respect to student learning, and in addressing any signs of practical difficulties in a more proactive manner. Student learning is a complex business, and these elements are relatively complex and, increasingly often in MYP schools around the world, are tackled by teachers whose experience may have largely derived from educational contexts in which such things featured rarely if at all. A greater need may exist than has perhaps generally been acknowledged for developing understanding of both how such aspects need to be addressed and, crucially, why.

The theory that 'one of the strengths of the MYP is that it provides a general framework and structure while at the same time liberating teachers from prescriptive curricular and summative assessment, thus allowing them to create challenging curriculums and new teaching methodologies' (Watts, 2002: 6) perhaps masks a gap to the practice, and to what is needed to bring that practice about, along with a gap in understanding how it may fit into the day-to-day realities of time, resources, understanding, and students' immediate need for the best quality learning they can experience. One may look for instance at interdisciplinary teaching and learning, and the claim that 'In the very beginning of its existence the MYP had been criticised in some quarters for the interdisciplinary nature of the programme and the perceived subsequent lack of disciplinary rigour in comparison to the IGCSE. However, those schools began to understand the MYP philosophy, and to use the disciplines through the areas of interaction to develop interdisciplinarity' (IB, 2010: 34). Anecdotal evidence from workshops and school visits indicates in fact that teachers continue, 20 years after the programme's adoption, to struggle with the requirement to implement 'a disciplinary programme, but with direction to teachers to seek interdisciplinary relationships through the areas of interaction' (IB, 2010a: 34), and struggle to negotiate a 126-page somewhat academically-written guide on the topic in seeking further guidance.

The launch of 'MYP–Next Chapter' in 2014 should hopefully begin to address some of these issues (and a rewritten interdisciplinary guide is certainly on the agenda), while articulation with the DP has represented one of the factors involved in shaping it. Time will tell if it does lend the guidance which should support a greater understanding, and consequently rigour, where that may currently be perceived to be lacking.

School administrators

The notion of understanding is also of significant importance in a number of ways in regard to school administrators. One such way lies in understanding of requirements which MYP brings with it and, indeed, the additional work involved in properly implementing a programme that is three years longer than the DP, contains less prescribed content, requires implementation of elements at times found difficult in the interdisciplinary, contextual and other learning it encompasses, and perhaps provides scope for a wider range of assessment practices. Many teachers of both MYP and DP will freely admit to finding the DP rather easier to deliver, and prefer to teach in the DP – exclusively, in many cases – for that reason. The issue is exacerbated further in some instances where DP teachers are remunerated at a higher rate than teachers of MYP. As a consequence, a perception of carrying out more work on which less value may be placed by other constituents such as school administrators, parents, and colleagues can prevail.

Yet there is certainly an argument that the core curricular and pedagogical understanding demanded of teachers within the MYP is greater than that demanded in DP, where a greater premium may be placed on perceived subject knowledge of teachers – though subject knowledge should also be of no small significance in an MYP scenario in which five years of curriculum must be constructed and populated in a manner which will engender meaningful and rigorous learning at each stage, as well as ensuring students are at the level they need to be in order to make a smooth transition into a corresponding DP course. There seems little logic in an approach which emphasises achievement at DP level and good university entry data, as few schools fail to do, yet does not make the most of five years of developing understanding and skills which are at the core not only of MYP subject objectives, but of DP ones also, and which could provide a significant boost to DP performance if such understanding and skills have been maximised at the point of entry. Part of the approach to this maximising of understanding and skills is acknowledgement of what such curriculum-building in MYP entails, and providing the structural support required, for instance in time, training, and personnel. Consideration might be given to appointing a curriculum specialist if that seems appropriate, and care should be taken not to assume necessarily that the MYP coordinator is able to carry out this role effectively without consideration of factors such as time and experience in this area. There is a need for direct accountability for the quality of curriculum, by someone with the resources (including time) and experience to take on the task of overseeing the process and monitoring and reviewing the various aspects of it properly, as needed.

There is a need too, with MYP, for understanding of the programme on the part of administrators, which allows for evaluation of the quality of the programme and curriculum at a first-hand level, and for informed judgements on the types of structures and support which may be needed to bring about the quality needed. Such structures/support may include positions and personnel, as indicated above, and provision of meeting time which will allow for purposeful curriculum planning, consciously targeted as needed at effective trans-programme articulation, planned to facilitate involvement of any MYP-only and DP-only teachers, and requiring knowledge exchange in terms of aspects such as objectives and assessment in both.

Informed professional development approaches meanwhile need to take into account implications of requirements in regard to MYP, where the IB requires only that one member of each subject group must be trained. The manner in which any professional development undertaken by individual teachers is subsequently made use of more widely within the school, therefore, and processes for ensuring this, become of greater significance. Professional development may also need to address how those who teach only in one of the programmes gain understanding of the nature and requirements of the other, in order to plan for and facilitate effective subject articulation. Alongside professional decision-making, meanwhile, lie a number of more ethos-based needs. One such is that of engendering trust in the programme among groups within a school community who may question a programme lacking in significant prescription and/or external assessment; parents represent one such constituency, but groups of DP-only teachers may be another – and perhaps even those charged with planning and delivering the MYP. Confidence and trust in the programme is much more likely to arise where informed leaders are among its advocates.

Greater articulation of pedagogy might also be considered, along with encouraging the supportive climate needed for this. Teaching approaches which match the learning targets will clearly be more effective than those which do not but, perhaps in the DP in particular – where a focus tends to be on grades, these may be used as the only real indicator of 'good teaching', and in essence may be the only things ultimately felt to matter to some constituents within a school community. There can seem little reason, therefore, for the teacher who enjoys good grades year on year to change very much of their approach, and certainly little incentive given the potential consequences in terms of reputation, role, and possibly even place within a school if that happened to be followed by those grades 'going down'.

The high stakes nature of DP examinations does very much militate against taking risks at this level and indeed can provide a temptation on occasion, as evidence of examination responses may suggest, for something akin to rote learning of 'thoughts' for answers where an independent response might really be called for. In literature examinations, for instance, one may see at times all students from a school choosing the same two (of a possible three) texts, and proceeding to call upon a very similar set of points and quotations, mostly in response to the same question, identified as that which best fits the information they have memorized. In reality such practice tends almost always to place a ceiling on the achievement of those in a higher ability range, while depressing achievement in general, since students find themselves dealing with material and ideas imposed from elsewhere, which are thus less-understood and hence less-developed than those they might well have generated themselves had they brought their own set of skills and understanding to the examination – at whatever level those may have been - and applied a more independent response. One also wonders how far a need to memorize information of momentary significance may hint at the value placed on development of the understandings and skills, as well as attitudes (there are many complaints of students who wish to be 'spoon-fed' at this level and beyond), which may well be needed for students to maximise their success in post-DP studies:

> The IB develops students that top universities want: students with expert subject knowledge; with the skills good students require – research, essay writing, footnoting; but above all, with the spirit of intellectual inquiry

and critical thinking, the ability to challenge, argue and ask questions. Universities are clearly aware of this: the offer rate and acceptance rate [in the UK] for IB Diploma students is notably above other post-16 qualifications (Ricks, 2013).

The DP, as has been seen, was designed from the outset to be about more than terminal examinations. Even for these examinations, however, practices – and perhaps ethos also – are of some significance in view of the principle that the most effective learning, and thus best grades at the end of the programme, will arise from the most effective facilitation of that learning by the teacher. Thus continuing development and understanding of teaching methodologies are important to support and promote within the programme. Teachers inclined to more 'traditional' methods across their courses may gradually introduce small-scale changes such as trying out a new visible thinking routine, or the use of an inquiry model in planning the path to a particular assessment which might well provide greater structure, direction and thoroughness to a process which may well already be happening. Such steps can enhance the learning process in DP, in a school culture which supports this, and where the relevant professional development is available if needed.

The role of administrators is thus crucial in a number of ways pertaining to curriculum, professional development, and ethos also, in the task of achieving effective articulation between the two programmes in a school.

Teachers

The IB places great emphasis on the notion of the 'lifelong learner', and teaching may be foremost among professions where that may particularly apply. Just over a hundred years ago, reading and writing skills were the preserve of a small elite; fast forward to the present and a plethora of educational theories abound, understandings of the brain move on apace, and the internet and technology have altered massively the focus of learning both in schools, and for life beyond. Education is a hugely dynamic environment, with the inevitability of change representing one of the few constants over the course of a teaching career; while acknowledgement of changing student learning needs over time, and willingness to develop one's own knowledge, understandings and skills to meet those needs, are prerequisites for any teacher.

Student learning is undoubtedly a complex business, in need of effort, time, and engagement to understand well, plan for, and deliver as effectively as possible. Complexity is thus inevitable in programmes such as the MYP in particular, but the DP also in many respects, which endeavour to meet varied learning goals. Understanding these, and engaging with them as needed for students to acquire such learning, must therefore be an expectation of any teacher choosing to take up a position in a school delivering such programmes, given that a teacher's first obligation is to the learning of his/her students, and to facilitating that as required.

This in turn calls upon understanding of the different types of learning involved in both programmes: that, for instance, there is more to DP than prescribed, knowledge-based content: 'The IB [DP] develops the future leaders the workplace needs – people who know how to collaborate and who know the value of teamwork, people with analytical ability, versatility, international understanding. The IB develops what a global society and a local community can't survive without – individuals who want to make a difference, who have developed the compassion and sense of public duty to contribute.' (Ricks, 2013) and that there should be more to MYP than its being 'a preparation for vocational study since it emphasises communication, problem solving, collaborative working, coursework assessment, integration with other subjects, real-life contexts etc.' (TES, 2013a).

For teachers there is the most crucial role of all to play in engaging with such a 'hugely dynamic environment', bringing structure and rigour to the programmes, and facilitating actual learning for students – and hence facilitating the success of various kinds which follows from there. The importance of such an undertaking is of the highest significance, the investment of time and effort required considerable. The scope for individual professional development, and indeed fulfilment, which may be derived from such engagement should, though, perhaps not be underestimated:

> If your programme's scope and sequence is articulated with a proper curriculum (...) and mapped backwards from all of your DP subjects (modelling assessment on internal and external DP assessment tasks, aligning DP and MYP objectives, etc.) you will have a brilliant programme. Your school's MYP will not in the least bit be compromised by doing this. A properly functioning IB continuum school can be truly amazing ... In my recent job search I looked for IB continuum schools exclusively (TES, 2013a).

Conclusion

While differences undoubtedly exist between the MYP and DP, it is clear also that differences exist in the needs of students within the age ranges these two programmes cover, and hence differences are also needed in the type of programme found at each level. Such were the drivers behind the programmes as they were originally developed, and the situation has changed little in that the DP must provide for university entrance access, and the mechanisms (most obviously formal external examinations) which go along with that, while less scope will self-evidently be found in a two-year as opposed to a five-year programme for implementing aspects such as exploring interdisciplinarity and inquiry.

The programmes must in the first instance, therefore, serve the needs of the students for whom they are intended, and inevitable differences arising from those needs will always pose certain challenges in transition between the two.

Nonetheless, a number of points of convergence between the two programmes exist also, among which are areas of learning extending beyond the subject-specific, which are of immense importance to students, as well as being valued more widely, including in many of the universities to which IB students aspire. Convergence may also be found, meanwhile, in the types of subject learning students should encounter, and in the teaching approaches which may be appropriate for those.

The MYP–DP 'gap' may thus be less cavernous in reality than comments can at times suggest, and may indicate a degree of scope for some reappraisal among individual practitioners and, perhaps, schools. That there are 'leaps' to be made is also clear, however, as acknowledged by an IB which has unquestionably directed quite considerable efforts in more recent times at addressing them. Crossing the 'gap' successfully requires all involved in the first instance to understand what the nature of the 'gap' actually is, and what kinds of input and participation might thus be needed on each part, in order that the transition process is managed in the manner ultimately best serving the interests of students.

For the IB, of crucial importance is how understanding of all aspects of the programmes is conveyed to teachers, in order for implementation to be as effective as possible. Philosophical and pedagogical approaches appear to be where uncertainty can arise, while greater scope may exist too for provision of guidance and resources for curriculum-building in schools, which may better ensure that rigour in MYP particularly is always, one might say, *de rigeur* in the programme's delivery in schools, and thus leads purposefully and effectively too into corresponding DP courses. For school administrators, understanding and valuing the programmes, and providing the support and leadership necessary for their positive and purposeful implementation, should clearly be expectations within schools which have, after all, made a proactive choice at some stage to adopt the MYP and DP. Meanwhile students have a right to expect wholehearted engagement from their teachers in whatever programme is being delivered in the classroom, along with the best pedagogical practices aligned with the particular learning they are seeking to acquire.

Perhaps ultimately, the crux of all lies in an awareness that, where IB programmes are concerned, understanding and articulating gaps in knowledge, conceptual understanding, skills and attitudes may not be the sole preserve of students.

References

Alberta Education (2004) Focus on inquiry. *A Teacher's Guide to Implementing Inquiry-based Learning.* Available online at: http://education.alberta.ca/media/313361/focusoninquiry.pdf (last accessed 22 September 2011).

Bunnell, T. (2011) International Baccalaureate Middle Years Programme after 30 years: A critical inquiry. *Journal of Research in International Education*, 10 (3), p. 261-274.

Chapman, M. (2011) Evolving the middle years curriculum in practice. In: Hayden, M. and Thompson, J. eds. *Taking the MYP Forward*. Woodbridge: John Catt Educational Ltd.

Codrington, S. (2002). The pain of curriculum change: The challenges of implementing the MYP. *IB World* 32, p. 18-21.

Dewey, J. (1933). *How we think: A rethinking of the relation of reflective thinking in the educative process.* New York: D. C. Heath.

Field, J. (2011) Subject-based, interdisciplinary, and transdisciplinary approaches to the MYP. In: Hayden, M., Thompson, J. eds. *Taking the MYP Forward.* Woodbridge: John Catt Educational Ltd.

First Monday (2002) Volume 7 Number 1 - 7: Finding Balance: *The Vices of our "Versus".* Available online at: http://firstmonday.org/htbin/cgiwrap/bin/ojs/index.php/fm/rt/printerFriendly/924/846 (last accessed 23 September 2011)

Hallinger, P., Lee, M., and Walker, P. (2011) Program transition challenges in International Baccalaureate schools. *Journal of Research in International Education,* 10 (2), p. 123-136.

Hayden, M. (2006) *Introduction to International Education.* London: Sage.

Hill, I. (2002) *The history of international education: an International Baccalaureate perspective.* In Hayden, M., Thompson, J., Walker, G. (eds) International Education in Practice: dimensions for national & international schools. pp 18-29 London, Kogan Page.

International Baccalaureate (2008a) *MYP: From principles into practice.* Cardiff: International Baccalaureate.

International Baccalaureate (2008b) *Towards a continuum of international education.* Cardiff: International Baccalaureate.

International Baccalaureate (2009) *The Diploma Programme: From principles into practice.* Cardiff: International Baccalaureate.

International Baccalaureate (2010a) *History of the Middle Years Programme.* Cardiff: International Baccalaureate.

International Baccalaureate (2010b) *MYP Coordinator's Notes: May 2010.* Cardiff: International Baccalaureate.

International Schools Review (2010) *Forums, Forum 1. From Questions about Search Associates to What's Happening at Various Schools: MYP – a Refutation.* Available online at: http://internationalschoolsreview.com/v-web/bulletin/bb/viewtopic.php?t=1322&start=45 (last accessed 5 February 2013).

ISAC (1991) Programme of International Secondary Education 11–16 years.

LinkedIn (2011) Forums: Which one do you prefer. *Cambridge, IGCSE program or IB, MYP Program?* Available online at: http://www.linkedin.com/groups/Which-one-do-you-prefer-3399563.S.45888791?view=&gid=3399563&type=member&item=45888791&trk=eml-anet_dig-b_nd-pst_ttle-cn (last accessed 9 March 2013).

Menino, T. in SearchQuotes (2012) *Thomas Menino quotes.* Available online at: http://www.searchquotes.com/quotation/Children_need_continuity_as_they_grow_and_learn./135399/ (last accessed 26 January 2013).

Online Curriculum Centre (2011) *Forums, MYP coordinators and implementation of the MYP: Teachers writing curriculum.* Available online at: http://occ.ibo.org/ibis/occ/fusetalk2/forum/messageview.cfm?catid=2424&threadid=368559&highlight_key=y (last accessed 25 January 2013).

Peterson, A. D. C. (2003) Schools Across Frontiers: *The Story of the International Baccalaureate and the United World Colleges.* Second Edition. Chicago, Illinois: Open Court Publishing Company.

Ricks, K. (2013) *The IB develops the students top universities want* in "The Independent", February 2013. Available online at: http://www.independent.co.uk/news/education/schools/the-ib-develops-the-students-top-universities-want-8503818.html?origin=internalSearch (last accessed 21 February 2013).

Times Educational Supplement (2013a) *Forums: Teaching overseas: MYP – a story.* Available online at: http://community.tes.co.uk/forums/t/475458.aspx?PageIndex=1 (last accessed 8 March 2013).

Times Educational Supplement (2013b) *Forums: Teaching overseas: MYP - Discuss.* Online: http://community.tes.co.uk/forums/t/646079.aspx (last accessed 12 March 2013)

Times Educational Supplement (2013c) *Forums: Teaching overseas: questions for people teaching MYP* Online: http://community.tes.co.uk/forums/p/646661/8023998.aspx#8023998 (last accessed 9 March 2013).

Watts, A. (2002) Adapting to change with the MYP. *IB World* 33, p. 6.